SENTENCE INITIAL DEVICES

SUMMER INSTITUTE OF LINGUISTICS
PUBLICATIONS IN LINGUISTICS
Publication Number 75

EDITORS

Desmond C. Derbyshire
Summer Institute of
Linguistics - Dallas

Virgil L. Poulter
University of Texas
at Arlington

ASSISTANT EDITORS

Alan C. Wares

Iris M. Wares

CONSULTING EDITORS

Doris A. Bartholomew
Pamela M. Bendor-Samuel
Robert Dooley
Austin Hale
Phyllis Healey

Robert E. Longacre
Eugene E. Loos
William R. Merrifield
Kenneth L. Pike
Viola G. Waterhouse

Jerold A. Edmondson

SENTENCE INITIAL DEVICES

Joseph E. Grimes
Editor

A Publication of
The Summer Institute of Linguistics
and
The University of Texas at Arlington

1986

© 1986 by the Summer Institute of Linguistics, Inc.
Library of Congress Catalog Card No. 83-051455
ISBN 0-88312-096-8

Copies of this and other publications of the
Summer Institute of Linguistics may be
obtained from
    Bookstore
    Summer Institute of Linguistics
    7500 W. Camp Wisdom Rd.
    Dallas, TX 75236

TABLE OF CONTENTS

Introduction

Joseph E. Grimes

The order of constituents in a sentence is not as arbitrary as was once thought. There is an internal logic behind constituent ordering. It is not the same for every language, but it responds to a surprisingly small number of factors. Different languages weigh each factor differently.

Typologies remained somewhat uncertain until this began to be more clear. One could question, for example, whether a particular language had a basic verb-initial constituent order on the grounds that a significant number of its sentences started with nominals rather than verbs. Once linguists began to be sensitive to the variety of reasons there are why a nominal might appear at the beginning of a sentence, however, they were able to see that such occurrences did not really weaken the validity of the basic pattern.

At the same time, the excitement of seeing how the ordering of constituents works in a few languages may have obscured understanding of its total communicative possibilities. Much of the early work on word order was directed towards languages like Czech and Russian where word order communicates relatively little about grammatical relations. In those languages constituents are usually ordered along an increasing gradient that represents how much unexpected information each one contributes to the communication. Recognizing that gradient explains a good deal about what comes first and what comes later.

Then attention turned to word order in English. In English much of the ordering depends on grammatical relations, but an important amount of information other than just grammatical relations is also communicated by it. Two other factors that influence order became prominent: the importance of sentence-initial position for connection

1

with the topic on the one hand, and the increase in communicative dynamism toward the end of the sentence on the other hand. But someone needed to ask, either on grounds of pure logic or of going out and listening to how other languages work, whether those were the only possibilities.

From South America comes the observation that there is at least one other option that has to be taken into account for understanding word order: communicative dynamism may decrease rather than increase during a sentence. In two unrelated languages, Gavião of the Tupi family and Xavante of the Gê family, we have good evidence that the least predictable part of what a speaker is saying actually comes at the beginning. Most sentences get into more and more predictable material as they go on. Even though other languages related to these organize their information in the more popular way of putting what can be presupposed before what is being focused on informationally, at least we see now that starting with high redundancy is not a necessary strategy for communication. These two languages seem to be enough, for example, to call into question claims about the universal psychological validity of beginning with what is known and going on to what is unknown.

As for other phenomena that are associated with sentence-initial position, the South and Central American data we offer here seem to line up fairly well with the way the rest of the world talks. Connectives and interrogatives come at the beginning of sentences. Topics are frequently set up there. The participants in discourse are brought on stage with sentence-initial devices when they occupy certain roles in the discourse, but sneaked in as noninitial constituents in other cases. Redundant clauses that glue paragraphs together have grammatical affinities that show they are at the beginning of complex sentences rather than at the end. Collateral information (the kind that tells what might be rather than asserting what is—questions and counterexpectations are typically collateral) often gets tagged as such on its first constituent.

The papers in this collection are the result of two seminars held in Brazil and in Colombia, in the fall of 1976 and the spring of 1977 respectively. They were organized at the initiative of the Summer Institute of Linguistics. The first was held at the field station operated by the Institute near Pôrto Velho. The second was cosponsored by the Department of Systems Engineering and Computation of the University of the Andes in Bogotá in connection with a lecture series I gave there on artificial intelligence models in the analysis of natural languages. The participants came from the sponsoring institutions and others. Drafts of several of these papers have appeared locally in Spanish or Portuguese; the English versions, however, merit presentation as a collection because of the view they provide on the way some imperfectly understood principles of language operate in languages that linguists have not heard much from yet.

New Information First

Constituent Order, Cohesion, and Staging in Gavião

Horst Stute
New Tribes Mission of Brazil

The order of constituents in Gavião clauses at first glance appears to be quite free. It is shown, however, that all variation of order, including the phenomenon of fronting, is accounted for by underlying semantic structures. These semantic structures control the surface structure of all clauses by way of rules. For making the parts of information cohere with each other, an information distribution rule is applied; and for having one set point to which the rest of information can be related, a topicalization rule is applied. The order in which these two rules apply is subject to changes, and this accounts for fronting. A suggested conclusion is that clause topics are always subjects.

A more general study of Gavião[1] discourse has been the ground for the clause analysis presented in this paper. After an outline of the inner structures of clause constituents is given, it is shown how constituents differ from particles, and then the structure of clauses is compared with that of sentences. Next, in sections 4 through 7, the order of clause constituents, as controlled by staging and cohesion, is analyzed and discussed. In section 8, the unusual characteristics of questions are considered. Finally, in section 9, some features of Gavião intonation, as it relates to discourse, are given.

1 Clause constituents

In Gavião clauses, noun phrases act as subject, verb phrases as

7

predicate, and adverbial modifiers, postpositional phrases, or dependent clauses as adjuncts. A verb phrase consists of either an intransitive verb or a transitive verb with its preceding object, which is a noun phrase. A postpositional phrase has the same structure as a transitive verb phrase, in that it consists of a postposition and its preceding object, a noun phrase. The following clause illustrates subject (S) and predicate (P), and also the three kinds of adjuncts (A). The third adjunct is a dependent clause containing the transitive verb phrase *evír tírí* 'cook your food'.

(1)   *e-gere en gújá e-hni ká e-vír tírí zàhr-á*
     2sg-sleep(P) you(S) well(A) 2sg-hammock in(A) 2sg-food burn
     1sg + simultaneous(A)-final
     'sleep well in your hammock while I cook your food!'

Noun phrases thus occur in subject position and also as objects of both verbs and postpositions. Noun phrase types cannot be described in detail here, but several are listed. The basic structure of a noun phrase is a noun, which may also be followed by adjectives. Pronominal prefixes are the most frequent elements that have noun-like reference. On rare occasions, however, such prefixes are substituted for by free pronouns. Verb phrases may be nominalized and thus constitute noun phrases. Recursive subordinate constructions, like 'the jaguar's head's bone', and coordinate constructions, like 'small children and adults', also constitute noun phrases. Embedded[2] constructions that constitute noun phrases are the relative clause and the complement clause.[3]

There is only one subject in a clause and usually one predicate, but adjuncts frequently occur two or three at a time with no definite limitation as to the possible number in one clause.

The occurrence of more than one predicate has special implications. One such implication is that only one of them can be a true predicate. The others (generally there are not more than two) function as adjuncts, though there is no indication of their status other than their position. In the following example, 'to take out his dreams' has the form of a verb phrase, but functions as an adjunct, stating the purpose of the main verb phrase.

(2)   *È tér alía máh* **a-kéjé-v** *piri a-vé-báta kíh betíhg atóh pí-á*
     kípo-á. (that connector sloth declar+past **3rd +
     reflexive-dream-nominalizer take=out** 3rd +
     reflexive-passive-fall repeatedly Betihg–tree high
     from-final hearsay-final) 'And then the sloth let himself fall
     repeatedly from a high tree to make himself stop
     dreaming.'[4]

2 Constituents and particles

Subject, predicate, and adjunct constitute the main body or nucleus of a clause. At least one of these constituents is necessary to make a predication.[5] In addition, there is in clauses a great variety of particles that mainly give modal information. These particles state various ways a clause is related to circumstances or to speakers and hearers. Thus, these particles are necessary for a clause to function in its context, and for a predication to constitute a speech act.

Besides differing in the kinds of information they give, constituents and particles also differ in distribution. Particles occur in fixed position and order, while there is no fixed order for the major constituents. In accordance with this fixity particles occur at the boundaries of clause constituents. For example, the particles that state the speaker's attitude toward what a clause predicates precede the subject, but these particles are partially supplemented by clause-final particles. In example 3 the initial particle *de* and the clause-final particle *kî* state not a common negative but something like 'the speaker holds as not true what the predication expresses'.

(3) ***de*** *e-zá-ka gakorá-la kíh* ***ki-á***
    particle 2sg-nondeclar-go hunt-plural frequent particle-final
    'I don't think you hunt frequently'

A few adverbial particles follow verb phrases. They are not adjuncts and may be included when verb phrases containing them are nominalized. One kind of information these particles give is frequency of the action, like *kíh* in the example above.

2.1 The auxiliary. The most important particle, which follows every subject or coalesces with it, is the auxiliary. The auxiliary carries a high semantic load. Besides showing which constituent is the subject, it gives information on tense and mode, and indicates the status of embedded clauses and the type of relation of dependent clauses. Also deictic information is stated by the auxiliary by a kind of auxiliary action: 'to come' and 'to go' as, for example, in the following clause:

(4) *gakorá tó-máa-ka àjùr ále-á*
    hunt 1pl=excl-declar + present-go today future-final
    'I am going to hunt today'

The time information that the auxiliary gives is frequently supplemented by additional particles, which occur only at the end of the clause, like *ále* 'future' in example 4.

2.2 Connectives. Simple conjunctions are particles, and other connectives are derived from particles but include real constituent information as well. The particles in a connective are the **demonstrative**, which comes first, and the **connector**, which comes last. Between them come words that together with the demonstrative form postpositional phrases, verb phrases, and noun phrases.

The textual demonstratives *è*, *mán*, and *méne* are the most common. While *è* refers in an unspecific sense to something previously mentioned, *mán* and *méne* are more specific anaphoric particles.[6] Examples of these connectives are given below. *è tér* and *è bó* are the conjunctions that mean 'and then'.[7] They are the specific time line connectives of narrative discourse.

> (5) *è bó tá-máh mató-á*
>   that connector 3pl-declar+past 3sg+'show-final
>   'then they showed it'

In examples 6 and 7, the demonstrative *mán* is the object of a postposition and a verb respectively, and in example 8 it constitutes by itself the subject noun phrase because it precedes the auxiliary. Less clearly in example 6, more clearly in examples 7 and 8, *mán* refers to a nominal in the preceding sentence.

> (6) *mán pí bó tá-máh mató-á*
>   that **after** connector 3pl-declar+past 3sg+show-final
>   'after that they showed it (what was mentioned before)'
> (7) *mán **mató** bó tá-máh-á*
>   that **show** connector 3pl-declar+past-final
>   'that one they showed'
> (8) *mán bó máh mató-á*
>   that connector declar+past 3sg+show-final
>   'that one showed it'

The next three examples begin with the other anaphoric particle *méne*, which relates the whole preceding sentence to the clause constituent that is constituted by the connective. In examples 9 and 10, it is the object of the postposition and the verb respectively, and in example 11, it constitutes the noun phrase subject.

> (9) *méne **ká** bó tá-máh mató-á*
>   that **in** connector 3pl-declar+past show-final
>   'therefore they showed it (what was mentioned before)'

(10) *méne **mató** bó tá-máh-á*
that **show** connector 3pl-declar+ past-final
'that they showed'

(11) *méne bó máh mató-á*
that connector declar+past show-final
'that showed it'

3 Clause and sentence boundaries

The clause and the sentence are basically not distinct in Gavião. There is no string of clauses that functions as a sentence; all dependent clauses have to be considered either as constituents of clauses because of possibilities of order within a clause, or as sentences that are bound semantically to a preceding clause but occur independently because they show all the characteristics of a sentence.

What constitutes a **sentence** is a clause or a clause followed by some minor elements. The end of the clause is signaled by the enclitic *-a* 'final', and some sentence particles or minor elements follow this enclitic. The most important sentence particle is *kípo* 'hearsay'. It signifies **verification** which means that the speaker is not eyewitness and that he has not received the information from an eyewitness. Example 12 is a sentence with an independent clause, and this sentence is followed immediately by sentence 13 with a semantically dependent clause acting as a secondary sentence.

(12) *Èna mán ká máh má aka-á **kípo** -á.*
that=manner relative in 3sg+declar+past one=other kill-final
hearsay-final
'In that situation he killed another one, they say.'

(13) *I ká sáhr-á **kípo** -á.*
river in 3sg+simultaneous-final **hearsay**-final
'It happened while he was in the river, they say.'

Other sentence particles that follow the clause include *màga* 'I tell you!', *abój* 'my friend!', and *djere-* 'poor guy!' One example follows:

(14) *È tér máh avi-á **djere**-á.*
that connector 3sg+declar+past die-final **poor=guy**-final
'Then he died, poor guy.'

Besides the particles, there is an important intonational factor that clarifies the boundaries of the sentence. Gavião has a two-level tone system, including high, low, and rising tone. The tone levels are perturbed by three kinds of downstep, causing the general key to drop at any point in the sentence. Only and always at sentence boundaries—including secondary sentences—the primary tone levels are picked up again, giving the effect of a real intonational break. The sequence of tones of sentence 15 is indicated by the line below it. The sentence that follows it starts high again.

(15) E tér máh xàlá tè-á kípo-á.
    that connector 3sg+declar+past 3sg+leave restrictive-final hearsay-final
    'Then he just left it.'

4 Information distribution and topicalization

The main phenomenon of Gavião clauses is the ordering of their constituents. It must be stressed that it is not the order of individual words but phrases that matters (Mel'chuk 1967). Within phrases, including object-verb sequences, word order is fixed.

Grimes's general concept (1975) that views language as consisting of four interrelated but distinct structures, namely sound, content, cohesion, and staging, is useful for Gavião clause analysis. While sound stands for the phonological structure, content refers to what is being said and how it is structured hierarchically. Cohesion expresses how the parts of clauses are put together for the benefit of the listener, who needs to keep track of the sequence of information.

One kind of cohesion device has to do with **information distribution** in a clause, i.e., with the distribution of information in constituents of the clause, not in particles. Halliday and Hasan's differentiation between **new** and **given** information (1976) is fundamental for information distribution in Gavião clauses. New and given have to do with predictability and are defined for Gavião as what the speaker regards as least predictable for new information, and as most predictable, for given information. This predictability of information is in reference (a) to the hearer in a statement and (b) to the speaker in a question.

Section 8 concerns questions and answers. For all other kinds of data, given, or predictable, information is what has been identified before, and what can be deduced from context, or simply what is common knowledge. New information is what the speaker regards as being new, or unpredictable, to the hearer.

Clauses generally do not contain only new, but also given information. The new is made to cohere with the given. That is to say, given information is already established in relation to time, location, and nominal identity, and new information is attached to it.

The fourth component of language is staging; it is concerned with expressing the speaker's perspective on what is being said and how he organizes what he wants to say. At clause level, staging has to do with topicalization. Each clause has one nominal constituent as **topic,** and all other constituents function as **comment** to that topic. To make a predication, thus, is to establish a point, a topic, and then say something about it.[8]

5 Unmarked clause structure

The sentences of a discourse that give the real steps of the event line show the unmarked, or basic, clause structure, with the normal ordering of constituents. There is, however, a threefold structure in which staging and the cohesive structure interact and lead to its resultant content structure. The three may be displayed as follows:

Staging:

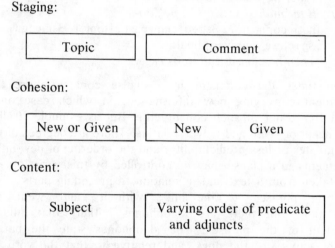

Staging structure and cohesive structure interact according to rules. These rules must be applied in structuring any clause. The topicalization rule that aims for an initial topic as starting point applies last in an unmarked clause structure and thereby determines the final surface structure: the topic occurs first, before its comment, and is always the subject in terms of content structure.

The information distribution rule that places new information in initial position applies before the topicalization rule and therefore cannot affect the placement of the topic. It controls, however, constituent order within the comment. That is to say, the constituents that contain new information come first after the topic, followed by the given information. The sequence of sentences that follows illustrates the unmarked placement of the topic and of new and given information. In example 17 the goal of the action, which is the dog mentioned in example 16, is last and is therefore given. In example 19 the location is stated first after the topic because it is new information, while the verb comes last because it is mentioned in example 18.[9]

(16) *Zàno máh a-pásala ávulu kaj-á.*
my=brother declar+past [topic] 3rd-be=angry=with [new] dog
goal [new]-final
'My brother was **angry** with the dog.'

(17) *È tér máh tágá kaj-á.*
that connector 3sg+declar+past [topic] hit [new] 3sg+goal
[given]-final
'Then he **hit** it.'

(18) *È pí bó máh pekáta-e kala-á.*
that after connector 3sg+declar+past [topic] 3sg+close=in-
nominalizer want [new]-final
'Later he wanted to **close it in.**'

(19) *È tér máh xi-savàhv ká pekáta-á.*
that connector 3sg+declar+past [topic] 3sg-cage in [new]
3sg+close=in[given]-final
'Then he closed it in **in its cage.**'

Sometimes the comment in a clause contains more than one
constituent conveying new information, in which case one would
expect free order of such constituents. But as example 20 illustrates,
the concept of given and new is relative. There are degrees of newness,
or of greater or less predictability, and the ordering of new-information
constituents in a clause may be controlled by this variation. Example
20 is taken from a text and in relation to preceding parts of that text
the three phrases 'to the hill', 'with it', and 'went' are new
information. But there are ideophones initially that influence the
placement of the phrases. The ideophones state the barking and
running activity of the dogs, and relative to that the verb 'went' is
given and is placed finally. The phrase 'with it' is also in some degree
predictable in relation to the ideophones and is placed second. 'To the
hill' is unpredictable and therefore first in the comment.

(20) *Xun xun xun, è tér tá-máń do koj xi-tá a-ka-á.*
ideophones=run=bark, that connector 3pl-declar+past [topic]
hill to [new] 3sg-with [slightly new] go [given]-final
'Bow wow, they (dogs) went with it (jaguar) to the hill.'

6 Marked clause structure: fronting

Gavião clauses show one consistent departure from unmarked
clause structure: the clause constituent that contains the least
predictable information is frequently fronted before the subject topic.
But of prominent and new information only one clause constituent,
either a predicate or an adjunct, can occur before the subject. Of the

examples that come next, 21 has an adjunct fronted and 22 a predicate. In example 23 a fronted predicate is the only constituent besides the subject.

(21) *ve kakúru ná pa-mága pèe máki magéré-á*
thing good postposition [new] lpl=incl-declar+present [topic] thing make in=morning-final
'it is good to work in the morning'

(22) *olixi sábéh máki tá-máh ivav ná-á*
cashew=tree bark make [new] 3pl-declar+past [topic] canoe postposition-final
'they made cashew tree bark into a canoe'

(23) *pèe máki máh-á*
thing make [new] 3sg+declar+past [topic]-final
'he worked'

6.1 Principles of fronting. The fronting of clause constituents or lack of fronting depends on the order in which the topicalization and information distribution rules are applied. In the marked structure, then, the information placement rule applies last and, therefore, to the result of the staging rule, causing fronting of one constituent.

Asking further why the topicalization and information placement rules apply in varying orders leads to still more basic principles. The order in which rules apply is conditioned by choices that a Gavião speaker has to make in structuring any clause. These choices are displayed in the following diagram:

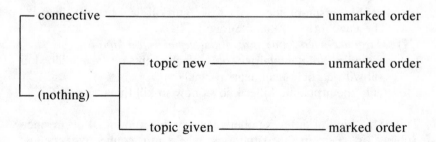

The first choice refers to the use of connectives. Connectives are topic introducers, always preceding the topic, except when they constitute the topic, as in examples 8 and 11 in section 2.2. If a connective is chosen, then there is no further choice, and the unmarked clause structure is used. If the first choice is not to use a connective, however, then a second choice must be made concerning the subject topic. Where the nominal phrase of the subject is new information, there is no change, and the unmarked structure occurs. If on the other hand the topic is given information, then the use of the marked clause structure with fronting of some new information is obligatory. In other words, when the topic is given information, then the information distribution rule overrules the topicalization rule and is applied last.

The initial sentences of seventeen short texts that do not begin with a connective show various kinds of subjects.[10] The subject of eight of these sentences is a prefix denoting a known referent like 'I', 'we', 'they', etc. In these cases some other element is fronted, as in example 24. The subjects of three other sentences are 'people', 'the old-timer', and 'the monkey killer'. All three are common knowledge and are considered to be given information; thus, as exemplified in 25, some element is placed before them. Five others have specific names of persons or tribes as subject topics. All these occur initially because they give new information, as in example 26. The subject of example 27 is similar to that of example 25, but it is new information because 'only' occurs with it. In Halliday's (1976) terms, 'armadillo killer only' is repudiative: it implies contrast and is, therefore, new and no fronting is carried out.

> (24) *Be tára **tá-ma-ká-á** kípo-á.*
>   path on **3pl**-declar+past-go-final hearsay-final
>   'They went to the path.'
> (25) *Ve-mi **aratígi-má-éhj** máh zav maâ-á kípo-á.*
>   skill-with **old=time-relative-pl** declar+past house build-final
>   'The old-timers knew how to make houses.'
> (26) *Pagûhj-éhj máh Seregúr aka-á kípo-á.*
>   **Pagûhj=person-pl** declar+past Seregúr kill-final hearsay-final
>   'The Pagûhj (tribe) killed Seregúr.'
> (27) *Mazój aká-r térte máa mazój aka ve-mi èna-á kípo-á.*
>   **armadillo kill-nominalizer only** declar+present armadillo kill
>   skill-with particle-final hearsay-final
>   'Only the armadillo killer knows how to kill the armadillo.'

This same kind of difference between fronting and initial occurrence of subject is seen in all situations where no connectives occur. Occurrence of connectives, however, is rarely a free choice for the speaker, but depends rather on the context into which the clause is to be placed. When an event is expressed in narrative or procedural discourse, a connective always has to be used; therefore, Gavião makes frequent use of connectives. On the other hand, not to use a connective is very common in the following situations: (1) in the type of text where the speaker reports what he sees few connectives are used; (2) sentences that give setting information, or commentaries on events, rarely occur with connectives; (3) all polar questions, imperatives, and most embedded and dependent clauses do not occur with connectives; and (4) simple individual statements like 'I am hungry' or 'John went fishing' are not given with connectives.

Gavião has the widely observed restriction that pronominal subject prefixes do not occur sentence initial because they are always given information. This is because topics, which are given information, do not occur initially, but are always preceded by some other element.

There is, however, one exception to the whole concept of fronting, including this restriction on the occurrence of prefixes in initial position. If no constituent of a clause contains any new information, then any subject, including a prefix, can occur sentence initial. The reason for this is logical, in that where there is no new information to be fronted, no fronting occurs. In fact, this exception supports the above analysis by showing that the restriction in subject prefix occurrence is not a mechanical restriction but a functional one. In example 28 the subject prefix is first. It is a paragraph-final clause whose constituents contain no new information. The constituents of this clause are stated only to relate them to the clause-final particle *káre* 'before a set point in time', which is the only new information in the clause. *Káre*, however, cannot be fronted because it is a particle with fixed position.

(28) *Ó-ma-ká zavpâjâ xàlá tè káre-á.*
      1sg-declar+past-go visit 3sg+leave restrictive yet-final
      'I went visiting people just leaving it (jaguar) there yet.'

6.2 Fronting and connectives. In comparing the structures of connectives and fronted constituents one realizes that they are almost the same, as illustrations in preceding sections show.[11] The constituent information in connectives is fronted information too.

Connectives and fronted elements are not the same because, first, in connectives it is not necessarily new information that is fronted and, second, connectives do have some special properties, for example, their connector *bó*.

6.3 Topic and subject. Even though in Gavião clauses any constituent that occurs before the subject has a special status, that is, it is fronted, nevertheless the speaker keeps the subject as the constituent that sets the stage in all clauses, even where one constituent occurs before it. This allows us to conclude that the clause topic and the clause subject are identical; that is, the subject is always topic and there are no topics that are not subjects.[12] The only exception to this is subject deletion, which is found occasionally in the marked clause structure, but never in the unmarked clause structure, and never if a connective is present. Deletion of the subject, however, does not mean that there is no topic in the clause, because, having been established earlier, it can be identified implicitly. Examples of this are 29 and 30; the topic in example 30 is implicit after having been established in example 29.

(29) *È tér ālīmé aká-r máa-ka ālīmé-éhj kábi-á kípo-á.*
      that connector monkey kill-nominalizer 3sg+declar+present-go
      monkey-pl for-final hearsay-final
      'Then the monkey killer goes after the monkeys.'
(30) *Tajaôhv aka baala-á kípo-á.*
      selected=one kill [deleted subject] first-final hearsay-final
      'First (he) kills a selected (monkey).'

6.4 Special kinds of fronting. Ideophones and quotations constitute a special kind of fronting because they may occur even before conjunctions, contrary to the general rule of fronting. Example 31 illustrates a quotation, while example 20 illustrates ideophones.

(31) *e-néva en-á, è tér xi-djaj máh kaj-á*
      2sg=eat   2sg+imperative-final,   **that   connector**   3sg-father
      declar+past 3sg+goal-final
      ' "Eat!" his father said to him.'

Gavião appears to have an extra structure for clauses that express adjectival and nominal states; in fact, however, it is not a distinct structure but a special kind of fronting. Clause 32 consists of only a subject, which is an unmarked structure of a noun phrase plus an auxiliary that could also be extended by a predicate and adjuncts. In clause 33 the adjective of the nominal phrase has been fronted as new information, while 'child' is in the position of given information.

(32) *buv xíxìr mága-á*
      child small declar+present-final
      'the small child' or 'the small child exists' or 'the child is small'
(33) *xíxìr, buv máh-á*
      small [new] child [given] declar-final
      'the child is **small**' or 'the child is a **small** one'

Adjectives may function as noun phrases, as illustrated in example 34. The fronted adjective in example 33 may therefore be considered a noun phrase too, having the English equivalent 'the child is a small one'. Other more complete noun phrase fronting is shown in examples 35 to 38.

(34) *xíxìr máh a-ala-á*
       small declar+past 3rd-fall-final
       'the small one fell'
(35) *buv xíxìr, e-máh-á*
       child small, 2sg-declar-final
       'you are a **small child**
(36) *gakorá-hr, zàno máh-á*
       hunt-nominalizer, my=brother declar-final
       'my brother is **hunter'**
(37) *zàno, gakorá-hr máh-á*
       my=brother, hunt-nominalizer declar-final
       'my **brother** is a hunter'
(38) *en, Xíko máh-á*
       you, Xíko declar-final
       '**you** are Xíko'

Such noun phrase fronting is common in Gavião. It is always accompanied by complementary signals. Between the fronted element and the rest of the clause there is an intonational break indicated by pause and by lack of morphophonemic change of consonants. Also the auxiliary of these structures occurs only in past tense form with a meaning that is probably without tense. None of these clauses may be extended further; the auxiliary is always the last item.

7 Repetition

In Gavião discourse there is repetition of sentences. A sentence may, for example, be repeated in order to add a particle or other constituent to it. Such repetitions do not seem to be corrections, but rather a means by which additions and slight changes are made. An example is given next: 40 differs from 39 only in that *i kábe ká* 'on the river Kábe' is deleted and *gólóá* 'a lot' and two particles are added to it.

(39) *Mán tára pí bó máh bolív-éhj abi aka i kábe ká-á kípo-á.*
       that=one on from connector 3sg+declar+past fish-pl kill+pl go
       river Kábe in-final hearsay-final
       'They went to kill fish on the Kábe River from the top of those (canoes).'

(40) *Mán tára pí bó máh bolív-éhj abi **góló̬á** aka kih èna-á kípo-á.*
      that=one on from connector 3sg+declar+past fish-pl kill+pl **alot**
      go frequent particle-final hearsay-final
      'They went to kill a lot of fish from the top of those (canoes).'

Such repetitions are problematic in that they depart from the general rules of information distribution. The only new constituent information in example 40 is *góló̬á,* but instead of being placed in first position after the subject, it follows some given information. The solution is this: in such repetitions there is no new ordering of information, but the new item is placed at the point where it could have been placed in the first occurrence of that sentence without any change of order. Thus it may be said that the two sentences together count as one unit of information.

8 Questions and answers

The information structure of a question and its answer departs from the general rules of information distribution. Concerning the question itself, the concept of more or less predictability of information is related not to the hearer but to the speaker. Gavião interrogative clauses illustrate this clearly, as seen in the examples below. In example 41 the interrogative marker is followed by a marked clause that has the predicate fronted before the subject. This kind of structure might be used, for example, when the speaker encounters the hearer on the trail, so that the subject and the auxiliary action of going are given information. This, of course, corresponds to the general rule that allows fronting only where the topic is given information. Question 42, for instance, can only be asked when it is predictable that the hearer is going to hunt, but the time is not predictable and therefore 'today' is fronted. Question 43, on the other hand, has an unmarked clause following the interrogative marker. This is the most common interrogative structure in that all information in the structure is considered to be unpredictable to the speaker. In questions like 41 and 42 the given information may also be left out, as 44 to 46 illustrate.

(41) *té **gakorá** e-zá-ka-á*
      interr **hunt** 2sg-non-declar+ present-go-final
      'are you going to **hunt?**'
(42) *té **àdjùr** e-zá-ka gakorá-á*
      interr **today** 2sg-nondeclar+ present-go hunt-final
      'are you going to hunt **today?**'

(43) *té e-zá-ka gakorá àdjùr-á*
      interr 2sg-nondeclar+present-go hunt today-final
      'are you going to hunt today?'
(44) *té máter ále-á*
      interr other=day future-final
      'tomorrow?'
(45) *té ă*
      interr this
      'this one?'
(46) *té póhj-á*
      interr big-final
      'is it big?'

Concerning the answer to a question, the following regularity can be observed: the information structure of the answer can be a repetition of the question structure, with no reordering of its elements, as the following illustrates. In example 48 there is a double answer to question 47; that is, the first 'yes' constitutes a clause by itself, and the second 'yes' occurs with other constituents. This is a common practice in Gavião.

(47) *Té tá-sá-volo a-neva kár-ále-á*
      interr 3pl-nondeclar-come 3rd+reflexive-eat yet-fut-final
      'Are they still coming to eat?'
(48) *Até-á, até tá-máa-volo a-neva kár-ále-á*
      yes-final, yes 3pl- declar+present-come 3rd+reflexive-eat yet-fut-final
      'Yes, they are still coming to eat.'

This kind of repetition in relation to questions is not quite identical with what was said about repetition in section 7. To ask a question is not normally to transmit information to the hearer, except insofar as it tells him what kind of information he is being requested to give. The information in questions and in their answers is basically the same, and they count as one unit. We may therefore define an **interrogative unit** of information as consisting of a question with its answer, and having the function of conveying information from the answerer to the questioner. Two directions are involved. In the question, the direction is toward the answerer; however, the main direction in which information moves is back toward the questioner. This may be illustrated as follows:

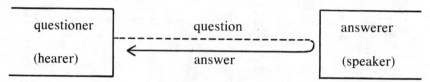

In the definition of predictability of information in section 4 the information structure of questions corresponds with predictability as seen by the questioner. That definition seems opposed to the general concept of cohesion since the questioner is usually viewed as the speaker, and cohesion is supposed to be concerned with predictability to the hearer only. Nevertheless, the definition is correct and according to general concept if, as shown above, the questioner is viewed as the ultimate hearer, the one who receives the information, even though he is the first that utters it.[13]

9 Information structure and intonation

In Gavião discourse two cohesive features are signaled by intonation. The first of these features is information blocking, which means that the information of an utterance is segmented into blocks. These blocks are bounded principally by pauses. Normally, the boundaries of blocks correspond with phrase boundaries, though not always. Whether the blocks are short or long (several constituents or a whole clause) depends on the rate at which information is introduced.

Blocking is used by a speaker to facilitate his hearer's comprehension of the content of the communication. At points where much new information is introduced, as is frequently the case at the beginning of a text, the information blocks are short and, in addition, they are frequently given at slower speed. On the contrary, sentences with little or no new information are uttered in long blocks and rapidly.

The other feature of intonation observed in Gavião discourse is not fully understood. It is intonational salience (stress, vowel length, and late release of stops) at some points, which may be termed points of prominence, though it is not known what kind of semantic prominence underlies them. The frequency of these points and the degree of salience varies from one text to another and surely has to do with the speaker's condition, that is, for example, how excited he is about the information he is conveying or how interesting he wants to make it for the hearer.

Most frequently points of prominence coincide with new information and thus supplement constituent ordering, which is the more general signal. The following examples are the first sentences of a text. (Diagonal lines indicate information blocking and underlining shows points of prominence.)

(49) *Baráj* maâ padére-éhj máh-á kípo-á abój-éhj.
Baráj take person-pl declar+past-final hearsay-final friend-pl
'People took Baráj away, my friends.'
(50) *Zerebãj-éhj* máh èna / maâ-á kípo-á.
spirit=like=person-pl declar+past particle / 3sg+take-final
hearsay-final
'The witches took him away.'
(51) *A-djaō sá-káhr* / táṁáh maâ èna kípo-á.
3rd=reflexive-play 3sg-dependent+simultaneous 3pl-declar+past
3sg+take particle hearsay-final
'While he was playing they took him away.'
(52) *Gonbe ádúr ká máh èna* / djigá **pâgâ-á.**
hut near in declar+past particle hunting=shelter make+pl-final
'He was near the hut making hunting shelters.'

Notes

1 The Gavião language has been classified by Aryon Dall'igna Rodrigues (1966) as
belonging to the Mondé family of the Tupi stock. Other languages of the Mondé
family are Mondé, Cinta Larga, Suruí, and Arara or Urukú.

Harald Schultz (1955) gives the name Digüt to the Gavião tribe and language, but
he was mistaken because that was only one of the names of his informant. The
Gavião number approximately 120 Indians living in various small villages around the
Pôsto Indigena Igarapé Lourdes, on the Igarapé Lourdes, affluent of the Machado
or Jiparaná River in the Federal Territory of Rondônia, Brazil. All Gavião speak
their mother tongue and about 15% are bilingual in Portuguese. They are
semiacculturated. The author is grateful to the National Indian Foundation
(Fundação Nacional do Indio) of the Brazilian Ministry of the Interior for giving
authorization to live among the Gavião since 1966 as a member of New Tribes
Mission of Brazil.

The data analyzed here were recorded on tape through the last eight years, but
transcribed principally during 1976. This paper was written at a linguistic workshop
held in Porto Velho by the Summer Institute of Linguistics. The author wishes to
thank Dr. Joseph E. Grimes of Cornell University and the Summer Institute of
Linguistics, who directed the workshop and gave theoretical and editorial
orientation during the preparation of this paper. Thanks are due also to the Summer
Institute of Linguistics for linguistic help and for making it possible for the author to
take part in the workshop. Also the author is indebted to his Gavião language
helper, Chambete B. Barros, with whom the data were checked.

Examples in this paper are written in ordinary Gavião orthography. The
consonants are **p, b, m, v** [ƀ], **t, d, n, r, s** [ts], **z** [dz], **l, x** [tṣ], **dj** [dẓ], **j** [ẓ], **k,** and
g. ([tṣ], [dẓ] and [ẓ] have laminal alveolar friction, articulated with the lamina of the
tongue, as opposed to [ts] and [dz], which are apical). Vowels are **i, e, a, o,** and **u**[ɨ].
Length of vowels is signaled by **h** after them. Tones are symbolized in combination
with the nasalization of vowels: ´ high oral, ` rising oral, ^ high nasalized, ˇ rising
nasalized, ‾ low nasalized, and no symbol for low oral.

2 Embedded clauses function as constituents of noun phrases and dependent clauses
function as constituents of the clause.

3 There are still other structures that function as noun phrases. Demonstratives are particles that occur with nominal phrases or that substitute for them, as in *ă kala màga* (this want I) 'I want this'. Numerals rarely occur with other nominals, but frequently substitute for them, as in *pàhdjakúv kala màga* (two want I) 'I want two'. Also structures such as *Zàno sevabá* 'My brother Sevabá' and *talóh pí xi* (ground from gruel) 'the gruel of the gourd' constitute nominal phrases. In constructions like 'I want to eat,' the verb 'eat' is always nominalized and functions as a regular object, but there are a few verbs that have as objects verbs without explicit nominalization, as in the clause below (this problem has not been solved satisfactorily yet): *gakorá matē màga* (hunt command 1sg+declar+present) 'I command you to hunt'.

4 A more detailed analysis might show that the meaning is 'got rid of his dreams by letting himself fall', in which case the falling is an adjunct predicate stating the instrument of the main verb phrase. Such adjunct predicates cannot be considered as separate clauses because they may be moved to various positions in the clause. Adjunct predicates are related to secondary sentences, which occur independently as sentences, but are semantically bound to the preceding sentence by stating information that could also be stated in adjunct form. Some kinds of information can thus be given in three different forms: as true adjuncts, adjunct predicates, or secondary sentences.

5 **Predication** refers to the combination of all clause constituents while **predicate** refers to the verb phrase, which consists of verb and object.

6 *mán* also relates embedded relative clauses to their slot in the noun phrase by representing it in that slot, though the actual clause directly precedes the demonstrative. This is similar to English clefting, as in **it is John who saw it** where the subject is represented by the embedded clause **it is John** and also by **who**. Both Gavião and English have this double representation. *méne* functions equally, but relates complement clauses to their slots in noun phrases.

7 As connectors no difference in meaning has come to light so far between the particles *tér* and *bó*. However, in other contexts *tér* has the meaning 'according to expectation' and *bó* has the meaning 'contrary to expectation'.

8 Some Gavião texts show also topicalization of whole discourses, paragraphs, and subsidiary paragraphs.

9 The boldfaced words in the gloss of examples 16-19 are where the intonational prominence comes in the corresponding English information structure.

10 One has to be careful in using initial sentences for evidence of semantic structure because they might prove to constitute special cases. What is shown in these examples, therefore, is not their contrast with other data in the same text, but rather how one differs from the other between texts.

11 In some cases it is doubtful whether items should be classified as connectives or as a fronted new information, e.g., *è ká* 'there', which is not always marked by a connector. It occurs as adjunct in other than initial position.

12 This conclusion differs from Gundel's work on staging (1974), which emphasizes the possibility of implicit topics that are distinct from subjects.

13 This is probably what the information structure of questions in English and other European languages is like. A quick observation seems to indicate two main facts. The first is that the placement of the information center (displacement in pitch) in questions shows that the questioner considers any information he himself cannot predict as being new. The second is that the information center of question and answer tends to fall on the same item.

References

Grimes, Joseph E. 1975. *The Thread of Discourse*. The Hague: Mouton.

Gundel, Jeanette. 1974. "The Role of Topic and Comment in Linguistic Theory." Ph.D. dissertation: University of Texas.

Halliday, M.A.K. and Ruqaiya Hasan. 1976. *Cohesion in English*. London: Longman.

Mel'chuk, I.A. 1967. "Ordre des Mots en Synthèse Automatique des Textes Russes." T.A. Informations 1:56-84.

Rodrigues, Aryon Dall'igna. 1966. "Classificaão da Língua dos Cinta Larga." *Revista de Antropología* 14:27-30.

Schultz, Harald. 1955. "Vocábulos Urukú e Digüt." *Journal de la Société des Américanistes* 44:81-97.

Focus and Topic in Xavante

Eunice Burgess

Information structure in Xavante differentiates new and given, and primary and secondary information. New primary information normally occurs preceding the predicate of a clause, and new secondary information and given information, within the predicate. The distribution of information in a multiple-clause sentence, and to some extent in a paragraph, parallels that of a single independent clause. Topic structure is established primarily by referential criteria. A topic is usually part of the given information in a clause, but it may be part of the new information in the opening clause of a discourse or paragraph. Marked topics are signalled grammatically; unmarked topics are not.

In this paper are described the information structure of Xavante[1] clauses, sentences, and paragraphs within the context of a discourse, the topical structure where it differs from information structure, and the surface structure as it affects, or is affected by, the information and topical structure.

The information structure differentiates new from given information, and primary from secondary information. The unmarked position for new information in a clause is the initial position. This affects the analysis of topical structure in that topic cannot be defined as the initial item of a clause if part of the definition of topic is that a topic is given information and anaphoric in reference to which new information is attached by a comment (Gundel 1974).

The topical structure involves the devices of fronting, tagging, pseudoclefting, topic interrogative, inflection, and the use of special pronouns.

The description of information and topical structure revolves principally around three relevant positions in the surface structure:

preceding, following, or embedded within the nuclear part of each level—that is, the predicate complex in the clause, the main clause in the sentence, and the body of the paragraph.

Many Xavante narratives are told in the form of an imaginary dialogue in which there are many repartee sequences which have some characteristics not found in monologue. Both styles are included in the description of the various kinds of structure.

1 Surface structure

1.1 Clause. Distribution of information and topicalization features are limited by certain constraints in the surface structure of clauses.

The grammatical subject is always the semantic agent in active clauses and the patient in stative clauses. This means that no other constituent can be subjectivized, there being no passivizing mechanism in the language.

The subject may be identified by a noun phrase. It is also identified by free person-aspect proclitics in all forms of transitive clauses, and in declarative active forms of intransitive clauses. In other forms of intransitive clauses, the subject is identified by person prefixes on the verb. The person-aspect proclitics and the person prefixes occur whether or not the subject is also identified by a noun phrase.

In transitive clauses the object may be identified by a noun phrase. If not, it is identified by a person prefix on the verb. Person and number suffixes on the verb agree with the subject of intransitive clauses, and with both subject and object of transitive clauses.

When both subject and object are identified by noun phrases, there is no overt distinction as to which is which either by affixation or by word order. If one noun phrase refers to an animate object and another to an inanimate, the animate one is usually the subject, and the inanimate one the object. If both are animate, or both inanimate, only context can disambiguate them. Their order relative to each other is determined by information or topical structure and not by surface structure.

The verb is most frequently the final element in a clause, although certain items of both new and given primary information may occur after the verb. Such items are usually marked off intonationally as separate information units. It is rare to find the verb as the first constituent of the clause unless it is the only constituent.

A predicate complex is the core of the clause. It is that part of the clause that begins with person-aspect proclitics and ends with the verb. The verb includes person prefixes and may have postposed modifiers together with person-number and modal suffixes. In the following examples the clause core is boldfaced: *Dzêmi-hãtê dza wê tsô ãwitsi*

(Jim-specifier **he will here them-for it-bring**) 'Jim will bring it (the plane) here for them'; *Toptö wahi* **matê** *titsa* (Toptö snake **it her-bit**) 'a snake bit Toptö'; i î-to *tse-di*, (her-eye **painful-is**) 'her eye is painful'; *da-tsipêtsê-u tê dza atsamrõ, hu'u-u* (people-dance-to **they will fly,** jaguar-to) they will fly to the dance, to the jaguar dance'.

1.2 Sentence. A sentence may consist of a single independent clause or a main clause plus one to three subordinate clauses. One or two subordinate clauses may precede the main clause, and one may either be embedded in or follow the main clause. The subordinating enclitic is usually last in the clause. The rhetorical relationships expressed by subordination are temporal succession, conditional, causal, and complement: *töibö ma tsiwi 'rê-pa ihö-rata-***wamhã***, ihö-teptsi tê oto tsiwi rom-dza'ra* (complete they collective plant-finish one-old **-when,** one-new they then collective thing-heap up) 'when they finished planting the old one (field), they then clear the new one'; *ĩ-pê'ēdze-tê-tsi tso ĩ-mori-***da*** *wa ta-ma tiña* (I-sad-**if**-only her-for I-go-**that** I her-to say) 'I said to her that I would go for her only if I were sad'; *ĩ-to datê ta-ma 'wa'ri-dâ, tê dza ti-wararê, hödze-ahâ-***wa*** (her-eye someone her-for operate-in order to, she future she-fly, pain-much-**because**) 'she will fly in order for someone to operate on her eye because it is very painful'.

2 Information structure

Information focus in a clause is that part that is new or informative. It is presented by the speaker to the hearer as not being recoverable from the verbal or situational context, or it is presented as new in relation to a particular predicate.

In Xavante there are two kinds of new information, primary and secondary. **Primary** information is that which the speaker identifies as essential to the development of the narrative. **Secondary** information is supplied by the speaker as explanation or background. It is information that helps the hearer understand the narrative, without being itself a crucial part of it.

Information that is not new is **given** information, which is recoverable from the verbal or situational context. Given information does not develop the narrative further but rather it provides a framework for handling new information.

2.1 Information structure in the clause. New primary information normally occurs before the predicate in a clause: *aro tê tsub-dza'ra* (**rice** they winnow-plural) 'they are winnowing rice'; *tsetsta-***na*** *ma ama aimatsitsi-dzahure* (**Friday-on** they there stay-both) 'they both stayed there on Friday'; *Batowi-ama tê ñamra* (**Batovi-at** he live) 'he lives at Batovi'. New secondary information normally occurs within the predicate: *dzahadu tê wêdêdzadadzöri tsada 'maña* (still they **coffin** him-for make) They are still making a coffin for him'. In the preceding example, the new secondary information was given to explain why a dead child was not yet buried.

In the same narrative, new secondary information tells as background what happened before the child died: *taha-dzô tê **mararo** ama îwa'redze 'mapra* (him-for she **at dawn** there **syringe** take), 'she took a shot there at dawn for him'.

New secondary information may also occur in a relative clause embedded within another clause constituent: *îi-hitebre tê îi-ma î-tsomrina wa uptsō* (**my-brother** he **me-to** that-give-with I wash) 'I wash with (the soap) which my brother gave me'; *a-tsihudu tsipedze têtê ama î-'öri dza wê öri* (**your-grandson knife he there that-take** future here bring) 'bring here the knife which your grandson took there'.

Given information normally occurs within the predicate: *te dza oto ōmemhā apetse* (they future soon **there** dance) 'they will soon dance there'; *tê natsi da-'rata ti-ñotō-dza'ra* (they repeatedly **them-by** they-sleep-plural) 'they slept near them'.

When all, or most of, the information is new, as in the opening clause of a discourse or paragraph, there may be more than one item of new information before the predicate, in which case their order in relation to one another is determined by which is the topic of the higher level unit. This topic precedes other new information. In the next example *Roberto* and *Cuiaba-u* both precede the predicate because they are both informationally new and primary. *Roberto*, the topic of the paragraph of which this is the first clause, comes first: **Roberto Cuiaba-u** *ma tô mo* (**Robert Cuiaba-to** he punctiliar go) 'Robert has gone to Cuiabá'. Similarly in *Toptö wahi matê titsa* (**Toptö snake** it her-bite) 'a snake bit Toptö', *Toptö* is the topic of the discourse.

When all the information in a clause is given information, such a clause is usually the final summary of a paragraph. For example, a paragraph beginning with *Eunice-nori-hā tê dza oto Batowi-u atsamrō* 'Eunice and another are flying to Batovi', which is developed by adding information as to companion, purpose, means of travel, and time of travel, ends with *tê dza atsamrō-dzahure* (they future fly-both) 'they will both fly', in which all information is given information.

Even though all the information in the final summary of a paragraph is given, if it is largely a repetition of the preceding clause, the word order of the first clause may be maintained in the repeated clause, in which case given information may occur before the predicate: *ti-mamau tê dza ama mo* (**her-father-to** (new) she future there go) 'she will go to her father', followed by *ti-mama-u tê dza ama ti-morirê, tahā* (**her-**

father-to she future there she-go, she) 'she will go to her father, she (will)'.

When a clause of given information is not final in a paragraph, it is reintroducing a topic or situation already mentioned but from which the narrator has digressed, and now wishes to return. In the next example the narrator has been talking about Nharinha flying, digresses into talking about Dominga staying, and then returns to Nharinha flying: *ê Nharinha tê dza oto wara* 'Is Nharinha going to fly?'; *tê dza oto wara* 'she is going to fly'; *Domingare-hã bete* 'what about Dominga then?' . . . (here follows the digression about Dominga) *Nharinha-tsi te dza wara* 'just Nharinha will fly'. In the last clause of this example *Nharinha* is given information but is reintroduced preceding the predicate as though it were new information. A further example of given information preceding the predicate after a digression is: *ê momo tê ai-mo* 'where are you going?'; *õwa, Bakairi-u wa mo* 'over there, to the Bakairi I am going'; *ê tihi-dzô* 'what for?'; *Bakairi ma 'matörö* 'a Bakairi has died'. Then follows a digression on whether it was an adult or child who died, and then: *ê ta-momo tê ai'aba'rei-wa'wa* (interrogative **that-where** you go-plural) 'is that where you went?'

Given information may also precede the predicate when it is linking secondary new information to preceding primary information: *ê ma tô apito tsabu* 'did the official visit him (the dead child)?'; *ma tô tsabu* 'she visited him'; *taha-dzô tê marare ama ïwa'redze 'mapra* (**him-for** she dawn there syringe take) 'she took a shot there for him at dawn'.

Both new and given information may follow the predicate. New information in this position may be added to new information preceding the predicate, as in **upa-dzama** *dza têtê dzuri,* **aro-dzama** (**manioc-also** future they plant, **rice-also**) 'they will plant manioc too, and rice'. Or it may make the new information preceding the predicate more specific, as in **da-tsipese-u** *tê dza atsamrõ,* **hu'u-u** (**people-dance-to** they future fly, **jaguar-to**) 'they will fly to the dance, the jaguar dance'. If the clause is in answer to a question, additional new information may follow the predicate, as in: *ê Nharinha tê dza oto wara* 'is Nharinha going to fly?', *tê dza oto wara* **Cuiaba-u, Nenehedzama** (she future soon fly, **Cuiabá-to, Nene-also**) 'she is going to fly, to Cuiabá, with Nene'; and in *ê mama-õ di* 'hasn't he a father?', *madzedi, ï-mama tsa'rêtse-õdi,* **ï-natsi** (no, his-father known-not, **his-mother-only**) 'no, his father is not known, only his mother'.

Given information may be highlighted by being placed after the predicate in a noun phrase that identifies an anaphoric reference earlier in the clause: *apö awaru-na wê tsitsa'rê* 'they came back by horse', *marare ma aihutu* 'they arrived at dawn'; *Negurê têtê tso tsimrõ,* **awaru-hã** (Nego he them-for them-led, **horses-that-is**) 'Nego led them for them, the horses, that is'. Or it may repeat for emphasis the new information preceding the predicate, as in *wa-wana ma tô ti-wawa-tsahöri-dza'ra*, *wa-wana* (**we-before** they completive they-cry-stop-plural, **we-before**) 'before we (got there) they stopped crying, before we (got there)'.

Given information may be deleted when it is in response to a content question. The information requested is supplied, and the rest of the clause is deleted: *ê 'wa ma āwitsi* (interrogative who he bring) 'whom did he bring?', *Donaudo* **'Donald'**. In a sequential information question, all given information except the question word may be deleted: *Uritiru-u tê dza 're tsamrā* (Uritiru-at he future continuative live) 'he is going to live at Uritiru', *ê tiha-dzô* (interrogative **what-for**) 'what for?'

The verb of a clause may be new or given information, but there is no grammatical difference in either case. When it is given, it is a repetition or a synonym of a verb that has already been used to describe the same situation: *ubure dza têtê a'â rom-dzuri* (everything future they there thing-**plant**) 'they will plant everything', *upa-dzama dza têtê dzuri, aro-dzama* (manioc-also future they **plant**, rice-also) 'they will plant manioc too, and rice'; *töibö ma tsiwi 're -pa ihâ'rata-wamhā* (complete they collective **plant**-finish old-field-when) 'when they finished planting the old field . . .'.

2.2 Information structure in the sentence. When a reason, condition, statement of purpose, or temporal succession is new primary information, it is encoded in a subordinate clause that precedes the main clause whether the main clause contains new information or only given information. The subordinate clause may contain some given information as well as new, but the rhetorical relationship to the information in the main clause is new: *têtê 'ri-pari-ptsi, tê dza oto mo* (**he build-finish,** he future then go) 'when he has finished building, he will go', *datê po'o-da, tê ti-wararê ama* (**someone operate-purpose,** he he-fly there) 'he flew there for someone to operate (on him)', *hödze-tê, tê dza ti-wararê* (painful-**because,** she future she-fly) 'she will fly because she is ill'.

When a subordinate clause contains new secondary information, it occurs within the main clause: *ta-dza tê ī-mama ī-'rata-ma têtê tso rop'rui-wa ī-'rada tsô mo* (that-why she, **her-father her-grandmother-to he her-for order-because,** her-grandmother her-for go) 'that's why, because her father told her to, her grandmother went for her'.

When a multiple-clause sentence is the final summary of a paragraph and, therefore, is all given information, a subordinate clause may precede the main clause paralleling the information distribution of a single independent clause (see 2.1). A paragraph which says that

'Nharinha is going to Cuiabá to have an operation on her eye which is painful' ends with the summary sentence: *hödze-tê, tê dza ti-warare, datê ta-ma 'wa'ri-da* (**painful-because,** she future she-fly, **someone her-for operate-purpose**) 'because it is painful, she will fly, for someone to operate on it'.

A subordinate clause containing only given information can also precede the main clause when it is acting as a link between paragraphs: *töibö ma tsiwi 're-pa, ïhö-'rata-wamhã, ïhö-tep-tsi tê oto tsiwi rom-dza'ra* (**complete they collective plant-finish** one-old-when one-new they then collective heap up-plural) 'when they finished planting the old (field), then they cleared the new one'.

A subordinate clause may follow the main clause when it is repeating, or making more specific, the information in a subordinate clause preceding the main clause, or one of the constituents of the main clause: *wa-pê'ēdze-ñere, wa dza da-dzo mapari-dza'rani, atsa wa-ama da-pê'ēdze-õ-ñere* (we-sad-since, we future them-for watch-plural, **reciprocal us-for they-sad-not-even=though**) 'since we are sad, we will watch for them, even though they are not sad for us in return'; *romhuri-dzo ma ta-watobro-ni apito-buru-u, wêdê têtê pahöri-mono-da* (work-for they they-leave-plural postman's-field-to, **trees they cut-purpose**) 'they left for work, to the postman's field, to cut down the trees'.

New information may be included in the answer to a yes/no question in a subordinate clause following the main clause: *ê ta-momo tê ai'aba'rei-wa'wa* 'is that where you are going?'; *ïhe, wa dza ama mo, tê tsabu-da* (yes, I future there go, *I him-see-to*) 'yes, I am going there to see him'.

If the information in a subordinate clause is in answer to a question for information, the main clause in the answer may be deleted: *Uritiru tê dza 're tsamrã* 'he is going to live at Uritiru'; *ê tiha-dzô* 'what for?'; *powawē têtê 'rê 'madö'ö-mono-da* (cattle he continuative watch-to) 'in order to look after the cattle'.

2.3 Information structure in the paragraph. The first sentence in a paragraph usually contains several items of new information. Further new information is added in the body of the paragraph, often one item per clause. The final sentence in a paragraph is often a summary one containing only given information. A clause containing parenthetical background information, i.e., new secondary information, may occur within the body of a paragraph. It is spoken with low level intonation which is in contrast to the intonation of the rest of the paragraph. The following example of a paragraph shows most of these features: *Eunitsi-nori-hã tê dza oto Batowi-u atsamrõ.* 'Eunice and another are going to fly to Batovi.' *ê 'wai-me* 'who with?' *Alitsi-hi-me* 'with Alice' *tê dza oto atsamrõ-dzahure* 'they will both fly' *Erena tê tsabu-dzahure-da, Erena-ha-u* 'to see Helen, to Helen's' *da-tsipetse-u tê dza atsamrõ, hu'u-u* 'they will fly to the dance, the jaguar dance' *(tê dza oto õmemhã apetse)* (parenthetical: 'they (the Xavante) will dance there') *hu têtê 'madö'ö-dzahure-da tê dza atsamrõ-dzahure* 'to watch the jaguar dance they will both fly' . . . *tê dza-atsamrõ-dzahure* 'they will both fly'.

2.4 General observations. A comparison of the information structure of the clause with that of the sentence reveals strong parallel features. As the information units in the clause are to the predicate, so those in subordinate clauses are to the main clause. To a lesser degree the paragraph also has some parallel features, the most notable being the parenthetical secondary information within the body of the paragraph and the greater volume of new information occurring at or near the beginning of the paragraph.

A comparison of the information structure of Xavante with that of English, as presented by Bayless and Johnson, shows some similarities and some differences. Their principle 1, "syntactic new information in one clause becomes syntactic old information for subsequent clauses," is only partially valid for Xavante. In summary final clauses of paragraphs, where all information is now old, the syntactic order of the preceding clause may be retained. The primary function of such a clause, however, seems to be not informative, but rather a signal that the speaker is concluding one topic and about to introduce another in the next clause. Where new information has followed the predicate in one clause, it may be put into the "proper" syntactic position for new information in the succeeding clause: *ê 'wa dza wê tsô äwitsi* 'who will bring it (the plane) here for them?'; **Dzemi-hã** 'Jim'; **Dzemi-hã** *tê dza wê tsô äwitsi,* **romhuriduridzep-amo-na** 'Jim will bring it here for them, **next Monday**'; **romhuriduridzep-amo-na** *tê dza wê tsô äwitsi* '**next Monday** he will bring it here for them'.

Their principle 2, "syntactic old information generally precedes syntactic new in the same clause," is not valid for Xavante. The reverse order is the case if the new information is primary. Both Halliday (1967) and Daneš (1974) propose a similar principle.

Their principle 3, "old information is generally found in subject position," is only partially valid for Xavante, because Xavante surface structure restricts the subject to being the agent of active clauses and the patient of stative clauses. If a series of active clauses has the same agent or a series of stative clauses the same patient, then the subject of the noninitial clauses is old information and is identified only by the obligatory person-aspect proclitics in the clause. If old information is other than the agent or the patient, then the subject may be new information and be identified by a noun phrase preceding the predicate complex. The surface constraints on what may be subject invalidate for Xavante their principle that "one function of surface-rearrangement rules (in English discourse) is to place old information, or a dummy NP instead of old information, in subject position."

Their principle 4, "the notions of old and new information operate at different structural levels," is valid for Xavante. In the next example *romhuri-u* and *romhuri-dzô* are postpositional phrases where the object in the second instance is old information, and only the postposition is new. *buru-u* and *apito-buru-u* have the same postposition *-u* but the object of the postposition is modified in the second instance by the possessor *apito*, which is new information: **Buru-u** *ma tô ta-dzömoridza'ra-ni*, **romhuri-u. Romhuri-dzô** *ma ta-watobro-ni*, **apito-buru-u.** (eld-to they punctiliar they-travel-plural, **work to. work-for** they they-leave-plural, **postman's-**eld to) 'They went to the field, to the work. They left for the work, to the postman's field.' The above examples show that part of a phrase may be new information and the rest of it old. In other words, new information does not have to be an entire constituent at clause level.

3 Topical structure

The question I wish to answer in this section is whether or not Xavante has a topic-comment structure for clauses that is different from the information structure already described.

The Prague school in their work on functional sentence perspective (Daneš 1974) mention three concepts that have to do with the topical structure of clauses, viz., given and new information, theme and rheme, and communicative dynamism. They affirm that known information is distinguished from theme because there exist instances where theme does not convey known information, although they acknowledge that such cases are the minority and are considered as marked themes. They then proceed to ignore the difference between known information and theme. They describe theme as the element of the sentence (usually the opening one) that links the utterance with the context and the situation; they also say that the theme carries the lowest degree of communicative dynamism in a clause.

Halliday (1967) divides the information structure of a clause into information, i.e., given and new; thematization, i.e., the sequence of elements; and identification, i.e., the patterns of clause structure. He defines theme as the first element in a clause or the point of departure for the clause as a message, and distinguishes marked themes from unmarked. Theme is distinguished from old information in that the former is what is being talked about now, while the latter is what was being talked about before. Gundel (1974), using the terms "topic" and "comment," says the topic is the element that names what the speech act is about. It is not necessarily the leftmost element or leftmost noun phrase in a clause, although this is probably its most common position. She further says that topic is always associated with given information and is necessarily a nonfocal element. She equates topical structure with information structure.

Gundel associates such syntactic devices as left dislocation, right dislocation, clefting, and pseudoclefting with the topic-comment structure of a clause. Bayless and Johnson associate the same devices with the information structure. Halliday associates them with identification, which is one part of total theme structure separate from considerations of new and given information and of theme and rheme.

In Xavante, the options in relation to order of constituents in a clause seem to be largely determined by information structure as has already been described. That structure involves not only new versus given information, however, but also primary versus secondary information. When given information occurs before a predicate complex, this could be called a case of fronting. Such fronting on the clause level usually functions where secondary new information has displaced given information, which then becomes the link between the secondary information and the preceding context. On sentence level, a subordinate clause that is given information may be fronted before the main clause both when the subordinate clause is the link between paragraphs and when the main clause introduces new information as the topic of a new paragraph. With interrogative clauses, there are some instances of fronting that seem to be genuine instances of marked topicalization, which occur as initial sentences of a discourse or paragraph: *pi'ō-nori-hã, ê momo tê ai'aba're* (**woman-plural** interrogative where they go) 'the women, where are they going?' *Donaudu, ê mame tê ñamra* (**Donald,** interrogative where he live) 'Donald, where does he live?' *buru-ama höiwahö tsetsta-na ĩ-tsipe, ê tiha ma tê bete āwitsi* (eld-at afternoon Friday-on who-arrive, interrogative what they then bring) 'the ones who arrived at the field on Friday afternoon, what did they bring?' The topic, which may be either new or given information, is fronted before the interrogative marker *ê*, which is normally the first element of an interrogative clause. By fronting, the topic is established, and then the question asked about it. The same sort of device is also used for rhetorical questions whose function is to intensify the quality of a descriptive. First, the topic is established and then it is described: *udzö-hã barana-hã, ê ĩ-ro'o-baihöirê* (**light night,** interrogative which-burn-many) 'lights at night, wow! are there ever a lot!'; *tiha u'ētē-'rarê, ê ĩ-tse-ōrê* (**thing cake-small,** interrogative that-delicious-not) 'the small cake thing, boy!, is that ever good!'

There are also some instances of tagging or right dislocation which seem to be instances of marked topicalization: *Negurê têtê tso tsimrō, awaru-hã* (Nego he them-for them-led, **horses-that=is**) 'Nego took them for them, the horses that is'; *ōhōta tê wê rop madö, ī-têdê-'wa-hã* (over there, he here look, **its-owner-that-is**) 'from over there he is looking this way, the owner that is'; *têtê 'ri-pari-ptsi, tê dza ama mo, Tsiriwaruwē-hã* (he build-finish-when, he future there go, **Tsiriwaruwē-that=is**) 'When he has finished building, he will go, Tsiriwaruwē, that is'. When tagging has a topicalizing function, it seems to be clarifying what is the topic, rather than singling out the topic to highlight it. In some instances two constituents are dislocated to the right: *dzahadu têtê tsada 'ri-pari-dza'ra-ōdi, Bakairi-hã, ī-tsa'wari-dzeb-da-hã* (incomplete they it-for it-build-finish-plural-negative, **Bakairi that is, its-empty-place-for-that=is**) 'they still haven't finished building it for it, the Bakairis that is, its storage place that is'. In the preceding example in the main part of the clause, there are three anaphoric references—to the agent (the Bakairis), to the beneficiary (the rice crop), and to the goal (the storage place). Only two of these are singled out following the predicate. The first of them, the Bakairis, seem to be topicalized. They have been the topic of a previous but not immediately preceding clause, and are now being reinstated as topic. The second element, the storage place, is new information but not topic. In other words, not all right dislocation has to do with topic structure. Given information is topicalized, and new information is not. In the next example, 'Nharinha' is old information, and 'by truck' is new. *Ī-mrōre-hã bete?* 'What about his wife?' *Cuiaba-u tê wara, Ñariñarê-hã, wedewara-nã* (Cuiabá-to she rode, **Nharinha-that=is**, truck-by) 'She went to Cuiabá, Nharinha that is, by truck'.

Another device for marked topicalization in Xavante is the use of the topic interrogative *bete* 'what about'. It is used when the speaker in dialogue wants to know something about a new topic that has come to his mind because of its situational association with the previous topic: *Domingare-hã bete* 'What about Dominga?' *Ī-mrō-hã bete* 'What about her husband?'

Pseudoclefting also occurs occasionally as a marked topic device. By this device a clause is made into an equative construction in which the comment occurs first followed by the the topic in the form of a relative clause, as in: *barana ī-dzömori-dze-hã* (night that-travel-time-that=is) 'the time that they traveled was at night'; *taha-tsi ī-'matsi-hã* (that=one-only which-full-that=is) 'that one only is the one which is full'; *buru-ama Tsabinohō-'rata ī-tsap-tsi, ī-tsa'wari-wawē hã* (field-at Sabino-near which-stand-only that-supply-big-that=is) 'the one which is at the field near Sabino's is the one with the big supply'. This use is similar to Halliday's identification structure. It is used with background or orientation information, rather than as part of the development of a narrative.

Another marked topic device is the use of free pronouns (as distinct from person-aspect proclitics in predicates). When this device occurs, the free pronoun is usually fronted or tagged: *wa-nori-hã,* *wa dza ama* *'wape-ni* (**we-group,** we future there it-carry) 'our group, we will carry it there'; *ti-mama-u tê dza ama ti-morirê ta-hã* (her-father-to she future there she-go, that-one) 'she will go to her father's, she will'; *tso tsai'uri, a-hã* (it-for climb, you) 'climb for it, you'.

The enclitic *-hã* is often used after a noun phrase when a constituent is topicalized in one of the marked ways already mentioned. This does not seem to be its only function, however; McLeod (1974b:71-73) describes its function in participant highlighting, marking change of agent, and as a device for building up suspense in a narrative.

The enclitic *-tsi* occurs with noun phrases that contrast with preceding topics. After a paragraph about Dominga, one text continues: *Ñariña -tsi tê dza wara* (Nharinha **-only** she future fly) 'only Nharinha will fly'.

Use of *-hã* or *-tsi* does not necessarily make a noun phrase topic of a clause; rather they serve to introduce elements that are part of the referential field of a succeeding clause. In the example in the preceding paragraph, the topic is still Dominga. It makes sense to assert that only Nharinha will fly in the context of talking about Dominga who stayed. In the next sentence, however, Nharinha is the topic. It makes sense to ask 'Why (will she fly)?' about Nharinha. The predicate complex has been deleted, but if it had been present, Nharinha would have been referred to by the person-aspect subject *tê* 'she': *ê tiha-dzo* (interrogative what-for) 'what for (will she fly)?'

In a clause in which all information is new, the first element is topic. In such clauses, the concept of identifying something and then saying something about it seems more relevant for establishing the topic than a question like 'About what does it make sense to make this assertion?' If the clause is intransitive, the subject is most likely to be the topic. If the clause is transitive, either subject or object may be topic, and their order relative to each other is determined by which is topic, the topic being the first element: *Litsi ma tê-dzada* (**Lici** she leg-burn) 'Lici burned her leg'; *Roberto Cuiaba-u matô mo* (**Robert** Cuiaba-to he go) 'Robert went to Cuiabá'; *Toptö wahi matê ti-tsa* (**Toptö** snake her-bite) 'a snake bit Toptö'. I disagree with Gundel when she says that no topic may be new information, and that in a sentence where all information is new, the topic is the temporal or local situation. This seems to me to fail in cases where the situation is not yet defined. I prefer to say that different criteria are needed for establishing the topic in sentences where all information is new than in other sentences.

In a clause that has an unmarked topic and where there is some given information, the topic is part of such information. Where there is more than one item of given information, there is no syntactic or morphological signal that singles out a single item as topic. If one considers such a clause in isolation and asks the question "About what does it make sense to make this assertion or ask this question?" it seems that any or all of the anaphoric referent could be topic. In context, however, reference is always to the referent most recently designated in the text as topic. To recognize that referent as the topic, therefore, does not break continuity with a previously established topic, even in the absence of a more explicit topic signal in the clause in question. How this operates can be seen by tracing the topic structure and referential field through the following short complete text.

In the following text each item of new information has a superscript number, and each succeeding anaphoric reference to that item has the same number. Where a reference has been elided, so that it is recognized by the absence of any overt signal, the number is placed in the position where the overt signal would occur.

1. *Toptö[1] wahi[2] matê[2] ti[1]-tsa.* (Toptö snake it her-bite) 'A snake bit Toptö.' 2. *Matêtê[2] [1]paihi[3]-dupto.* (it her-arm-swell) 'It arm-swelled her.' 3. *Nharinha[4] tê[4] [1]tso mo, têtê[4] [1]wa'ri-da ti[2]-wi.* (Nharinha she her-for go, she inject-for it-against) 'Nharinha went to her, to give her a shot against it.' 4. *Matê[4] [1]paihi[3]-watsitsi.* (she her-arm-tied) 'She tied her arm.' 5. *I[2]-tse matê[4] ti[2]-wi [1]ama tsõ'rã.* (its-poison she it-from her-at stop) 'She stopped its poison from spreading at her.' 6. *Mãdarê[5] têtê[1] i[5]-tsa'rare-dzo [1]mori-dza, matê[2] ti[1]-tsa.* (mango she which-pile up-for go-as, it her bite) 'As she was going for the mangoes she had piled up, it bit her.' 7. *I[1]-mama[6] tê[6] [1]ama ti[6]-wawa.* (her-father he her-at he-cry) 'Her father is crying over her.' 8. *Tê[6] [1]ama 're tsadari.* (he her-at continuative wail) 'He is wailing over her.'

In sentence 1, all the information is new. Both subject and object are nominal constituents and precede the predicate. In terms of information content, one would say that the text is about Toptö rather than the snake, and for that reason *Toptö* precedes *wahi* in the first clause and is established as topic. In sentence 2, there are two anaphoric references, the subject and the object, referring back to the snake and Toptö respectively. If it were asked, "About what does it make sense to make the assertion 'it arm-swelled her'?" the answer could equally well be either Toptö or the snake, unless one concluded that Toptö is topic by reason of having been topic of sentence 1. In sentence 3, a new participant, Nharinha, is introduced as subject of both the main and the subordinate clauses and there are anaphoric references to Toptö as referent in the main clause and as object in the subordinate clause, and to the snake as referent in the subordinate clause. In sentence 4, the anaphoric references are to Nharinha as subject and to Toptö as object. In sentence 5, there are references to Nharinha as subject, and to the snake and Toptö as referents. In sentence 6, there is reference to Toptö as subject of the relative clause and the subordinate clause, and as object of the main clause, and to the snake as subject of the main clause. In sentence 7, a new participant, 'her father', is introduced as subject by a kinship term which relates him to Toptö, and another reference to Toptö as referent. In sentence 8, there is reference to 'father' as subject and to Toptö as referent. Continuity of Toptö as referential topic is assumed throughout each sentence of the text since no other marked topic occurs.

To sum up this section, Xavante information structure and topical structure are largely but not completely overlapping. Topic is defined referentially rather than grammatically, although there are grammatical signals in the case of a marked topic. Two criteria are needed to establish an unmarked topic. In a clause containing only new information, the topic is the element that identifies an existing object about which the rest of the clause says something. In a clause containing given information, the topic is that element about which it makes sense to make an assertion or ask a question. Where there is ambiguity as to what the topic is, continuity of a previously established topic is assumed.

Notes

1 Xavante is a Gê language spoken by approximately two thousand people in northeastern Mato Grosso, Brazil. The data on which this paper is based were collected during various field trips between December 1958 and May 1962, made possible at that time under a contract between the Summer Institute ofLinguistics and the Museu Nacional of Rio de Janeiro, with permission to live on the Posto Indígena Simoés Lopes being granted by the then Serviço de Proteção aos Índios. I wish to thank my colleagues Ruth McLeod and Joan Hall for access to their data, and Joseph Grimes and Ivan Lowe, both of the Summer Institute of Linguistics, for their help, advice, and criticism.

Xavante has 10 consonants, 8 oral vowels, and 4 nasalized vowels. These phonemes are represented in the orthography used in this paper as follows: Consonants /p/ *p;* /t/ *t;* /ʔ/ *';* /b/ *b, m;* /d/ *d, n;* /dz/ *dz;* *ñ;* /ts/ *ts;* /w/ *w;* /r/ *r;* /h/ *h.* Vowels /i/ *i;* /e/ *ê;* /ɛ/ *e;* /ɨ/ *y;* /a/ *a;* /o/ *ô;* /ɔ/ *o;* /ə/ *ö;* /ĩ/ *ĩ;* /ɛ̃/ *ẽ;* /ã/ *ã;* /ɔ̃/ *õ.* For a fuller description of the phonological system see McLeod (1974a). Morphemes within a phrase are joined by hyphens in the examples.

References

Bayless, Richard L. and Linda K. Johnson. Ms. "A Function of Surface
    Rearrangement Rules in English Discourse: Old and New Information."
    University of Michigan.
Daneš, František. 1974. "FSP and the Organization of the Text." In *Papers on
    Functional Sentence Perspective*, ed. by F. Daneš. Janua Linguarum,
    Ser. Minor 147. The Hague: Mouton.
Gundel, Jeanette. 1974. "The Role of Topic and Comment in Linguistic
    Theory." Ph.D. dissertation: University of Texas.
Grimes, Joseph R. 1975. *The Thread of Discourse*. The Hague: Mouton.
Hale, Austin and David Watters, eds. 1973. *Clause, Sentence, and Discourse
    Patterns in Selected Languages of Nepal: Part 2, Clause.* Summer
    Institute of Linguistics Publication 40. Norman, Oklahoma: SILUO.
Halliday, M.A.K. 1967. "Notes on Transitivity and Theme in English, Part 2."
    Journal of Linguistics 3:199-244.
Levinsohn, Stephen H. 1975. "Functional Sentence Perspective in Inga."
    Journal of Linguistics 11:13-37.
McLeod, Ruth. 1974a. "Fonemas Xavânte." Série Lingüística, Publicações do
    Summer Institute of Linguistics 3:131-52.
——. 1974b. "Paragraph, Aspect and Participant in Xavánte." *Linguistics*
    132:51-74.

Connectives

Sentence-initial Elements in Brazilian Guaraní

Robert A. Dooley

In Guaraní narrative, the sentence constituents that can occur initially and precede the independent clause are of two types: referential connectives and dependent clauses. Referential connectives, like English *after that*, make pronominal reference to some preceding passage. Sentence-initial dependent clauses are predominantly those that restate the preceding clause.

These sentence-initial elements serve two text-forming functions: primarily, to increment the basic content framework by adding new material to it with specific relational ties; and secondarily, to indicate the onset of hierarchical groupings of sentences. Ties within the basic content framework, either temporal or causal, are indicated by elements present in both referential connectives and dependent clauses.

The hierarchical groupings within a narrative are paragraphs and episodes. The morpheme *rami* appearing in referential connectives can indicate hierarchical onsets. But also, temporal ties tend to be indicated paragraph initially and causal ties paragraph medially. This pattern apparently reflects a general principle of text construction in Guaraní: the relationships presented between successive hierarchical units of a narrative are predominantly temporal, while the relationships presented between successive sentences within a paragraph are predominantly causal, with temporal sequence implicit.

1 Introduction and overview

The nature of the content and hierarchical structures of a narrative, and the relationship between the two, are important questions for the analysis and formation of texts. In Guaraní, some light is shed on these

45

matters by the sentence constituents that occur sentence initial and precede independent clauses.[1] Such a sentence-initial element serves one or both of two text-forming functions: to indicate a content relationship between the sentence at hand and what has preceded it, or to indicate the onset of some hierarchical grouping of sentences. The content relationships thus indicated are of either the temporal or the causal type; the hierarchical groupings are either paragraphs or episodes.

From the distribution of sentence-initial elements the following pattern emerges: the content relationships indicated across paragraph and episode boundaries are predominantly temporal, while those indicated between successive sentences within a paragraph are predominantly causal. This principle of text organization incorporates two distinct views of narrative: (1) that a narrative is basically a report of a temporal sequence of past events (Longacre 1976:199ff.), and (2) that a narrative paragraph is a passage whose events and states (including inferred states) are "joined into a complete causal chain" (Schank 1974:11).

In this section a broad overview of the relevant factors is presented. These ideas are developed, along with examples, in subsequent sections.

1.1 All sentences in Guaraní narrative are of the form

$$(1) \quad \left\{ {\text{Referential} \atop \text{connective}} \right\} \quad \left\{ {\text{Dependent} \atop \text{clause}} \right\}^{n} \quad \text{Clause} \quad \left\{ {\text{Dependent} \atop \text{clause}} \right\},$$

where

$$(2) \quad {\text{Dependent} \atop \text{clause}} \quad = \text{Clause} \quad {\text{Clause} \atop \text{subordinator.}}$$

Theoretically, there seems to be no maximum value for n in the above formula for sentences, but a value of $n = 3$ is not only adequate for most texts but rarely invoked.

Thus, the only sentence constituents that can occur sentence initial and precede the independent clause are referential connectives and dependent clauses.[2] **Referential connectives** are conjunction phrases that, like English *because of that*, make pronominal reference to the preceding context. Of the dependent clauses, by far the most common type that occurs sentence initial consists of dependent clauses that restate some previous clause. Other common types are those that report the fulfillment of a preview or establish a new calendric temporal setting.

This study of sentence-initial elements focuses on referential connectives, discusses dependent restatements less fully, and hardly mentions other types at all. The proportion of time devoted to each type of sentence-initial element corresponds roughly to its frequency of occurrence: referential connectives are initial in 46% of all narrative sentences, dependent restatements are initial in another 11%, and dependent clauses of all other types are initial in only 8%. The remaining sentences (35%) begin with an independent clause.

1.2 As already mentioned, two different ways of organizing a narrative are useful in describing sentence-initial elements: organization by content relationships, and groupings of sentences into hierarchical units.

A first approximation of the content organization of a narrative is that it consists of events in a temporal framework. Most narratives, however, include, in addition to the events, occasional descriptions of states, particularly those states that enable subsequent events in the sense of rendering them reasonably possible or well motivated. The presence of such states in a narrative indicates the existence of a causal framework along with the temporal framework (Schank 1974). Not only do states enable events, but events can result in states, and events can make possible subsequent events by means of intermediate and often unexpressed states. The temporal framework and the causal framework have, of course, many elements in common. Taken together, they make up a skeletal framework that incorporates all the basic content relationships found in a narrative. This **content framework**, then, is defined informally as all the events and states in a narrative, including those states that must be inferred, connected together with temporal or causal relationships that are either indicated explicitly or are readily inferrable.[3]

As a narrative progresses, its content framework is incremented, or successively built up, as new events and states are added to the content framework that already exists. These new elements must be connected to the existing framework by ties of either the temporal or causal type.

As to its hierarchical structure, a Guaraní narrative is made up of episodes, episodes of paragraphs, and paragraphs of sentences. The following types of episodes are relevant to the discussion: an obligatory introduction consisting primarily of participant information; passages within the body of the narrative that end with some sort of resolution; an optional summary of the story; and an optional application or moral.

Episodes other than those in the main body of the narrative usually consist of only a single paragraph. Hence, in speaking of paragraphs as distinct from episodes, I am referring to paragraphs within the main body of a narrative. Such a paragraph is roughly defined as a grouping of sentences that is bounded by discontinuities in temporal or locational setting or by changes in participant interaction, but that is internally continuous in all three of these respects. This paper assumes rather than proves the existence of episodes and paragraphs, but this assumption is shown to be reasonable in that it makes possible descriptions of sentence-initial elements that are both simple and well motivated.

1.3 The primary function of sentence-initial elements is to indicate specific content relationships between new material and the existing content framework, particularly when new material is in a sentence subsequent to the point in the content framework to which it is to be connected. This is the same function that conjunctions serve in English; that is, to indicate "a specification of the way in which what is to follow is systematically connected to what has gone before" (Halliday and Hasan 1976:227).

The new material in each instance is the event or state reported by the independent clause of the sentence in which the sentence-initial element is found. If the event or state in the independent clause is not informationally new, there is ordinarily no other sentence constituent preceding it.[4]

The particular point in the existing content framework to which new material is tied by sentence-initial elements is indicated within the sentence-initial elements themselves. For referential connectives, for example, the anaphoric pronoun refers to the part of the existing content framework that is to serve as the point of connection. In paragraph-medial cases, this point of connection is always the independent clause of the preceding sentence, but in paragraph-initial cases it is with rare exception the entire paragraph or episode immediately preceding. For dependent restatements, the point of connection is the clause from the preceding context that is being restated. In almost all cases this is the independent clause of the preceding sentence. Hence, no matter which of these two types of sentence-initial elements is being considered, the point of connection it indicates includes at least the preceding independent clause.

A sentence-initial element indicates not only the point in the existing content framework to which new material is connected, but also the particular content relationship the connection manifests. This is done by the clause subordinators that are final in both referential connectives and dependent restatements. In Guaraní, clause subordinators are of two types: temporal and causal. There are no clause subordinators, for example, that mean 'in the same location as' or 'in the same manner as'. This restriction to temporal and causal relationships is, of course, implied in the claim that by means of these clause subordinators the kind of content framework defined in 1.2 is to be built.

Clause subordinators, of course, do not have to occur in sentence-initial elements in order to indicate explicit content relationships between new material and the existing content framework. This happens whether they are used in sentence-initial elements, as already discussed, or in other dependent clauses. There is, however, the following difference. In the case of a referential connective or dependent restatement, the old material to which the new is connected is in a preceding sentence or, more specifically, in the passage indicated by *ha'e* or the restatement. In contrast, other types of dependent clauses do not point outside the sentence in indicating the place where the new material in the following independent clause is to be connected. Instead, the dependent clause itself, as soon as it is uttered, becomes the old material to which the new is connected.

> 'After that the king said thus: "Don't you know (which is) your bed?" he said. **When he (the king) showed it,** he (the other) went to bed.' (The dependent clause, shown in boldface, is the point to which the following independent clause is logically connected.)

It still requires explanation why a dependent clause, which in general is not connected to the preceding content framework in any explicit way, can be treated as part of the content framework as soon as it is uttered, and new material accordingly connected to it. This is only possible because, as substantiated in 3.1, dependent clauses tend to encode information that is to some degree recoverable from the preceding context. For this reason, their connection to the content framework can be left unexpressed, being understood as part of their general recoverability. Dependent restatements are then just the limiting case of the recoverability that tends to be true for dependent clauses in general.

1.4 All referential connectives and dependent restatements function as described above, building up the existing content framework by means of either temporal or causal ties. Some paragraph-initial referential connectives serve an additional function that, for the class of sentence-initial elements as a whole, is secondary, namely, to indicate the onset of a hierarchical grouping. This function can be signaled by purely formal means; that is, referential connectives that include medial *rami* 'like, as' generally occur paragraph initial.[5] But semantic features can indicate hierarchy as well; that is, referential connectives that denote temporal ties also generally occur paragraph initial.[6] When formal and semantic signals are both present in a referential connective, in the case of temporal referential connectives that include medial *rami*, not just paragraph onset but episode onset is indicated.

1.5 In sections 2 and 3 referential connectives and dependent restatements are considered in some detail. Section 4 summarizes the inferences drawn from sentence-initial elements regarding the content and hierarchical structure of a narrative.

The primary corpus from which this analysis is developed consists of six narrative texts, each by a different speaker. Among these six speakers there is considerable variation in the choice and usage of sentence-initial elements, and the present study represents only the part common to all their narrative styles. Other narrative texts have been consulted occasionally. Nonnarrative discourse is not treated here.

2 Referential connectives

A referential connective takes the form

(3) *ha'e (rami)* Clause subordinator

where the set of clause subordinators is, with exceptions to be noted later, the same as that in formula 2. The three positions in this construction can in a general sense be said to correlate with three text-forming phenomena: *ha'e* with anaphoric reference, *rami* with hierarchical grouping, and the clause subordinators with connections within the context framework.

2.1 The anaphoric pronoun *ha'e* occurs in many types of constructions. It can refer to persons, things, locations, temporal settings, or the content of clauses or larger units. Within a referential connective, however, *ha'e* refers to at least a whole proposition. Specifically, if *ha'e* is paragraph-medial, its referent is the content of the preceding independent clause; if it is paragraph-initial, its referent is the content of the largest hierarchical grouping that immediately precedes it.[7] Rarely in paragraph-initial cases *ha'e* refers to the largest hierarchical grouping before the one immediately preceding.

These rules are the simplest generalizations that can be drawn consistent with the data, in the following sense. Although in any given instance, given the facts of the story and the specific temporal or causal relationship being indicated, more than one referent may be logically possible for *ha'e*, yet always included in those possible referents is the one given by the above rules. Moreover, no other possible referent is inherently more likely than the one given above.

For example, in all paragraph-medial cases of referential connectives no factual errors or contradictions arise if the referent of *ha'e* is taken as the independent clause of the preceding sentence.

'So his grandfather removed all the clothes from the youngster. **That after** (*ha'e gwi*) he took him to bathe him there.'

For paragraph-initial referential connectives, however, it is often insufficient to suppose that *ha'e* refers to the previous independent clause only. In one narrative, for example, the final section within the body of the text tells how in a test of bravery a jaguar lost its nerve. The final sentence in the section reports how the jaguar was killed. Then follows a summary section, beginning with the sentence

'**That like after** (*ha'e rami rire*) the jaguar is no longer brave.'

The point of the statement is that, because one jaguar lost its nerve long ago, today all jaguars are cowardly. Thus, in this and similar examples the pronoun *ha'e* cannot refer to only the content of the preceding independent clause and still allow the content relationship denoted by the referential connective to have a reasonable application within the narrative. In such paragraph-initial cases, a reasonable content relationship does become possible if *ha'e* is understood as referring to the content of the largest hierarchical grouping (paragraph or episode) that immediately precedes it.

The scope of the reference of *ha'e* that is given by the rules of this section can occasionally be corroborated by a dependent clause which, appearing subsequent to a referential connective, represents the referent more specifically. For instance, following the previous example is this sentence:

'**Because Tupã** [a folk hero] **came emitting lightning and thunder,** the jaguar is no longer brave.'

The dependent clause above is a summary of the episode preceding the former example. Because its position in the sentence corresponds to that of the referential connective in the former example, and since the independent clauses are exactly the same, the obvious inference is that *the dependent clause is a kind of expansion of the referent of ha'e rami.*

Actually, it is more common to find such an expansive dependent clause in the same sentence as the referential connective, between it and the independent clause, and in an appositional relationship to it. When this is so, the two clause subordinators must be the same or have the same meaning.

> 'So after crying remorsefully, he cut his own throat. **That in=consequence=of** (*ha'e vy*), **because** he cut his own throat (*vy*), he killed himself.'

The preceding example shows a clausal expansion of *ha'e* occurring paragraph medial and restating the preceding independent clause. The earlier example is of a clausal expansion of paragraph-initial *ha'e*, which summarizes the preceding episode. In this way, in every case where clausal expansions of *ha'e* are found, they verify the rules given for identifying the referent of *ha'e*.[8]

As mentioned, the referent of a paragraph-initial *ha'e* can refer to the paragraph or episode preceding the one immediately preceding the referential connective. Only one clear example of this phenomenon has been found (paragraph onsets are noted by indentation).

> 'After that her mother put a flower into her hand. And she said thus: "Throw it at the one you like the best," she said. And so, as she was about to throw it she said thus: "I am just going to throw it at that one," she said, and she threw it at the ugly negro.
> **'That in=response=to** (*ha'e rã*) her younger sisters laughed derisively at the ugly negro.
> **'That in=response=to** (*ha'e rã*), because the old man was angry with his daughter, he said thus: "There are so many good looking young men, but you throw the flower at this one," he said.'

Since the father is responding in anger to his daughter's throwing the flower, it is clear that the *ha'e* at the beginning of the third paragraph refers to the events of the first paragraph. Although this type of referential skipping complicates the general rules being considered, it also provides the narrator with a useful device. In the above example the last two paragraphs are indicated as standing in the same content relationship to the first paragraph, even though only one can be adjacent to the first in linear arrangement.

2.2 Before the optional element *rami* is considered, the clause subordinators that occur at the end of referential connectives are discussed. There are six such clause subordinators: *jave* 'during', *rire* 'after', *gwi* 'after', *vy* 'in consequence of', and *ramo* and its shorter form *rã* 'in response to'.[9]

Two modifications need to be made to formula 3 with respect to these clause subordinators. First, although *ha'e rami jave* 'that like during' occurs, **ha'e jave* does not. The postpositional phrase *ha'e jave py* 'that time-span in' occurs in its place with *jave* being used as a nominal, possibly because *jave* is more readily understood as a nominal than as a clause subordinator. Second, although *ha'e gwi* 'that after' occurs, ** ha'e rami gwi* does not. The reason for this noncooccurrence is perhaps hierarchical, and is explained in note 12.

Two types of temporal relationships are indicated by the clause subordinators under discussion: simultaneity and sequence. Simultaneity is indicated by *jave:*

> 'She was going sadly down the path. **That like** during (**ha'e rami jave**) a youngster cried noisily in the hole where a palm tree had once been.'

The far more common type of temporal relationship is sequence. This can be indicated by either *rire* or *gwi*.

> 'And so the girl came there. **That after** (**ha'e rire**) her mother put a flower into her hand.'

> 'He put it away. **That after** (**ha'e gwi**) he went.'

Note that the difference between *rire* and *gwi* is not in meaning but in hierarchical function.

The nontemporal clause subordinators in referential connectives are *vy*, *ramo*, and *rã*. The subordinator *vy* in a referential connective is glossed 'in consequence of'. It is used when the new material being added to the content framework is routinely fulfilling cultural expectations in some sequence of actions. This expectation can have been set up by any one of the following three factors: cause and effect relationships as culturally perceived, even though perhaps not actually experienced; familiar patterns of action commonly experienced within the culture; and patterning or preview established by the preceding context. These three sources of expectation are illustrated in the following three examples:

> 'When he arrived there, he didn't know what to do with the sheep. So the sheep were all there outside. **That in=consequence=of** (**ha'e vy**) the king, being angry, said thus: "Don't you know to put the

sheep there in the pen?'' he said.' (Although there are no kings and few sheep in Guaraní culture, it can be projected from cultural experience that if a king's sheep were running loose, he would be angry and want them penned up.)

'At that time a youngster cried noisily in the hole where a palm tree had once been. **That like in=consequence=of** (*ha'e rami vy*) when the old woman looked, she became very happy.' (The Guaraní are very affectionate towards babies even when they cry, so this happiness would be considered culturally routine.)

'So he (the negro) spoke to him. "Here is money. If I die first, as may happen, put the money on top of my grave," he said. "After I am buried," he said. "But don't let me be laid out," he said. "Stand me up. Then put the money on top of my head," he said. Afterwards, eight days later, the negro died. **That like in=consequence=of** (*ha'e rami vy*) the owner of the goat put the money on top of his head.' (The expectations set up earlier in the text are fulfilled as previewed.)

The element *ramo* and its short form *rã* in a referential connective do not in contradistinction to *vy* indicate that an action is contrary to cultural expectations, but instead relate to a different facet of causation.[10] These elements are glossed 'in response to', where response is considered to be a volitional reaction to some stimulus. The stimulus is that event or state reported in the preceding independent clause, and is most commonly direct speech by another person. When the stimulus is direct speech, the response can be either a conversational reply or a nonverbal response such as compliance or noncompliance to a request.

'When he arrived home he said thus: "Look, grandmother. I found a companion," he said. **That in=response=to** (*ha'e ramo*) his grandmother said thus: "Fine. You both go again. Kill a lot of birds," she said.'

'Then, "Bring it. Let me see it," his grandfather said. **That in=response=to** (*ha'e rã*) he didn't want to show it to his grandfather.'

Occasionally the stimulus is not in quoted speech, in which case again the response may be either verbal or nonverbal.

'So he didn't want to leave his son-in-law's house. He stayed there constantly. **That in=response=to** (*ha'e rã*) his daughter said thus to her father in anger: "Go bring mother. Let mother stay here too," she said.'

'When he arrived there where the house had stood, around the hole of the corner post frogs were croaking. **That in=response=to** (*ha'e rã*) the old king sat listening.'

Since response is understood as volitional, the independent clause of a sentence with *ramo* or *rã* in its referential connective has an agent as its subject.[11] On the other hand, with any of the other clause subordinators in referential connectives, both agentive and nonagentive subjects occur freely in the independent clause.

'Afterwards, after he went to the negro's house, as he was coming back, he forgot the path. **That like in=consequence=of** (*ha'e rami vy*) it got quite late.'

When *vy, ramo,* and *rã* occur in dependent clauses instead of in referential connectives, they have structural rather than semantic meaning. In a dependent clause, *vy* indicates that two clauses have the same subject, while *ramo* and *rã* indicate that they have different subjects. The two clauses whose subjects are being compared are the dependent clause in which the subordinator occurs, and the clause adjacent to it in the direction of the independent clause, which may be and often is the independent clause itself. Formula 1 gives the range of possibilities for these two clauses.

'So (because) the old man was angry with his daughter (*vy*) **same=subject,** he said thus: "There are a lot of good-looking boys but you throw the flower at this one," he said.'

'So (since) the jaguar is not brave (*ramo*) **different=subject,** nowadays we can really kill it.'

'(Since) (as) he listened (*rã*) **different=subject** the sheep was bleating at the base of the slope (*rã*) **different=subject,** he ran to there.'

It is not clear how these structural meanings in dependent clauses are related to the semantic meanings that *vy, ramo,* and *rã* have in referential connectives. A relationship does seem to be indicated by the fact that, when they occur with referential connectives, the structural meanings of these elements are correct in predicting the subject about 90% of the time, where the two clauses being compared are those on either side of the referential connective. It should also be pointed out that, although these clause subordinators in dependent clauses do not indicate any specific semantic relationship between the clauses of that sentence, some temporal or causal relationship always exists in actual fact. Within a dependent clause other means are available, besides the clause subordinator itself, for indicating a specific temporal or causal relationship.[12] Not surprisingly, these content relationships that exist alongside *vy, ramo,* and *rã* obtain between the same two clauses whose subjects these clause subordinators compare. Thus, in the preceding example, the first dependent clause has its content relationship with the second dependent clause rather than directly with the independent clause. However, since most sentences contain no more than one dependent clause, most dependent clauses have their content relationship with the independent clause.

When a clause subordinator is used as part of a referential connective, as has been noted, it indicates a particular semantic relationship between the independent clauses of two sentences, and this relationship is either a specific temporal type or a specific causal type. The particular semantic relationship indicated, however, is not completely determined by the actions in the narrative itself. The speaker often has a true choice as to which semantic relationship to present, since several such relationships could plausibly be claimed to hold between two sentences. Quite similar patterns can be presented in different lights, as the following three expressions of exasperation show.

'Afterwards he was standing outside. **That in=consequence=of** (*ha'e vy*) the king said thus: "Don't you know that here is where you always come in and sit?" he said.'

'It was already late at night but he was still (sitting) there. **That after** (*ha'e gwi*) the king said thus: "Don't you know (which is) your bed?" he said.'

'The ugly negro was walking around outside not really knowing what to do. **That in=response=to** (*ha'e rã*) the old woman said thus: "You too go take a bath . . . ," she said.'

The point is that the relationship between two consecutive sentences is whatever the speaker chooses to make it, and it can be predicted from the context only within broad limits.

2.3 Besides adding new material onto the existing content framework, referential connectives can also indicate the onset of hierarchical units.[13] This second function accounts for about 70% of all paragraph-initial sentences that begin with referential connectives, compared with 47% of all sentences in general. Paragraph onset is signaled by referential connectives in one of two ways: by the presence of medial *rami,* or by the presence of a clause subordinator that indicates a temporal relationship.

The postposition *rami* 'like, as' in a referential connective has the anaphoric pronoun *ha'e* as its grammatical head, and *ha'e rami* 'that like' denotes something more vague than *ha'e* does by itself. This suggests that *ha'e rami* in a referential connective might refer to more than just the preceding independent clause, thereby raising the possibility that the referential connective is functioning on a level higher than the purely intersentential. This explanation is only conjectural at this point, and is not pressed, but the fact remains that *ha'e rami ramo* and *ha'e rami rã* occur only paragraph-initial, while *ha'e ramo* and *ha'e rã* are under no such restriction.

Referential connectives with *vy,* on the other hand, occur almost exclusively paragraph-medial. With *vy,* therefore, *rami* can serve little hierarchical function, so that there is no contrast between *ha'e vy* and *ha'e rami vy.* In fact, the two forms do not cooccur within a single narrative; a speaker uses one exclusively of the other. In rare cases when a speaker does use *vy* in a paragraph-initial referential connective, however, it may be significant that *ha'e rami vy* is the form he uses.

The second type of referential connective that occurs regularly at paragraph onsets is the one that indicates temporal relationships, as figure 1 shows. This is actually part of a more general phenomenon, which is that temporal relationships are seldom indicated other than at the beginning of paragraphs. This phenomenon is related to the fact that paragraphs, as defined in 1.2, are internally continuous as to temporal setting, but at their boundaries often have temporal gaps. These gaps are what must be noted, because indications of temporal relationships are associated with paragraph boundaries, particularly with paragraph onsets since time settings must be established for paragraphs. Similar comments apply as well to locational setting and participant orientation, the other two parameters in terms of which paragraphs are defined, since specification of location and explicit reference to participants are most commonly found at or near paragraph onsets.

Initial constituent of sentence	Paragraph-initial sentences	Paragraph-medial sentences
Temporal referential connective	38 (47%)	10 (5%)
Causal referential connective	17 (22%)	59 (32%)
Dependent clause	15 (19%)	35 (20%)
Independent clause	10 (12%)	78 (43%)
	80 (100%)	182 (100%)

**Fig. 1. Initial sentence constituents
and sentence position within paragraphs**

The ten paragraph-medial instances of temporal referential connectives that are noted in figure 1 all occur in a single narrative, and all are realized by *ha'e gwi* 'that after'. In that text temporal sequence is denoted by two referential connectives: *ha'e gwi*, which occurs only paragraph-medial and *ha'e rire*, which occurs only paragraph initial. So, in that one text hierarchical information can be inferred from the particular referential connective used to indicate temporal sequence. In all other texts only one of these two expressions appears at all, and then only paragraph initial, so that the very presence of a referential connective indicating temporal sequence implies hierarchical information.

Policy options such as these for a narrative as a whole are presented as a systemic network in figure 2, with square brackets indicating alternative options. The numbers key this network to one presented later.

When *rami* is present in a referential connective that also indicates a temporal relationship, two signals of hierarchical onset are thereby present. Accordingly, *ha'e rami jave* 'that like during' and *ha'e rami rire* 'that like after' are found only at episode onsets. Because of this hierarchical stairstep effect, *rami* (except when it cooccurs with *vy*) can be understood as giving a referential connective a hierarchical significance one level higher than it would have otherwise.[14]

2.4 Because temporal relationships can indicate hierarchical information, the speaker's choice whether to indicate hierarchy is not entirely independent of his choice as to what type of semantic connection to indicate. For example, if for a given sentence he decides to indicate temporal sequence, he must also thereby indicate the onset of either a paragraph or an episode, unless by having selected policy 3 (see figure 2) for the text as a whole he has allowed himself the possibility of indicating temporal sequence paragraph medially. Figure 3 is a systemic network that shows such interdependencies between the speaker's options for a given sentence, assuming that for that sentence he has already made the decision to use some referential connective. In figure 3 the policy options previously displayed in figure 2 for a narrative as a whole are indicated with broken lines, with numbers matching those in figure 2.

Branching (where one alternative is of the form "Indicate X" and the other is of the form "Do not indicate X" or "Indicate Y") is actually an abbreviated representation. The more complete representation would have preceding branching with alternatives "X is the case" and "X is not the case", followed by the branching that is actually furnished. If X is not the case, then necessarily "Do not indicate X" or "Indicate Y" is selected. Only if X is the case does the narrator have a true choice between "Indicate X" and "Do not indicate X" or "Indicate Y".

From the various options indicated as numbers in figure 2 and letters in figure 3, it is possible to determine in most cases the particular form of the referential connective that is to be used. This information is presented in figure 4.

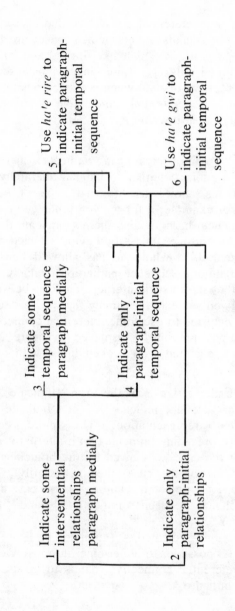

Fig. 2. Policy options in force throughout an entire narrative

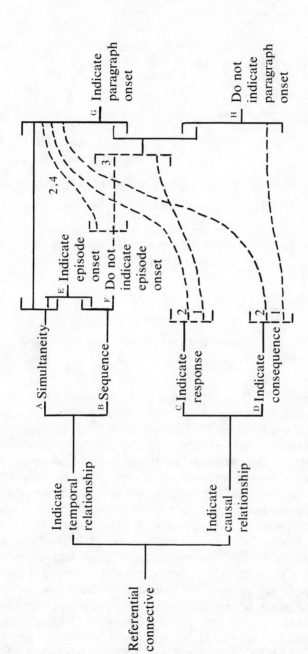

Fig.3. Options for the referential connectives in a given sentence

Options in figure 2	Options in figure 3	Referential connective(s)
	A G	*ha'e rami jave*
	A E	*ha'e jave py*
	B E	*ha'e rami rire*
5	B F G	*ha'e rire*
6	B F G	*ha'e gwi*
3	B F H	*ha'e gwi*
	C G	*ha'e rami ramo, ha'e rami rã, ha'e ramo, ha'e rã*
1	C H	*ha'e ramo, ha'e rã*
	D G	*ha'e rami vy*
1	D H	*ha'e rami vy, ha'e vy*

**Fig. 4. Referential connectives resulting from options
in figures 2 and 3.**

3. Dependent restatements

A restatement reports again the content of a previous clause, called
the *protostatement*.

3.1 The distribution of restatements and protostatements in the
structure of a Guaraní sentence (see formula 1) follows a distinctive
pattern. With few exceptions, a protostatement is the independent
clause of the sentence immediately preceding the sentence where the
restatement occurs.[15] Restatements, on the other hand, are encoded as
dependent clauses in the majority of cases. This pattern, with a
dependent clause restating the independent clause of the previous
sentence, is discussed in Grimes 1975 as linking, and has been studied
in several geographically diverse languages (Grimes and Glock 1970,
Lewis 1972, McCarthy 1965, Stout and Thomson 1971, Thurman ms.)
That restatements occur predominantly in dependent clauses is a
special case of a more general principle at work in Guaraní, namely,
that event and state information recoverable from the preceding
context tends to be encoded in dependent clauses, and information not
thus recoverable tends to be encoded in independent clauses.[16] Figure 5
shows this tendency statistically. In this figure, fulfillments are to be
understood as reports of whether and how earlier previews are fulfilled.
Since contraexpectancies are counted as fulfillments, the content of

fulfillment clauses is only partially recoverable from the preceding context.

	Restatements	Fulfillments	Clauses of all other types
Dependent clauses	40 (85%)	25 (40%)	36 (15%)
Independent clauses	7 (15%)	37 (60%)	200 (85%)
	47 (100%)	62 (100%)	236 (100%)

Fig. 5. Encoding in dependent and independent clauses

It is relevant to the scope of this paper that dependent restatements are in almost every case sentence initial. The few exceptions to this regularity are those restatements that occur following a referential connective and expand its pronominal reference, as discussed in 2.1.

3.2 A dependent restatement builds new material onto the existing content framework in much the same way that a referential connective does. The main difference is in the way the two constructions point out the part of the content framework to which the new material is to be connected. Whereas a referential connective does this by means of pronominal reference, a dependent restatement repeats the point of connection. These two means of representation are in syntactic correspondence within their respective constructions; that is, a referential connective has *ha'e (rami)* (formula 3) where a dependent restatement has a clause that restates (formula 2).

The elements in final position, the clause subordinators, are essentially the same for both constructions. Dependent restatements, and dependent clauses in general, have available a somewhat greater selection of clause subordinators than are discussed in 2.2 for referential connectives, but the differences are minor.[17] There are also meaning differences for some clause subordinators that appear in both constructions. *vy, ramo,* and *rã* are discussed in 2.2, and *gwi,* in its rare occurrences as a clause subordinator, seems to indicate some kind of causal relationship instead of temporal sequence. Once these differences have been noted, however, it can still be said that clause subordinators in any construction connect new material to the existing content framework, and the connection is either temporal or causal.

3.3 As to hierarchical function, restatements are not as closely related to paragraph boundaries as are referential connectives. While it is true that restatements can occur paragraph initial as well as paragraph medial, less than 10% of all narrative paragraphs do, in fact, begin with a dependent restatement. This is to be compared with the 70% of narrative paragraphs that have an initial referential connective.

The scarcity of paragraph-initial dependent restatements could well be due to the very specificity with which restatements relate to their preceding contexts. The pronominal reference of a referential connective is by comparison a less specific way of representing anaphora; therefore, when it is used paragraph initially it can conveniently be taken to refer to an entire paragraph or episode. This is especially true, as noted in 2.3, when *rami* is present. Since, on the other hand, a dependent restatement represents exactly the previous independent clause, information with regard to broad hierarchical units is more difficult to infer from it.[18]

For dependent restatements, a more characteristic position is sentence initial in the second sentence of a paragraph.

> 'Afterwards, when the appointed day arrived, from very early in the morning the young men were all arriving. *As they arrived,* the ugly negro was walking around outside, not really knowing what to do.'

This position within a paragraph is the case in about half of all occurrences of restatements.

This tendency should be considered in view of the many kinds of information that are commonly found in paragraph-initial sentences. As in the preceding example, the initial sentence is often heavy with nonevent information; that is, besides the anaphoric, hierarchical, and semantically connective information usually provided by the paragraph-initial referential connective, there are often adjuncts of temporal or locational setting and explicit identification of participants. Amid all these details, the event information encoded in the independent clause could well become lost to the hearer. By restating this event information at the beginning of the next sentence, the speaker ensures that this loss, if it has indeed taken place, is not permanent.[19]

3.4 The close and many-sided relationship between dependent restatements and referential connectives is here summarized. First, the two constructions are internally parallel in syntax, each composed of two constituents, namely, some representation of anaphora followed by a clause subordinator.[20] For this reason, the two constructions sometimes appear in apposition within a sentence, that is, with the dependent restatement expanding the meaning of the referential connective, as discussed in 2.1.

Second, the two constructions both have as their primary function the connecting of new material to the existing content framework by means of a temporal or causal tie. The point of connection is the anaphora they represent; the content tie is indicated by the clause subordinator; and the new material is in almost every case found in the independent clause.

Third, aside from the rare instances when a dependent restatement occurs in apposition to a referential connective, the two constructions are in a paradigmatic relation with one another; they serve as alternate choices for the sentence-initial element.

The principal basis on which a speaker makes his choice between these two constructions seems to be simply that dependent restatements represent anaphora more specifically than do referential connectives. Thus, paragraph initial, where the speaker wishes to refer broadly to the content of the preceding paragraph or episode, a dependent restatement would be less useful than a referential connective. On the other hand, when the second sentence of a paragraph is meant to remind the hearer of the event information of the paragraph-initial sentence, the specificity of a dependent restatement is required.

One other observation is made without explanation. When *haé* in a referential connective refers to a clause, that clause can encode either an event or a state. A clause that is restated, however, can encode only an event.

4 Content and hierarchy

The usage and meaning of sentence-initial elements suggest general observations concerning the organization of Guaraní narratives in terms of both content and hierarchical structure. These observations, discussed in some detail throughout the paper, are here summarized.

First, sentence-initial elements suggest the basic form the content and hierarchical structures have as separate entities. The most basic type of content relationship between the events and states of a narrative can be inferred from those relationships obtaining between sentences, which are either temporal or causal. Although other content relationships can be indicated by other means, these two intersentential types can be taken as the more basic.

Hierarchical groupings of sentences are also signaled by sentence-initial elements, by certain referential connectives in particular. In this way, two levels of hierarchy emerge: paragraphs and episodes. Paragraph onsets are signaled by a referential connective in one of two ways: by the presence of either *rami* or a temporal clause subordinator. When these two elements are both present, the onset of an episode is being indicated.

With regard to hierarchical units, two points are made. First, these hierarchical groupings are not defined in terms of surface signals, but, as shown in 1.2, they are defined by semantic parameters. Thus, their boundaries can be located with some certainty by semantic criteria alone. Formal surface signals, once they have been recognized at semantically unambiguous boundaries, can afterwards be used to clarify those boundaries where semantic criteria are more difficult to apply. Second, not all paragraph and episode boundaries are indicated as such by referential connectives. Some are indicated by other surface manifestations of the defining semantic criteria, such as verbs of motion or expressions of distance that indicate change of location. The claim being made in this paper is that those referential connectives that do indicate paragraph or episode onsets occur only at those onsets, and therefore are reliable as hierarchical indicators whenever they occur.

Sentence-initial connectives, in addition to indicating the nature of the content and hierarchical structures separately, also point to a relationship between the two structures. Content relationships between consecutive paragraphs or episodes tend to be temporal, while between consecutive sentences within a paragraph relationships tend to be causal. This reflects that, in narrative at least, temporal gaps are one, and possibly the main, defining feature of paragraph boundaries, while internally a paragraph is the realization of "a complete causal chain" of events and states (Schank 1974:11).

Notes

1 Guaraní is a language of the Tupí-Guaraní family spoken by approximately two thousand persons in the states of Rio Grande do Sul, Santa Catarina, Paraná, and São Paulo in southern Brazil. Related dialects of Guaraní are found in Argentina, Paraguay, and Bolivia. This study is based on field work carried on during 1975 and 1976 at the Posto Indígena Rio das Cobras, Paraná, under the auspices of the Summer Institute of Linguistics in cooperation with the Fundação Nacional do Indio and the Museu Nacional. This paper was prepared during a linguistics workshop held in Porto Velho, Rondônia, Brazil, in 1976. The author is greatly indebted to Joseph E. Grimes, who conducted the workshop, for many helpful ideas and suggestions.

2 Some sentence-initial phrases are constituents of the initial clause rather than of the sentence as a whole, and for this reason are not under discussion in this paper. Such phrases, including *ha'e py* 'in that place' and *ha'e rami* 'in that manner', do not even occur consistently in clause-initial position. There are other initial sentence constituents, such as *aỹ ma* 'now then', that do not occur in narrative.

3 In order for one element to cause another, it must temporally precede the other. (Purpose clauses are only an apparent exception.) This would suggest that the

causal framework might be a substructure of the temporal framework. States, however, are not usually incorporated in the temporal framework (Litteral 1972), especially those states that have to be supplied by the hearer from cultural or anaphoric factors. Nor can the temporal framework be a substructure of the causal framework, for one event can precede another without causing the other. Nevertheless, the two frameworks are closely connected, and can be considered as intersecting partially ordered sets whose orders agree on their common elements, in the sense that if A causes B, then A precedes B.

4 There are only two counterexamples in the corpus. One is 'After that he went to take a bath. As he grabbed the soap *he went*.' The other is the third example in 2.1, which, because of hierarchical considerations, is irregular in other respects. The converse of the general rule does not hold. If an independent clause is sentence initial, the event or state it reports can be either new or given information.

5 In this paper, Guaraní is analyzed as having six vowels, /i/, /ɨ/ (written *y*), /u/, /e/, /a/, /o/, and fourteen consonants: /p/, /t/, /š/ (written *x*), /k/, /kʷ/, /ʼ/ (glottal stop), /m/ (written *mb* preceding oral vowels), /n/ (written *nd* preceding oral vowels), /ɲ/ (written *nh* preceding nasal vowels and *j* preceding oral vowels), /ŋ/ (written *ng*), /ŋʷ/ (written *gw*), /v/, /r/, /h/. (Since this paper was written, [h] has been reanalyzed as subphonemic and some changes have been made in the orthography.) Nasalization is regressive throughout a word whose final syllable is written either with /˜/ or with one of the nasal consonants /m/, /n/, /ŋ/. Nasalization is also regressive from a nasal consonant /m/ (or *mb*), /n/ (or *nd*) or /ŋ/ (*ng*). Stress is on the last syllable of a noun or verb phrase unless indicated otherwise by an acute accent ´.

6 Minor exceptions to this and the preceding sentence are discussed in 2.3.

7 An alternative analysis would be to say that the referent of ha'e is indeterminate in such cases, but includes at least the preceding independent clause. A third analysis would be to disregard the referential function of *ha'e*. This third analysis would be similar to that of Halliday and Hasan 1976 for English, who state that "in analytical forms such as *after that* we respond to the cohesive force of the phrase as a whole rather than singling out *that* as an anaphoric element on its own" (p. 230). To these writers, the analysis adopted in the present paper would not be a viable option, for paragraphs are defined graphically instead of semantically: "The paragraph is a device introduced into the written language . . ." (p. 296).

8 Dependent clauses following referential connectives often expand other elements of the connective besides the pronominal reference. Commonly, at the beginning of a paragraph and especially of an episode, a referential connective of temporal sequence is followed by a dependent clause specifying the extent of elapsed time.

9 *jave* also occurs as a substantive, meaning 'a span of time'. *gwi* is commonly a postposition meaning 'from the source or origin of', 'due to the effects of', 'since the time of', or 'than' in comparisons. *rire* can also be a postposition, meaning 'after'. The meanings that *gwi, vy, ramo,* and *rã* have when they occur in dependent clauses are different from those listed here, and are discussed later.

10 *ramo* is the form used in written texts. In oral texts *ramo* tends to be used in paragraph-initial referential connectives, and *rã* tends to be used elsewhere.

11 Only one exception to this agent-as-subject restriction has been found; it might indicate that the gloss 'in response to' is being conceived too narrowly: 'He untied his (grandson's) hand that was wrapped up. **That in=response=to** *(ha'e rã)* his hand was a beautiful gold.'

12 If the dependent clause reports an event, then certain markers in that clause can indicate that the event temporally precedes the event or state reported in the following clause. These markers include the aspect expressions *ma* 'already', *jevy* 'again', *rai* 'almost', and *-pa* 'completely' following the verb, and *-ve* 'more'

following the clause subordinator. A verb like -vaē 'arrive' with a definite cutoff point in its underlying time set can also have the effect of indicating temporal sequence with respect to the following clause. In the absence of such indicators of temporal sequence, some causal relationship is in fact present, perhaps with a temporal relationship as well. A causal relationship is usually prominent when the dependent clause reports a state instead of an event. With most instances of vy, ramo, and rã, however, both temporal sequence and causality are, in fact, the case, and often neither is more prominent than the other.

13 Bridgeman (1966) reports the same phenomenon in Kaiwa, another Brazilian Tupí-Guaraní language.

14 This view of rami explains the nonoccurrence of *ha'e rami gwi. ha'e gwi 'that after' occurs either paragraph initial or paragraph medial; it is hierarchically distinct from ha'e rire 'that after' only when paragraph medial. Since rami invests a form with hierarchical significance on the next higher level, then *ha'e rami gwi would presumably indicate paragraph onset, or perhaps episode onset, as well as temporal sequence. But indicating paragraph onset, it would be both hierarchically and semantically indistinguishable from ha'e rire, and indicating episode onset it would be likewise indistinguishable from ha'e rami rire. Thus, *ha'e rami gwi would not be functionally unique in any context.

15 The exceptional cases, which comprise less than 5% of all restatements, are either the second or third restatements in a series, or restatements of a narrative summary.

16 One speaker encodes only 40% of his restatements as dependent clauses, as compared with 85% for all speakers taken together. But this is only a reflection of his reluctance to use dependent clauses of any type (an average of .17 per sentence, as compared with .44 for all speakers taken together).

17 reve, usually a postposition 'with', is used but rarely as a clause subordinator indicating some type of simultaneity. It is possible that rami can also be used as a clause subordinator.

18 There are dependent clauses, though not restatements, that occur paragraph initial and summarize the content of the preceding paragraph or episode. These occur in about 5% of all paragraphs.

19 There is another consequence of this type of crowding of information in paragraph-initial sentences. The speaker often encodes in the initial independent clause of a paragraph events with either minimal functional value with respect to the story itself (such as motion with change of setting) or high recoverability from the preceding context (this may account for those few restatements that do occur paragraph initial). Encoding such information in that position is a means of insuring that, if such information is actually lost to the hearer, the loss will not be important.

20 In Asurini, another Tupí-Guaraní language of Brazil, all dependent restatements with ramo as clause subordinator are obligatorily transformed into the referential connective a'e ramo (Harrison 1975:87). Harrison (p. 20) glosses this referential connective as 'como conseqüência de', that is, 'as a consequence of', and says that the anaphoric pronoun a'e refers to the preceding sentence. Were it not for the fact that ha'e in Guaraní can refer to more than the preceding sentence, referential connectives in Guaraní could largely be accounted for by transformations of the type Harrison cites, except optional.

References

Bridgeman, Loraine Irene. 1966. "Oral Paragraphs in Kaiwa (Guarani)." Ph.D. dissertation, Indiana University.

Grimes, Joseph E. 1975. The Thread of Discourse. The Hague: Mouton.

Grimes, Joseph E., and Naomi Glock. 1970. "A Saramaccan Narrative Pattern." *Language* 46:408-25.

Halliday, M.A.K. and Ruqaiya Hasan. 1976. *Cohesion in English*. London: Longman.

Harrison, Carl H. 1975. Gramática Asuriní. Série Lingüística No. 4. Brasília: Summer Institute of Linguistics.

Lewis, Ronald K. 1972. "Sanio-Hiowe Paragraph Structure." *Pacific Linguistics* A-31.

Litteral, Robert. 1972. "Rhetorical Predicates and Time Topology in Anggor." *Foundations of Language* 8:391-410.

Longacre, R.E. 1976. *An Anatomy of Speech Notions*. Lisse: Peter de Ridder.

McCarthy, Joy. 1965. "Clause Chaining in Kanite." *Anthropological Linguistics* 7:59-70.

Schank, Roger C. 1974. *Understanding Paragraphs*. Technical Report 5. Castagnola, Switzerland: Instituto per gli Studi Semantici e Cognitivi.

Stout, Mickey, and Ruth Thomson. 1971. "Kayapó Narrative." *International Journal of American Linguistics* 37:250-56.

Thurman, Robert C. MS. "Chuave Medial Verbs."

Coreguaje Dependent Verb Suffixes

Dorothy Cook

Clauses with dependent verbs function in Coreguaje to provide time setting, the sequence of events leading up to the main event of a sentence, or the circumstances under which the action or state denoted by an independent verb comes about. They also express the cause or condition upon which an independent predication is contingent. When used as links between sentences the dependent clauses repeat or paraphrase a previous verb, especially in narrative where the link shows progression in time or space. The categories governing these verb suffixes are time, contingency with sequential or overlapping connection, and same or different subject, or else general time or circumstances.

1 Discourse function

In Coreguaje, dependent verb clauses are used in approximately 50% of the sentences found in texts,[1] which are of the narrative, hortatory, and explanatory discourse types.

1.1 Relations within a sentence. Dependent clauses function within a sentence to provide the time setting, express the sequence of events leading up to the main event of the sentence, or state the circumstances in which the action of the independent verb takes place or its state is effected. Such clauses also express the cause or condition upon which the carrying out of the independent predication is contingent. They do not repeat or paraphrase verbs of preceding clauses or sentences except when the dependent clauses are used as links between sentences. (Linkage is discussed in section 1.2.) In the unmarked order dependent clauses precede independent clauses; however, a dependent clause can follow an independent clause. The following examples show the various functions of dependent clauses within a sentence.

Time setting:

(1) *Cнн'н abe-**rнmн** cнн'н i-cheja oracha mama huн'e jobo ba'i-**rнmн** re'o-ja'-che cнн'н ba'i-si'-cн-a'-mн.*[2]
I early-**general=time** I this-place Maticurú new house village be-**general=time** good-appear-circum I be-compl-masc=nom-stat-masc+sg+cont[3]
'Earlier, during the time Maticurú was a new village, I lived well.'[4]

Sequence of events:

(2) *Sai-ja-'-mн cнн'н. **Rani** cнa-ra cнн'н.*[5]
go-intent-stat-masc+sg+cont I. **come** tell-det+sg I
'I will go. After I come back, I will teach you.'

Circumstantial:

(3) *Gu'a-**che** cu'i-si'-cн-a'-mн cнн'н.*
be=bad-**circum** travel-compl-masc=nom-stat-masc+sg+cont I[6]
'I traveled badly.'

Causal:

(4) *Co'rehuajн-**je**-jн co'rehuajн cнн'o-re che'cho-me cннcнna mнsanнcona-re.*
Coreguaje-**causal=verbal**-temp+nonseq Coreguaje words+pl-obj teach-pl+cont we you+pl-obj
'Because we are Coreguajes, we teach you Coreguaje words.'

Condition:

(5) *Cнн'н jěca sai-ja-'-mo. Sai-ma'-**to** mн'н-bi jŭ'je-jai-jн'н.*
I firewood go-intent-stat-fem+sg+cont. go-neg-**conting+nonseq** you-counterexp split-movement-imp
'I will go for firewood. If I don't go, you go and split it.'

1.2 Linkage. A further use of dependent clauses is to link sentences of a discourse—a function where the dependent clause explicitly relates the action or state of one sentence to that of the following sentence. Dependent clauses thus provide cohesion within a discourse, and they may contain new information. Independent clauses related by linkage present only those actions or states that show temporal or logical progression in the flow of the discourse. Where there is no linkage, however, there is no progression. Independent clauses not linked to the ones preceding them amplify what has just been said, add comments, or expound what has been stated previously. The one exception to this is when linkage is not used where the peak of a narrative discourse occurs.

Linkage is used with highest frequency in narrative discourse because of the nature of narratives, which are always actions with progression in time and space, rather than explanations of particular points or exhortations.

A dependent clause is considered a link when its verb recapitulates the final verb in the immediately preceding clause or a verb that occurs earlier in the same discourse, as shown in the examples below. The verb of a linking dependent clause may be a paraphrase of the final verb of the preceding clause or a generic verb, such as *cho'o-* 'do' or *ba'i-* 'be'. In both cases the link has the additional function of summarizing the action or state expressed by the preceding sentence or sentences.

The following is an example of a recapitulative link to the final verb in the immediately preceding sentence:

(6) *Cho'o-che cho'o bi'ni chura ta'ni jo'e hua'i sai-ja-na-'-me. Hua'i sani hua'i jña jainнco-re jña sнcho ãi-ja-na-'-me cниснпа hua'i.*
work-circum work+temp+seq finish+temp+seq now but again fish go-intent-pl=nom-stat-pl+cont. fish **go+temp+seq** fish get+temp+seq many-obj get+temp+seq smoke+temp+seq eat-intent-pl=nom-stat-pl+cont we fish
'After finishing doing our work, then we'll go fishing again. After having gone fishing and getting a lot, we will smoke and eat it.'

The following is an example of a recapitulative link to a final verb in a clause not immediately preceding the dependent clause link:

(7) *Tĩ'a-ja-'-тн. Cнēñe ba'i-сн-'-тн. Tĩ'a un día Florencia cнн'н ba'i-ja-'-тн chosa'aro нин'e jobo un día.*
arrive-intent-stat-masc+sg+cont near be-masc=nom-stat-masc+sg+cont. **arrive** one day Florencia I be-intent-stat-masc+sg+cont Florencia house village one day
'I will arrive. It (Florencia) is near. Having arrived, I will be in Florencia for one day.'

The following are examples of a paraphrase link (the verb of the dependent clause *che're-* 'rip' is a more specific way of stating the action of the final verb *gahua-* 'fight' of the previous clause):

(8) *Gahua-sō-guha aso-me rebana. Cā-ña che're-sō-ju huani-sō aso-me majabāi chi'a.*
fight-intensifier-punct reportative-pl+cont they. Cloth-pl rip-**intensifier-temp+nonseq** hit-intensifier reportative-pl+cont relatives only)
'They just began fighting. Ripping clothes, the relatives only were hitting one another.'

(9) *Pedro-ni Juan gahuн-na rebaн-'te rūso huēa-sō-ra chini aso-mн. Cā'a ta'ni rebaн Pedro huani aso-mн rebaн-'te. Sāi aso-mн rebaн. Cā'a cho'o-jн-na rebaн campesino chosa'aro cho'o-si'-cн chнcнna ña-si'-cн rani aso-mн rebaн.*[7]
Peter-obj John neck-locative him-obj choke+temp+seq kill-intensifier-det+sg wanted reportative-masc+sg+cont. that but he Peter hit reportative-masc+sg+cont him-obj. do=in=return-reportative-masc+sg+cont he. **that do-temp+nonseq-diffsubj** he peasant Florencia work-compl-masc=nom we see-compl-masc=nom came reportative-masc+sg+cont he
'John choked Peter and wanted to kill him. However, Peter hit him. He did it in return. As they were doing that, a peasant who had worked in Florencia, whom we had seen, came.'

In addition, free conjunctions *cā'a ta'ni* (that but) 'however' and *cā'a-je-cн-na* (that-causal=verbal-temp+nonseq-diffsubj) 'because of that' are also used as linking devices to explicitly relate sentences. These free conjunctions are used in only approximately 10% of the sentences found in text material.

The next two examples illustrate the use of free conjunctions *cā'a ta'ni* 'however' and *cā'ajecнna* 'because of that':

(10) *Macaрн curi sa-mн chн'н. Cā'a ta'ni gu'a-che beo-che cu-sa chн'н re'o-ja'-che.*[8]
little=bit money take-masc+sg+cont I. **that but** be=bad-circum be=not-circum travel-det+sg I be=good appear-circum
'I am taking a little bit of money. However, I will travel well (without problems).'

(11) *Co'rehuajн-a'-mн chн'н. Cā'a-je-cн-na co'rehuajн chн'o chн'н gutu-cн ba'i-cн-'-mн chн'н.*
Coreguaje-stat-masc+sg+cont I. **that-causal=verbal-temp+nonseq-diffsubj** Coreguaje words+pl I speak-temp+nonseq be-masc=nom-stat-masc+sg+cont I

'I am a Coreguaje. Because of that I habitually am speaking Coreguaje words.'

1.3 Suffix Categories. Following is a chart of the suffixes presented in this paper.[9] There is neutralization of the suffixes for contingency nonsequential and contingency sequential when the subject referred to is the same.

	Temporal		Contingency		General Time	Circumstantial
	Non-sequential	Sequential	Non-sequential	Sequential		
Same subject	-jʉ[10]	∅	-ni	-ni	-rʉmʉ	-che[13]
Different subject	-jʉ+na	-rena[11]	-to	-rʉ[12]		

1.4 Parameters. The parameters that govern the use of Coreguaje dependent verb suffixes are the following:

Temporal. This parameter refers to the relative time relationship between the action of a dependent clause and the action of the next clause, whether it be another dependent clause or an independent clause. The relationship may be sequential or nonsequential.

Sequential. This parameter signifies that the action of a dependent clause is completed before the action of the next clause begins. The sequence may be tight or loose, depending on the time span between the two actions. There may be a lapse of time between the two actions or one action may immediately follow the other.

Nonsequential. This parameter refers to the partial or complete overlap in time between two or more actions.

Same or different subject. This parameter concerns whether there is a change of subject between a dependent clause and its related independent clause.

Contingency. This parameter refers to whether the action or state of an independent clause is dependent on that of a dependent clause. It carries an 'if' or 'when' idea, and it is not always clear which meaning is intended, except when clarified by the context. (This is explained in the section on the contingency suffixes.)

General time. This parameter signifies that there is a time span during which at one point the action of the independent verb occurs. The duration of the time may be one day or many years or more. Causality is not a component of this parameter; change of subject also is not significant and, therefore, is not marked or implied.

Circumstantial. This parameter concerns the way in which an action is carried out or the circumstances surrounding that action. The subject of a dependent clause may be the same as that of the independent clause or it may be different. However, it does not require a change of subject suffix. The temporal relationship with the independent clause is either nonsequential or sequential.

2 Internal composition

In this section the verb suffixes and their usage are presented. These suffixes include temporal nonsequential {-jи}, temporal sequential {-rena}, contingency nonsequential -to, contingency sequential -ru, general time -rнтн, and circumstantial -che, and they are presented below in that order.

2.1 Temporal nonsequential. The temporal nonsequential verb suffix {-jи} expresses temporal overlap between the dependent clause in which it occurs and the independent clause of the same sentence. The overlap is coterminous, which means the action of the dependent clause and the action of the independent clause begin and end at the same time. The following example illustrates coterminous overlap:

(12) *Beore huн'-ña jobo ña-ju rai-si-na-'-me chнcнna.*
all house-pl village look-**temp+nonseq+samesubj** come-compl-
pl=nom-stat-pl+cont we
'While looking at all the villages, we came.'

This overlap is not incompatible with a causal relationship, though it does not assert causality. "Causal Relation (CAU) is defined as a relation which expresses one variable (the effect) as a function of another variable (the cause)" (Frederiksen 1975). In other words, the action of the independent clause could actually be a result of the action of the dependent clause, but the speaker is not calling attention to it. To call attention to a causal relation one uses the causal verbalizer suffix -je, which is discussed in section 2.2.

The following example implies causality:

(13) *Chura cho'o-che-'te ba-тн chн'н huн'e. Ba-cи chija'iro chн'н huн'e cho'o-ra chii-тн chн'н.*
now work-circum-obj have-masc+sg+cont I house. have-
temp+nonseq+samesubj tomorrow I house work-det+sg want-
masc+sg+cont I
'Now I have work to do on the house. As long as I have work, tomorrow I want to work on the house.' Or, 'Now I have work

to do on the house. Because I have work, tomorrow I want to work on the house.'

The relationship between clauses is never causal when the independent verb is *ba'i-* 'be, live'. The verb stem *-jн ba'i-* forms a close-knit progressive verb phrase, which emphasizes the progressive aspect of the action that takes place not in a moment but over a long period of time.

The following is an example of a progressive verb phrase:

(14) *Cã'a-re chнcнna asa oi-jн ba'i-me chнcнna bãi.*
that-obj we hear+temp+seq cry-**temp+nonseq+samesubj** be-pl+cont we people
'We heard that and we people are crying.'

The aspect suffixes *-si* 'completive' and *-ja* 'intentive' do not cooccur with {*-jн*} because the temporal nonsequential relationship {*-jн*} expresses is semantically incompatible with the lack of temporal overlap implied by both aspect suffixes.[14]

The suffix {*-jн*} can be followed by *-na* to denote a change of subject between the dependent and the independent clause.[15] (Exceptions to this principle are given in sec. 2.3, where *-na* is described.) Examples 15 and 16 illustrate the use of *-na*:

(15) *Iracusa guaso-mн rebana-re iracusa cã-ña-re ju'i-jн-na.*
whites+pl caused=to=think-masc+sg+cont them-obj whites+pl cloth-pl-obj wear-temp+nonseq-**diffsubj.**
'It causes you to think like whites because you wear their clothes.'

(16) *Iracusa cã-ña-re ju'i-jн co'rehuajн ba'i-che huesн-me i-hua'-na chĩ-hua'-na.*
whites+pl cloth-pl-obj wear-**temp+nonseq+samesubj** Coreguaje be-circum know=not-pl+cont this-creature-pl child-creature-pl
'Because these children wear white people's clothing, they don't know how to be Coreguajes.'

2.2 Causal verbalizer. The causal verbalizer suffix *-je* explicitly expresses causality. It occurs on nouns, noun phrases, nominalized verbs, time words, demonstratives, and adverbs. *-je* is used when the action of the independent verb is the result of the state or condition that is implied by the dependent verbalized form. When a state or condition is involved, it is expressed by the nonverbal property of the stem that *-je* follows, which can include nominalizations. *-je* serves to incorporate this nonverbal expression into the verbal morphology required by other dependent clause mechanisms.

-je is always followed by the dependent temporal nonsequential suffix {*-jн*}, which is the category most consistently compatible with causality, as seen in the following examples:

(17) *Majabāi ba-co-**je**-co ña-ra chi-ni sai-ja-goso-mo que-cheja majabāi.*
relatives+pl   have-fem=nom-**causal=verbal**-temp+nonseq+samesubj look-det+sg   want+temp+nonseq+samesubj go-intent-prob-fem+sg+cont that-place relatives+pl
'Because she is one who has relatives there, she will probably go in order to visit them.'

(18) *Cā'a ta'ni iracusa ña-to chн'н capita-'-тн. Capita-**je**-cн Bogotá chн'н sai-bi'ra-cн ba'i-тн chн'н.*
that but whites+pl look-conting+nonseq+diffsubj I chief-stat-masc+sg+cont.   chief-**causal=verbal**-temp+nonseq+samesubj Bogotá I go-begin-temp+nonseq+samesubj be-masc+sg+cont I
'However, when whites look, I am chief. Because I am chief, I am about to go to Bogotá.

(19) *Cho'o-che cho'o-ra chii-тн chн'н romi chн'н йsн-rнтн-**je**-cн-na i-rнтн chн'н.*
work-circum work-det+sg want-masc+sg+cont I women+pl I sun-general=time-**causal=verbal**-temp+nonseq-diffsubj   this-general=time I
'I want to do work, women, because now it is summertime.'

Potentially *-je* could be followed by the temporal sequential suffix {*-rena*}, which is also compatible with a causal relation. However, sequential relationships can also be shown by aspect in the verbalized form. When *-je* occurs on a nominalized verb, then, if the state or condition expressed by the nominalized form has ceased to exist by the time of the action of the independent verb, the completive aspect suffix *-si* must follow the verb stem and precede the nominalizer, as in *rai-si-na-je-jн* (come-**compl**-pl=nom-causal=verbal-temp+nonseq) 'because they are ones who came'. On the other hand, if the state or condition expressed by the nominalized form is anticipated at the time of the action of the independent verb, then the intentive aspect suffix *-ja* must follow the verb stem, as in *rai-ja-na-je-jн* (come-**intent**-pl=nom-causal=verbal-temp+nonseq) 'because they are ones who will come'. Examples 20 and 21 illustrate the use of *-si* and *-ja* with causal verbalizer *-je* on nominalized verbs:

(20) *Ja'cн-re co'rehиajн ba-**si**'-**cн-je**-cн chн'н chн'н rebaн Tama beo-cн-'-тн chн'н.*

father-obj Coreguaje have-**compl-masc=nom- causal=verbal**-
temp+nonseq+samesubj I I myself Tama be=not-masc=nom-
stat-masc+sg+cont I
'Because I am one who had a Coreguaje father, I am not a
Tama.'

(21) *Cã'a-ja'-ñe ba'i-**ja-и-je**-cн reван tao garuni-**ja-и-je**-cн йgua
abe-rитн-na tĩ-н bani aso-тн reван.*[16]
that-appear-circum be-**intent-masc=nom-causal=verbal**-
temp+nonseq+samesubj he eagle turn= into-**intent-masc=nom-
causal=verbal**-temp+nonseq+ samesubj also early-general=time-
temp=contrastive different-masc=nom was reportative-
masc+sg+cont he
'Because he was one who would be like that, because he was
one who would turn into an eagle, he was also really different
before.'

-*si* and -*ja* cannot, however, occur on nouns. Therefore, in order to
show aspect on a verbalized form whose stem is not a nominalized
verb, *ba'i-* 'be' must be used following a noun, adjective, or adverb.
Ba'i- 'be' is followed by aspect suffixes, nominalized with -*cн*
'masculine', -*co* 'feminine', or -*na* 'plural', and then verbalized in order
to fit the dependent stative format, as in the following example:

(22) *Gu'a cнн'o i'ca-cн ta'ni йgua i'ca aso-тн **bãi ba'i-si'-cн**-je-
cн.*[17]
be=bad words+pl speak-masc=nom but still spoke reportative-
masc+sg+cont **person be-compl-masc=nom**-causal=verbal-
temp+nonseq+samesubj
'He was one who spoke bad words (hard to understand);
however, he still spoke because he was one who had been a
person.'

Often *ba'i-* 'be' is used with a noun even though the aspect suffixes
do not occur. This use of *ba'i* is to emphasize the progressiveness of
the state or condition, as shown in the following example:

(23) *Cнлсна-'te gobierno presidente cнлсна-'te soi-н aso-тн
chuo-hua'-na ba'i-na-je-jн-na.*
us-obj government President us-obj call-temp+temp+nonseq
reportative-masc+sg+cont **poor-creature-pl be**-pl=nom-
causal=verbal-temp+nonseq-diffsubj
'The President is calling us because we are ones who are
poor.'

2.3 Change of subject. If there are subjects in the dependent clauses of a sentence that are different from the subject of the independent clause, the verb of each dependent clause must indicate change of subject. *-na* is the change of subject suffix that occurs with {*-jн*}, which without *-na* means the subject is the same. The dependent contingency verb suffixes *-to* and *-ru* inherently show change of subject; therefore, an overt change of subject suffix is not necessary. General time suffix *-rнтн* and circumstantial suffix *-che* are never followed by the change of subject suffix *-na* since they do not make a distinction between same and different subjects.

Example 24 below shows the change of subject suffix *-na* following the temporal nonsequential suffix { *-jн* }. Example 25 illustrates change of subject inherently expressed by the contingency nonsequential suffix *-to*.

(24) *Chēa-**cн-na** chн'н chнri ña-si'-cн-a'-тн.* grab-**temp+nonseq-diffsubj** I turn=around+temp+seq+samesubj look-compl-masc=nom-stat-masc+sg+cont
'As he (a spirit) was grabbing me, I turned around and looked.'

(25) *Chн'н jēca sai-ja-'-mo. Sai-ma'-**to** тн'н-bi jēca jū'je-jai-jн'н.* I firewood go-intent-stat-fem+sg+cont. go-neg-**conting+nonseq+diffsubj** you-counterexp firewood split-movement-imp
'I will go for firewood. If I don't go, you go and split some.'

In a sentence of three clauses in which the first two are dependent, if the first and third clauses have subject A and the second clause has subject B, there is a change of subject suffix only on the verb of the second clause, not on the first clause. The subject of the second clause must be made explicit unless it has been mentioned previously in the discourse and there is no possibility of misunderstanding or the context makes it obvious as to what the subject is.

In example 26 the subject of the second dependent clause is not made explicit, however, since the narrator was fishing and it is assumed that it is the fish that were not biting:

(26) *No'i bi'ni ācue-ma-bн-**na** mani cāi-bi'ra-si'-cн-a'-тн chн'н.*[18]
fish=with=line+temp+seq+samesubj finish+temp+seq+samesubj eat-neg-temp+nonseq-**diffsubj** go=up+temp + seq+samesubj sleep-begin-compl-masc=nom-stat-masc+sg+cont I
'I finished fishing and because the fish weren't biting, I went up and began to sleep.'

In example 27 the subject, *gerente* 'agent', of the second dependent clause is made explicit.

(27) *Нин'е jobo-'te gu'a-hua'-na-re jojo-cн ba-sa chi-ni reбaн gerente curi īsi-н-**na** huaca co-goso-тн reбaн.*
house village-obj animal-creature-pl-obj raise-temp+nonseq+samesubj be-det+sg want-conting+nonseq+samesubj he agent money give-temp+nonseq-**diffsubj** cow receive-prob-masc+sg+cont he
'He wanted to raise cattle in the village and probably because the agent gave him money, he bought a cow.'

If a subject other than that of the independent clause is used in the same sentence in two separate dependent clauses, each of the dependent clauses must indicate change of subject, even though the subject of both dependent clauses is the same. The second dependent clause, which occurs immediately following the first in all the examples found to date, is in apposition to the first clause.

In each of the following two examples (28 and 29), the second dependent clause, which is in apposition to the preceding dependent clause, is more specific.

(28) *Cнн'н-re i-cheja oracha cнн'н ba'i cheja cнн'н-bi ba'i-н-**na** capita-bi ba'i-н-**na** ba'i bāi cнн'н jē'e huesн-na bāi i-cheja rai-me cнн'н-re.*
me-obj this-place Maticurú my be place I-counterexp be-temp+nonseq-**diffsubj** chief-counterexp be-temp+nonseq-**diffsubj** be people+pl I even know=not-pl=nom people+pl this-place come-pl+cont me-obj
'Because I am here and am chief, important people who I don't even know come to me.'

(29) *Reba bāimia-н chi-si-рнтн tī'a-**to** mes de septiembre el fin de septiembre tī'a-**to** cниснna bāi beore sai-ja-goso-me.*
that moon-masc say-compl-general=time arrive-**conting**+**nonseq**+ **diffsubj** month of September the end of September arrive-**conting** +nonseq+**diffsubj** we people+pl all go-intent-prob-pl+cont
'When the month they talked about arrives, the end of September, all of us will probably go.'

2.4 Temporal sequential. The temporal sequential suffix {-*rena*} expresses a temporal sequential relationship between the dependent clause in which it occurs and the next clause in the sentence, whether that is another dependent clause or the independent clause. The action of the temporal sequential clause is completed before the action of the next clause begins. There can be a lapse of time between the events or close sequence with one event occurring immediately preceding the

next. Like {-jн}, {-rena} is not incompatible with causality. The change
of subject suffix -na is obligatory with {-rena}, which never occurs
without -na. When there is change of subject, the stem of regular verbs
is used with no affixation and the stem of radical-changing verbs is
changed by the replacement of the final syllable with -ni.

Example 30 illustrates a temporal sequential clause where there is
no change of subject. Radical-changing verb mai- 'come up' becomes
mani, and it is the stem of regular verb tī'a- 'arrive' that alone signifies
the temporal sequence. Implied causality is also illustrated in the next
examples:

(30) **Mani tī'a** hн н'e bнa-cн-'-mн.
     come=up+temp+seq+samesubj   arrive+temp+seq+samesubj
     house rest-masc=nom-stat-masc+ sg+cont
     'I come up, arrive, and rest in the house' or 'Because I come
     up and after I arrive, I rest in the house.'

Of the following two examples, 31 illustrates a temporal sequential
clause where there is change of subject. The verb of the dependent
clause is regular verb sa- 'take', which is followed by {-rena} and does
not undergo any change. However, the verb of the dependent clause in
example 32 is radical-changing verb rai- 'come', which is shortened to
ra- preceding the temporal sequential suffix. Causality is also implied in
these examples:

(31) Cнн cнn a-'te señoritas romi-chī cнн cнn a-'te na'i-guha-to-na
      San Antonio hн н'e jobo sa-**rena** cнн cнn a sai-si-na-'-me.
      us-obj señoritas women+pl-children+pl us-obj get=late-punct-
      conting+nonseq-temp=contrastive San Antonio house village
      take-**temp**+**seq**+**diffsubj** we go-compl-pl=nom-stat-pl+cont
      'When it was just getting late the young women took us to San
      Antonio and we went' or 'When it was just getting late, and
      because the young women took us to San Antonio we went.'
(32) Cнн'н cho'oje-н ra-**cнna** ña-ra cнн'н.
      my younger = brother - masc come-**temp**+**seq**+**diffsubj** look-
      det+sg I
      'My younger brother came and I will visit with him' or
      'Because my younger brother came, I will visit with him.'

The completive aspect suffix -si does not cooccur with {-rena}
because the completive aspect is inherent in the suffix, making use of
-si redundant. However, the temporal sequential form of the verb bi'ni-
'finish' is often used as an auxiliary verb following the main verb of the
clause to make the completive aspect explicit. In example 33 bi'ni-

occurs following radical-changing verb *āi-* 'eat', which changes to *āni*. In example 34 *bi'ni-* follows regular verb *cho'o-* 'work'.

(33) *Ani **bi'ni** sai-ja-'-mo chɯ'ɯ.*
eat+temp+seq+samesubj **finish+temp+seq+samesubj** go-intent-stat-fem+sg+cont I
'After I finish eating, I will go.'

(34) *Ūsɯ-rɯtɯ tī'a-to cho'o-che cho'o **bi'ni** chɯcɯna co'rehuajɯ goɯ sai-na-'-me chɯcɯna sɯribɯ.*
sun-general=time arrive-conting+nonseq+diffsubj work-circum work+temp+ seq+samesubj **finish+temp+seq+samesubj** we Coreguaje turtles+pl go-pl=nom-stat-pl+cont we downriver
'When summertime arrives, and after we have finished doing our work, we Coreguajes go downriver for turtles.'

2.5 Contingency nonsequential. The contingency nonsequential verb suffix *-to* expresses an 'if' or 'when' relationship between the dependent clause in which it occurs and the independent clause of the same sentence. It is not always clear which meaning is intended. *-to*, though not basically temporal, is compatible with a temporal relationship because it can have the meaning of 'when' with the implication of temporal overlap. Likewise, {*-jɯ*} and {*-rena*}, though not basically implicative, are not incompatible with the contingency relationship because they can imply causality.

Examples 35 and 36 can imply either an 'if' or a 'when' relationship between the dependent and independent clauses, and they involve temporal overlap as well:

(35) *Bōse ro'i ba-**to** rɯa gu'a-tɯ bōse ro'i.*
merchandise pay have-**conting+nonseq+diffsubj** very be=bad-masc+sg+cont merchandise pay
'When (or if) you have debts, it is bad.'

(36) *Cā'a ta'ni chɯ'ɯ bāi jū'i-**to** oi-ɯ ba-sa chi-tɯ chɯ'ɯ.*
that but I people+pl be=sick-**conting+nonseq+diffsubj** cry-temp+ nonseq+samesubj be-det+sg want-masc+sg+cont I
'When (or if) people are sick, I want to be crying for (concerned for) them.'

Any potential ambiguity as to whether the contingency clause implies an 'if' or a 'when' relationship with the independent clause can often be cleared up by the context, as shown in examples 37 and 38. In example 37 a 'when' relationship is implied; however, in example 38 an 'if' relationship is implied because of the addition of *re'o-* 'good' preceding *ñata-* 'dawns'. This implies that it may not be a good dawn and therefore the action of the independent clause will not be carried out:

(37) *Chija'iro ñata-to cho'o-jữ'ʜ.*
      tomorrow dawns -**conting**+ **nonseq** + **diffsubj** work-imp
      'Tomorrow when it dawns, work.'
(38) *Chija'iro re'o ñata-to cho'o-jữ'ʜ.*
      tomorrow good dawns-**conting+nonseq+diffsubj** work-imp
      'Tomorrow if it dawns nice, work.'

If the action or state of the independent verb is stative completive, -*to* always implies 'when', never 'if', as shown in examples 39 and 40:

(39) *Chʜ'ʜ chī-hua'-ʜ ña-cʜ aine-cʜ ba'i-to ai bāi i-ja'-che ba'i-si-na-'-me būicũti bāi.*
      I   child-creature-masc   look-temp+nonseq+samesubj   grow=up-
      temp+nonseq+samesubj   be-**conting+nonseq+diffsubj**   old
      people+pl   this-appear-circum   be-compl-pl=nom-stat-pl+cont
      Granario people+pl
      'When I as a child was growing up and observing, this is the way the old people (our ancestors) of Granario lived.'
(40) *Sai-to ma'a carretera ma'a rʜ'tʜhua-'te īsi cuānʜ ũi-si'-cʜ-a'-mʜ.*
      go-**conting+nonseq+diffsubj**   path   road   path   edge-locative
      pineapples+pl piles+pl lie-compl-masc=nom-stat-masc+sg+cont
      'When we went, there were piles of pineapples lying by the edge of the road.'

The 'if' relationship is made explicit when the counterfactual suffix -*ra'a* is used with the independent verb of the sentence whose dependent clause contains -*to* to indicate a special kind of contingency.[19] This is illustrated in example 4l, which is the statement by a man just after he had been knifed by another man:

(41) *Hua'ti ba-ni ũgua-ja'-che tējño-ra'a-mʜ chʜ'ʜ mʜ'ʜ-re.*
      knife   have-**conting+nonseq+samesubj**   same-appear-circum   cut-
      counterfac-masc+sg+cont I you-obj
      'If I had a knife (but I don't), I would cut you in the same way.'

In example 42 the speaker is talking about a time during his youth when many were sick with measles. A large number had died as a result, but he lived. He states the condition on account of which he had survived, which was that God had refused to let him die:

(42) *Dios ūse-ma¹-to cɥɥ¹ɥ jūni-sō-ra¹a-si¹-cɥ-a¹-tɥ cɥɥ¹ɥ.*
God prevent-neg-**conting+nonseq+diffsubj** I be=sick-intensifier-**counterfac**-compl-masc=nom-stat-masc+sg+cont I
'If God hadn't prevented it (but he did), I would have died.'

The contrastive suffix *-na* can occur after *-to*; however, further study would be necessary for the reason for this to become clear. *-na* never occurs after *-ru*.

Example 43 below is from a story about a lazy boy who kept telling his sister's husband that he was going into the jungle with him. However, whenever it was time to go, the lazy boy wouldn't go. One day the brother-in-law came back from the jungle and told his wife and her younger brother, the lazy boy, about some *huansoco* fruit that had fallen from a tree and was all over the ground. It is at this point that the contrastive suffix *-na* follows *-to* on *cɥa-* 'tell'. The brother-in-law's having told about the fruit is that which motivates the lazy boy finally to go to the jungle, whereas previously he had always promised to go but never did. Again, further study is necessary to verify this.

(43) *Cɥa-to-na hɥa-ɥ maja-a¹cho cho¹o-je-ɥ a¹cho cɥɥ¹ɥ sani ācuera chura ta¹ni chija¹iro.*
tell-conting+nonseq-**contrastive** in-law-masc his-sister younger=brother-masc sister I go+temp+seq+ samesubj eat-det+sg now but tomorrow
'When the brother-in-law told them (and not before), "Sister, tomorrow, however, I will go and eat the fruit," the lazy boy said.'

In example 44 it could be that people thought their sister's coming was a result of their having been thinking about her more than usual, and therefore *-tona* occurs:

(44) *Rɥa guasa-jɥ ba¹i-to-na tɥ¹ɥ cɥɥcɥna-¹te rai-mo a¹cho.*
much think-temp+nonseq+samesubj be-conting+nonseq-**contrastive** you us-obj come-fem+sg+cont sister
'When we are thinking about you (more than under ordinary circumstances), you come to us, sister.'

2.6 Contingency sequential. The contingency sequential verb suffix *-ru*, like *-to*, expresses an 'if' or 'when' relationship between the dependent clause in which the suffix occurs and the independent clause of the same sentence. *-ru* differs from *-to* in that it expresses a sequential relationship rather than temporal overlap. In other words, the condition expressed by the *-ru* clause has to be an action or state completed prior

to the action or state of the independent clause. There is the same
ambiguity as to whether it means 'if' or 'when', and the distinctions are
made explicit in the same ways as mentioned for -to. -ru can also occur
with the counterfactual suffix -ra'a.

Example 45 illustrates the use of -ru with counterfactual suffix -ra'a
when there is a change of subject:

(45) *Neato toachochин ra-tu i-cheja ba'i-mane-ra'a-mo chн'н.*
      yesterday plane come-**conting+seq+diffsubj** this-place be-neg-
      counterfac-fem+sg+cont I
      'If the plane had come yesterday (which it didn't), I wouldn't
      be here.'

Example 46 illustrates the use of -ru when there is no change of
subject:

(46) *Rна hua'i jña-ni chнcнna sucho-na-'-me chнcнna*
      much fish+pl get-**conting+seq+samesubj** we smoke-pl=nom-stat-
      pl+cont we
      'When (or if) we get a lot of fish, we then smoke it.'

-to and -ru can both be followed by the counterfactual suffix -'te. In
such cases, -'te seems at times to express a contrary-to-fact condition
similar to that expressed by -to and -ru clauses when the counterfactual
suffix -ra'a occurs with the independent verb, as illustrated by the
following examples:

(47) *Curi ba-to ĩsi-ra'a-mo.*
      money   have-**conting+nonseq+diffsubj**   sell-**counterfac**-
      fem+sg+cont
      'If you had money (which you don't), I would sell it to you.'
(48) *Curi ba-to-'te ĩsi-mo chн'н mн'н-re.*
      money   have-**conting+ nonseq+diffsubj-counterfac**   give-
      fem+sg+cont I you-obj
      'If you had money (which you don't), I would sell it to you.'
(49) *Chija'iro re'o ñata-ru cho'o-jũ'н.*
      tomorrow good dawns- **conting+ seq+diffsubj** work-imp
      'If tomorrow dawns pretty, work.'
(50) *Chija'iro re'o ñata-ru-'te cho'o-jũ'н.*
      tomorrow good dawns-**conting+seq+diffsubj-counterfac** work-
      imp
      'If tomorrow should dawn pretty (which I don't expect it will),
      work.'

In text material, -*to'te* and -*ru'te* never occur when -*ra'a* occurs
with the independent verb. When several different adult speakers of the
language were asked, it was not possible to elicit this combination from
them; they would not accept it. However, recently two teenage
speakers said it was acceptable, which would indicate that the system
may be in flux at this point.

(51)   *Curi ba-ni co-ra'a-mн cнн'н.*
       money have-**conting+nonseq**+ **samesubj** buy-**counterfac**-
       masc+sg+cont I
       'If I had money (which I don't), I would buy it.'

(52)   *Curi ba-ni-'te co-ra'a-mн cнн'н.*
       money have-**conting+nonseq**+ **samesubj-counterfac** buy-
       counterfac-masc+sg+cont I
       'If I had money (which I don't), I would buy it.'

2.7 General time. The general time suffix -*rнmн* denotes a temporal
relationship between the dependent clause in which it occurs and the
independent clause. It provides the time setting for the action or state
expressed by the independent verb, just as other time words do, such
as *chura* 'now', *na'a bani* 'later', or *chija'iro* 'tomorrow'.

(53)   *Cā'a gātнcha bāi cнн'н-re cu'i-**rнmн** cнн'н-re cнa-si-na-'-me*
       cнн'н-re.
       that Putumayo people+pl me-obj travel-**general=time**
       me-obj tell-compl-pl=nom-stat-pl+cont me-obj
       'The people of the Putumayo, during the time I was traveling
       there, told me that.'

In example 54 the second general time clause is both in apposition
with and more specific than the first general time clause:

(54)   *Cнн'н abe-**rнmн** utija'o huн'e ba'i-**rнmн** maestra che'cho-si'-e-*
       re cнa-ra.
       I early-**general=time** paper house be-**general=time** teacher
       teach-compl-circum-obj tell-det+sg
       'I will tell you what the teacher taught us during the early time
       (days), during the time I was in school.'

-*rнmн* is followed by the temporal contrastive suffix -*na* in order to
show temporal contrast between the time word or clause where it
occurs and another time word or clause explicitly mentioned in the
same text or implied by the context.[20]

In example 55 the speaker is drawing attention to a time when it was very cold. It may imply a contrast between what the traveler would have liked the weather to be and the way it was, rainy and cold.

(55) *Rна sнsн-rнmн-na снисна-'te sa-si'-сн-a'-mн rē-нин.*
       very cold-general=time-**temp=contrastive** us-obj take-compl-
       masc=nom-stat-masc+sg+cont motor-shape
       'During a very cold time the motorboat took us.'

Then in example 56 the travelers were supposed to have boarded a plane early in the morning but were delayed because of rain. In this case contrast is implied between the time when they were scheduled to board the plane, which is not mentioned in the text, and the time they actually did board it:

(56) *Satena-нин tui-si-na-'-te снисна осо ñata-si-rнmн-na.*
       Satena-shape board-compl-pl=nom-stat-pl+cont we rain dawns-
       compl-general=time-**temp=contrastive**
       'We boarded the Satena plane following a rainy dawn (rather than the scheduled time).'

The completive aspect suffix *-si* can occur immediately preceding *-rнmн* to indicate the period of time after which another event takes place. *-rнmн* with *-si* differs from the temporal sequential suffix {*-rena*} in that {*-rena*} refers to the completion of an action or state, not the period of time following that action. For example, *reван sai-si-rнmн* 'the time after he had gone' refers to the period of time after the action of going, while *reван sa-сна* 'after he went' refers to the action itself.

(57) *Cā'a-ja'-ñe снн'н сho'o-si'-сн-a'-mн mнsaпнсoпa sani-sō-si-*
       rнmн.
       that-appear-circum I do-compl-masc=nom-stat-masc+sg+cont
       you+pl go-intensifier-**compl+general=time**
       'That is what happened to me during the time after you had gone away.'

2.8 Circumstantial. The circumstantial suffix *-che* is used with dependent verbs to fulfill various functions. One function is to indicate that the verb where it occurs modifies circumstantially the action expressed by the independent verb. This modification is the same as that of an adverb that modifies the action or state by describing the circumstances surrounding them. The subject of a *-che* clause may be the same as or different from that of the independent clause and does not require a change of subject suffix.

(58) *Gu'a chн'o jē'e i'ca-ma'-ñe gu'a chн'o asa-ma'-ñe bāi ba'i-si-na-'-me.*
be=bad words+pl even speak-neg-**circum** be=bad words+pl hear-neg-**circum** people+pl live-compl-pl=nom-stat-pl+cont
'The people lived without speaking bad words and without listening to bad words.'

-che also may be used to amplify what has been said in the previous sentence. For example, a sentence in which *-che* occurs may have the same independent verb or clause as the previous sentence, but additional information is presented in the dependent clause formed by using *-che*. A *-che* clause may also be a repetition of the dependent clause of the preceding sentence with a slight change in the independent clause. This is seen in example 60 below.

In example 59 the dependent *-che* clause amplifies the action of the preceding independent clause:

(59) *Chн'н chosa'aro chн'н sai-si'-cн-a'-тн. Gu'a-**che** guasa-ma'-ñe chн'н sai-si'-cн-a'-тн chн'н.*
I Florencia I go-compl-masc=nom-stat-masc+sg+cont. be=bad-**circum** think-neg-**circum** I go-compl-masc=nom-stat-masc+sg+cont I
'I went to Florencia. I went without thinking badly (without expecting problems).'

In example 60 the *-che* clause is a repetition of the dependent *-che* clause of the preceding sentence:

(60) *Beo-**che** quince pesos нco jñaca ro'i-si'-cн-a'-тн chн'н rна ro'i jñaca. Beo-**che** ro'i-sō-si'-cн-a'-тн chн'н.*
have=not-**circum** fifteen pesos medicine needle pay-compl-masc=nom-stat-masc+sg+cont I much pay needle. have=not-**circum** pay-intensifier-compl-masc=nom-stat-masc+sg+cont I
'Not really having much money, I paid fifteen pesos for an expensive injection. Not really having much money, I spent it all.'

-che can also be used to make a verb into an inanimate noun, just as the nominalizer suffix {-cн} makes a verb into an animate noun. *-che* can be preceded by the aspect suffixes *-si* 'completive' and *-ja* 'intentive'; thus, if *-che* is preceded by *-si*, it becomes *-si'e*. This form expresses the state resulting from an action that has already taken place, as in *cho'osi'e* 'that which was made'. If it occurs with *-ja*, *-che* indicates a state that will exist in the future as a result of an action, as

in *cho'ojache* 'that which will be made'.

Example 61 shows the use of circumstantial *-che* with the completive aspect suffix *-si*:

(61) *Uja cuаnн īsi cuаnн tн'se-si'-e rubн cā'a tī'a ña-jн ba'i-to rani ācue-jн'н īsi chнcнna-'te iracusa co ājño-si'-cн-a'-mн.*
big piles+pl pineapples+pl piles+pl cut=off-**circum** just that arrive+temp+seq+samesubj look-temp+nonseq+samesubj beconting+nonseq+diffsubj come eat-imp pineapples+pl us-obj white buy+temp+seq+samesubj feed-compl-masc = nom-stat-masc+sg+cont
'When we arrived and were just looking at the big piles of pineapples that had been cut off the stalk, he said, "Come and eat pineapples." The white bought pineapple and fed it to us.'

A verb nominalized with *-che* can be followed by the object suffix *-re*, like any noun or nominalized verb, as shown in example 62:

(62) *Cā'a-ja'-ñe ba'i cheja bāi te'e-н meno jē'e beo-cн cā-ña meno jē'e beo-**che**-'te choa-si'-e-**re** ju'i-н bani aso-mн.* that-appear-circum be place person one-masc dirt even be=not-temp+nonseq+samesubj cloth-pl dirt even be=not-**circum-obj** wash-compl-**circum-obj** wear-temp+nonseq+samesubj was reportative-masc+sg+cont
'In a place like that (without water) there was one man who wasn't dirty, who wore clothes that were not dirty and that had been washed.'

There are several specialized usages of *-che*. If the verb stem of the dependent clause in which it occurs is the same as the verb stem of the independent clause of the same sentence, the action expressed by the independent verb is greatly intensified, as shown in the following example:

(63) *Rнa huai-**che** huani-sō aso-me.*
much hit-**circum** hit- intensifier reportative-pl+cont
'They were really hitting a lot.'

It is possible in a given sentence to have two circumstantial dependent clauses, formed by use of *-che*, which are in contrast. The contrast relates to actions or states, and it is always between negative and positive. Contrast can also be expressed by the use of lexical opposites like *re'oja'che* 'well' and *gu'ache* 'badly'.

For example, the contrast in 64 is between sitting and standing while riding in a bus:

(64) *Garo-sai-huн cнисипа ñu'i-ma'-ñe ruibн писа-che sai-si-na-'-me cнисипа.*
car-go-shape we sit-neg-**circum** just stand-**circum** go-compl-pl=nom-stat-pl+cont we
'We went in the bus without sitting but just standing.'

And example 65 illustrates the use of lexical opposites to express contrast:

(65) *Gu'a-reba-che ba'i-mane-ra re'o-ja'-che.*
be=bad-emphatic-**circum** be-neg-det+sg good-appear-**circum**
'I will not live badly but well (good-appearing way).'

Another use of *-che* is as a complement in a negative desiderative verb phrase. First of all, a positive desiderative verb phrase is formed as follows: *Na-ra chii-тн cнн'н.* (look-det+sg want/say-masc+sg+cont I.) 'I want to look' or ' "I'll look," I said. ' The two translations are possible because the verb *chii-* can mean either 'want' or 'say'. Also, the second translation is valid because *ñara* 'I'll look' can occur as an independent clause without *chiiтн* 'I want/say'.

The negative of the above would be:
Na-mane-ra chii-тн cнн'н. (look-neg-det+sg want/say-masc+sg+cont I) 'I wanted to not look' or ' "I won't look," I said.'

In the above verb phrases it is never the independent verb that is negative. In order to make the independent verb negative the dependent verb must be formed with *-che* rather than with *-ra*, as in the following:
Na-ñe gue-тн cнн'н. (look-**circum** want=not-masc+sg+cont I) 'I don't want to look.'

Another basic difference in the three verb phrases immediately above is that in the first two the verb *chii* 'want, say' must always be the independent verb. However, in a *-che* verb phrase the independent verb can be any verb that is either inherently negative or negativized. Further, a *-che* word or clause may be the complement of another dependent *-che* clause or word. This is illustrated in examples 66 and 67. In example 66 *-che* is used as the complement of a negative independent verb:

(66) *Asa-che gue-si'-cн-a'-тн cнн'н-re.*
hear-circum want=not-compl-masc=nom-stat-masc+sg+cont
me-obj

'He didn't want to listen to me.'

In example 67 *gu'ache* 'be bad' is the complement of the negativized verb of a dependent clause:

(67) *Gu'a-che guasa-ma'-ñe cнн'н sai-si'-сн-а'-тн cнн'н.*
be=bad **circum** think-neg-**circum** I go-compl-masc=nom-stat-masc + sg+cont I
'I went not thinking badly (not expecting problems).'

3 Conclusion

In this paper I present the Coreguaje dependent verb suffixes—their categories, their parameters, and their internal composition. It is seen that dependent clauses play a very important role in sentence and discourse structure, functioning to express temporal and logical relationships between clauses and sentences. Without dependent clauses the flow of speech would be very dry and uninteresting. A narration would lack the details that give life to the story or the listener needs to know in order to understand what is being said. Therefore, a knowledge of the usage of dependent clauses is necessary for an understanding of the language as a whole.

Notes

1 Coreguaje is spoken by five hundred or more people of that same name. They live in various villages located on the Orteguaza River and its tributaries in the Intendencia de Caquetá in Colombia, South America. The present analysis is based on texts given by members of this language group who live in the village of Maticurú. Coreguaje is a member of the Western Tucanoan language family.

2 The Coreguaje transcription reflects a sound system consisting of the following: voiceless aspirated stops /p/,/t/,/k/(written with *c/qu* as in Spanish); voiceless unaspirated stops /b/,/d/(rare),/g/,/'/(glottal); alveolar tap /r/; fricatives /s/,/h/(written *j* as in Spanish); nasals /m/,/n/,/ñ/,/jñ/ (voiceless alveopalatal); semivowels /w/(written *hu*), and /dy/(written *ch*); vowels /a/,/e/,/i/,/o/,/u/,/ʉ/ (high central unrounded); and their nasalized counterparts written with ˜. *ch* and *ñ* neutralize to *ñ* when occurring in a suffix contiguous to a nasalized vowel. The symbol *h* is used between *u* and another vowel to signify a syllable break as opposed to a diphthong.

3 The abbreviations of category labels used in glosses are circum circumstantial, compl completive, conting contingency, cont continuative, counterexp counterexpectancy, counterfac counterfactual, det determinative, diffsubj different subject, fem feminine, imp imperative, intent intentive, masc masculine, neg negative, nom nominalizer, nonseq nonsequential, obj object, pl plural, prob probability, punct punctiliar, samesubj same subject, seq sequential, sg singular, stat stativizer, temp temporal, and verbal verbalizer.

4 In the formation of independent verbs, tense is not the determining factor. An action or state is either continuative or stative. A continuative action is one that is continuing either actually or in effect. An independent verb is formed by a verb stem followed by the gender suffixes *-тн* 'masculine' or *-mo* 'feminine', or the

number suffix -*me* 'plural'. In the singular there is no distinction between persons; the only distinction is between masculine and feminine. The plural is the same for all persons and both genders. There are three types of statives: completive, habituative, and intentive. The completive stative is formed according to the following sequence: verb=stem-compl-nom-stat-gender=suffix, as in *sai-si¹-cи-a¹-mи* 'I went' or 'I am one who went'. The stative habituative is formed as follows: verb=stem-nom-stat-gender=suffix, as in *sai-cи-¹-mи* 'I habitually go' or 'I am one who habitually goes'. The stative intentive is formed thus: verb=stem-intent-nom-stat-gender=suffix, as in *sai-ja-na-¹-me* 'we will go' or 'we are ones who will go'. In the stative intentive singular the nominalizer is dropped and the resulting form is *sai-ja-¹-mи* 'I (masculine or feminine) will go' or 'I am one who will go'.

5 There are two classes of verbs, regular and radical-changing, like *cho¹o-* 'work' (regular) and *sai-* 'go' (radical-changing). Radical-changing verbs may undergo one of two stem changes, depending on what suffixes immediately follow them. One change is a simple shortening of the stem by loss of the final syllable, and the other change consists of the final syllable's being replaced with -*ni*, For example, radical-changing verb *ba¹i-* 'be' becomes *ba* or *bani;* *ñe¹e-* 'wear beads' becomes *ñe* or *ñeni;* *sai-* 'go' becomes *sa* or *sani;* *see-* 'ask' becomes *sē* or *sēni;* and *chii-* 'say' becomes *chi* or *chini.*

6 Coreguaje aspect suffixes are -*sō* 'intensifier', -*reba* 'emphatic', -*jai/-ja/-jani* 'movement', -*cai/-ca/-cani* 'benefactive', -*guha* 'punctiliar', -*gojño* 'passive', -*te¹e* 'frustrative', -*goso* 'probability', -*ma¹/-ma/-mane* 'negative', -*ra¹a* 'counterfactual', -*si/-si¹* 'completive', -*ja/-ja¹* 'intentive', and the gender suffixes -*mи* 'masculine' and -*mo* 'feminine', and the number suffix -*me* 'plural'.

7 The object suffix -*re* has an alternate form -*¹te*. The object suffix is not obligatory.

8 The determinative suffixes are -*ra* 'singular' on regular verbs, -*sa* 'singular' on radical-changing verbs, and -*ñu* 'plural' for both verb types. There is no distinction of person or gender in the singular or in the plural. This suffix is used to express a strong determination to perform an action. It is also used along with the verb *chii-* 'want, say' to form a desiderative verb phrase meaning 'I want to. . .'.

9 I wish to express thanks to Dr. Joseph E. Grimes for his invaluable help in the analysis of the suffixes of Coreguaje and in the preparation of this paper. I am grateful to the Coreguaje people of the village of Maticurú who so willingly teach us their language and have provided the text material on which the analysis of this paper is based. Also, the analysis of the dependent verb suffixes was greatly aided by the concordance made on the IBM 1410 computer at the University of Oklahoma under the Linguistic Information Retrieval Project of the Summer Institute of Linguistics and the University of Oklahoma Research Institute, and sponsored by Grant GS-1605 of the National Science Foundation.

10 -*jи*} represents the suffix set -*(c)и* 'masculine singular', -*(c)o* 'feminine singular', and -*jи* 'plural'. There is no gender distinction in plural. These suffixes can be followed by -*na* to denote a change of subject. -*(c)и* 'masculine' and -*(c)o* 'feminine' are homophonous with the animate nominalizers in the singular. However, the plural nominalizer is -*na,* so the two sets differ. Furthermore, the nominalized forms cannot be followed by the change of subject suffix -*na,* and the {-*jи*} suffix cannot be followed by the object suffixes -*re* and -*ni*. Also {-*jи*} does not occur with aspect suffixes -*si* 'completive' or -*ja* 'intentive', but the nominalized form can include either. Although the two sets are clearly distinct in their overall properties, some ambiguities occur.

11 {-*rena*} represents the suffix set -*c(и)na* 'masculine singular', -*(c)ona* feminine singular, and -*rena* 'plural' for regular verbs and -*tena* 'plural' for radical-changing verbs. This set of suffixes is used when there is a change of subject in the next clause. They differ from temporal nonsequential {-*jи*} in that {-*rena*} never occurs

without the change of subject suffix *-na*. However, if there is no change of subject, only the verb stem is used for regular verbs, and the stems of radical-changing verbs are changed by replacing the final syllable with *-ni*.

12 *-ru* has an alternate form *-tu*. *-ru* occurs on regular verbs and *-tu* occurs on radical-changing verbs. The two-syllable stem of a radical-changing verb is shortened by dropping the second syllable preceding this suffix. If there is no change of subject, *-ni* is added to regular verbs and replaces the final syllable of radical-changing verbs.

13 The circumstantial suffix *-che* has an alternate form *-e* following the aspect suffix *-si* 'completive'. It also has an alternate form *-ñe* because *ch* and *ñ* neutralize to *ñ* when occurring in a suffix contiguous to a nasal vowel.

14 The completive suffix *-si* and the intentive suffix *-ja* have alternate forms *-si'* and *-ja'*.

15 *-na* is the change of subject suffix that occurs on {*-jи*}, which without *-na* means no change in subject. The dependent contingency verb suffixes *-to* and *-ru*, discussed later in this paper, inherently mean change of subject; therefore, no overt change of subject suffix is necessary. The general time suffix *-rиmи* and the circumstantial suffix *-che* do not distinguish same or different subject.

16 The nominalizer suffixes *-cи* 'masculine' and *-co* 'feminine' change to *-и* and *-o* after *-ja* 'intentive' in this construction.

17 Verb stems without affixation function as modifiers preceding nominals as in *gu'a chи'o* 'bad words'.

18 The temporal nonsequential suffix {*-jи*} following the negative suffix becomes *-bи*.

19 *-ra'a* can occur in an independent clause when there is no *-to* or *-ru* dependent clause. The condition that would normally be expressed by a dependent clause is implied but not overtly mentioned. The *-ra'a* clause expresses an action or state that would have happened if something had not intervened to prevent it, for example, *Tиā'i-ra'a-si'-cи-a'-mи chи'и*. (fall-**counterfac**-compl-masc = nom-stat-masc+sg+cont 1). 'I almost fell' or 'I would have fallen'; however, whatever prevented the fall is not mentioned.

20 The temporal contrastive suffix *-na* can be distinguished from the change of subject suffix *-na* in that the former occurs on *-rиmи* 'general time', which never makes a distinction between same or different subject. It is also different from the plural nominalizer suffix *-na* in that the temporal contrastive suffix *-na* on *-rиmи* never occurs with the counterexpectancy suffix *-bi* or the object suffix *-re*, which occurs on nominalized forms and other nouns, while plural nominalizer *-na* does occur with *-bi* and *re*.

Reference

Frederiksen, Carl H. 1975. "Representing Logical and Semantic Structure of Knowledge Acquired from Discourse." *Cognitive Psychology* 7:371-458.

Higher-level Conjunctions in Karitiâna

Rachel M. Landin

This paper describes the conjunctions that function at levels higher than the sentence in Karitiâna.[1] The rhetorical relations expressed by these conjunctions apply in all types of texts so far recorded, that is, speeches, historical narratives, and folk tales.

Following Halliday and Hasan (1976), I see the conjunctive relation as a semantic one, specifying the way in which what follows is systematically connected to what has gone before. They suggest four categories of conjunctive relation: additive, adversative, temporal, and causal.

To account for the higher-level conjunctions present in the Karitiâna data, only the categories additive, temporal, and causal are needed.[2] The additive conjunction is *atūm* 'and'. The temporal conjunctions are *a'ot* 'meanwhile', *amuk* 'afterwards', and *apip* 'then'. The causal conjunctions are *atukit* 'therefore' and *māsōg* 'and so'.[3]

Interclausal link		Above sentence link	
tūm	'also'	*atūm*	'and'
'ot	'while'	*a'ot*	'meanwhile'
muk,mu	'after'	*amuk*	'afterwards'
tukiri	'if'	*atukit*	'therefore'

Table 1

Four of the above conjunctions are derived from their corresponding interclausal link words by the addition of the prefix *a-* 'deictic reference', as shown in table 1.

1 Additive conjunction

atūm 'and' expresses the rhetorical relation of simple addition.

"Ako-pip a-or-oko" māsōg ka-ʹa-t atūm nukusuk īm-putup-tuso ʹot māsōg nāka-tata ōm Pōhūwūmā
many-place you-get-again then narrative-say-past **and** ant him-hurt-continuous while then narrative-go it=seems Pōhūwūmā
' "We will get you all again," they said. And while the ants were hurting him, Pōhūwūmā went.'

2 Temporal conjunctions

aʹot 'meanwhile' expresses a temporal relation of simultaneity with a durative sense. While one action is continuing in time, another action takes place, whose boundaries are within those of the first action:

```
While _____A_____
Then              a'ot    B
```

Amuk ka-pā-oko-t sepa. Aʹot nā-pisoyya-t sarut epeʹop taso opʹit.
afterwards narrative-weave-again-past basket. **meanwhile** narrative-apply=pepper-past they=say tree=hole man youth
'Afterwards he wove another basket. Meanwhile the young man put pepper in the hole in the tree.'

amuk 'afterwards' expresses the temporal relation of succession with completion, in the sense that, when one event is complete, the other takes place. Thus a time gap is implied, which can be of short or long duration.

```
First___A___   then  amuk    B
```

Amāg amāg goko amāg amāg giyo amuk nā-uru-oko-t gōgōrōgō tu.
plant plant cassava plant plant corn **afterwards** narrative-come-again-past summer big
'They planted cassava, they planted corn. Afterwards the dry season returned.'

apip 'then' is used to express a relationship of sequence between events, but without the completive aspect implied by the use of *amuk*. When *apip* is used the temporal relation between the propositions is a much looser one, and a time gap is not necessarily implied.

"ay sara tu a u" i-puʹeso "sara tu a u" apip nāka-hot-∅ i-puʹeso.

"you cayman large you eat" his-people "cayman large you eat"
then narrative-go-past his-people
' "The large cayman ate you, it ate you," said his people. Then
they went.'

3 Causal conjunctions

atukit 'therefore' expresses the causal relationship 'because of A
therefore B'. Sequence of time is implied only in the sense that the
second proposition follows logically from the occurrence of the first; no
examples found so far permit any possibility of ordering except 'A,
then B'.

*Nāka-u-t iso Ohēy mop māsorokõnh **atukit** nā-omuk sarut Isoason
ta mēm-oko.*
narrative-eat-past fire Ohēy no-more cinders **therefore** narrative-
be=ashamed they=say Isoason to enter-again
'The fire ate Ohēy, he was no more, only cinders. Therefore
Isoason was ashamed to return.'

In its use as a conjunction, *māsõg* 'and so' expresses the semantic
relationship of reason and result. The result proposition always follows
the reason proposition.

*Mūnhūm sakūn uyya-taka-pukuy-i. Kanat uyya-taka-m'a-i **māsõg** i-
pu'u-i õwā.*
three sacks we-emphatic-pull=up-future. much we-emphatic-make-
future **and=so** they-eat-future children
'We will pull up three sackfuls. We will make a lot. And so the
children will eat.'

The above use of *māsõg* is found in all types of texts. However,
there are further uses of *māsõg* that are restricted to the narrative
folktale genre. These are of two types as follows.

3.1 When there has been a break in the event line, such as when
background information has been given, or a conversation reported, the
resumption of events is usually indicated by the occurrence of *māsõg*
on the first event clause.

*"Mõnā tūm i-amo-tuso pāmpi hu" iri'ay **māsõg** ka-hoto õm anuk
sarut se tūm.*
which way he-climb-continuous sky question say **link** narrative-go
it=seems intend they=say water way

' "Which way does one climb up to the sky?" he asked. Then it seems he went by way of the water.'

3.2 When there is a change of subject from the one who has been responsible for the events of the previous clauses to some other participant, this subject change may be indicated by the presence of *māsōg*.

*"Non" iri'ay. Māsōg ka-tat. Māsōg ka-hori i-anikiy taso. I-anikiy i-anikiy guw i-anikiy guw i-anikiy guw otām iri'ay **māsōg** ka-hana ōm sarut.*
ready he=say then narrative-go **then** narrative-go him-behind man. him-behind him-behind hidden him-behind hidden him-behind hidden arrive he=say **then** narrative-speak it=seems they=say
' "It is ready," he said. So then he went. The man went behind him, behind him, behind him, hidden behind him, hidden behind him, hidden. "We've arrived," he said. Then it seems he spoke, they say.'

The foregoing example gives three occurrences of *māsōg*. The first is an instance of its use after conversation to indicate a return to the event line, and the second and third show its use to indicate a change of subject.

One example exists of *māsōg* cooccurring with *amuk* where there is a return to the event line (calling for *māsōg*) and also a time break from the previous events (calling for *amuk):*

*"Ka-pip ta-ator-i u-o opok, opok aka tukiri" māsōg ka-'a-t sarut. Māsōg kahut i ipi pip māsōg nā-atot-∅ i-o opok. **Māsōg amuk** nāka-kata-wak.*
"this-locative emphatic-take-future my-head Indian, Indian be if" then narrative-say-past they=say. then thus he say locative link narrative-take-past his-head Indian. **then afterwards** narrative-sleep-want
' "The Indians will take away my head in it, if there are Indians!" he said. And so, in the place where he said, the Indian did take his head. Then, afterwards, they wanted to go to sleep.'

Notes

1 The Karitiâna language is spoken by approximately seventy-five people resident on the Pôsto Indígena Karitiâna in the Territory of Rondonia, Brazil. The language belongs to the Tupi stock, and to the Arikêm language family (Rodrigues 1968). The data on which this study is based were collected during the period September 1972 to August 1976. Many Karitiâna Indians have served as language helpers, and my

debt to them for their cooperation is very great. The present paper was written at a field workshop in linguistics held under the auspices of the Summer Institute of Linguistics in Porto Velho, Rondônia, Brazil, from September to December 1976. and directed by Joseph Grimes.

2 For a description of the interclause link words see my previous paper "A preliminary report on Karitiâna sentence structure" on file with the Summer Institute of Linguistics in Brasília.

3 The orthography used throughout this paper is based on a phonemic analysis by the present author and David Landin on file with the Summer Institute of Linguistics in Brasília. The Karitiâna phonological system consists of five oral vowels /a,e,i,o,u/ and their nasalized equivalents. The vowel symbolized *u* has the IPA value [ɨ]. There are thirteen consonants /p,t,s,k,'/; /w,r,y,h/; /m,n,nh,g/. The consonant /'/ has the IPA value [ʔ]. The continuants /w,r,y,h/ have nasalized allophones adjacent to nasalized vowels. The nasals have the phonetic values [m, n, ñ, ŋ] adjacent to nasalized vowels, [mb, nd, ñdy, ŋg] preceding oral vowels, and [bm, dn, dñ, gŋ] following oral vowels. Stress is not predictable, but it has not been symbolized in the orthography.

References

Grimes, Joseph E. 1975. *The Thread of Discourse*. The Hague: Mouton.

Halliday, Michael A.K. and Ruqaiya Hasan. 1976. *Cohesion in English*. London: Longman.

Longacre, Robert E. 1972. *Hierarchy and Universality of Discourse Constituents in New Guinea Languages: Discussion*. Washington, DC: Georgetown University Press.

Rodrigues, Aryon Dall'Igna. 1968. *As Linguas "Impuras" da Familia Tupi-Guarani*. XXXI Congresso Internacional de Americanistes.

Topic

Staging in Teribe Discourse

Carol Koontz Schatz

Teribe, a language of the Republic of Panama, has three clear levels of topicalization: clause, paragraph, and discourse. This article deals mainly with clause and paragraph topicalization. The topic of a clause is the nominal element that occurs clause initial. Various devices are available for placing the desired element in clause-initial position. The topic of a paragraph is the first participant that is overtly referred to and actually plays a role in the events or ideas discussed within the paragraph. Paragraph topics are established and maintained by manipulating the various options available for clause topicalization.

When a speaker of any language tells a story, describes how to do something, or performs any of a number of other linguistic activities, he creates a discourse. Underlying any such discourse are three sets of relationships: content organization, cohesion, and staging (Grimes 1975:112-13).

Content organization has also been called semantic organization or cognitive structure. It has to do with the semantic concepts present in a discourse and their relationships to each other.

Cohesion relates new information to information that is already known. At any point in a discourse there are things that the speaker assumes his hearer knows. He assumes this because he has just told him, because the things are part of a shared cultural heritage, or because they are part of the real-life situation shared by speaker and hearer at the moment. As the speaker progresses through his discourse, he carefully ties each new piece of information to the accumulated stock of information already given or assumed in the discourse. The devices he uses to do this are called cohesion relationships.

Finally, **staging** expresses the speaker's perspective on what is being said. It includes the mapping of semantic themes to surface

103

structure as grammatical topics. Grimes has chosen a theatrical metaphor to describe the processes involved here:

> Clearly the marking of thematization is related to a semantic factor of PROMINENCE. It is as though stage directions were given to the spotlight handler in a theater to single out a particular individual or action, or as though one actor were placed close to the audience and another off to the side (Grimes 1975:327).

The primary concern of this paper is this matter of staging techniques, or topicalization procedures, in Teribe[1] discourse. Basic to the discussion is the premise that the speaker's perspective is superimposed on the entire discourse and, thus, that topicalization principles are everywhere at work, whether they result in marked or unmarked topics. Since the relationships operating within a discourse are at least partially interdependent, it is occasionally necessary to refer to features of content and cohesion, which enter into establishing and maintaining topics within a discourse.

Teribe discourse manifests three clear levels of topicalization: clause, paragraph, and discourse. The first section of this paper is devoted to topicalization at the clause level. The second describes how clause topics are manipulated to establish and maintain topics at the paragraph level. Topicalization at the discourse level is not discussed in detail but is mentioned several times in section 1.2 as it relates to clause-level topicalization.

1 Clause topics

The topic of a Teribe clause, whether or not it is overtly represented, is always clause initial, immediately following any connectives that may occur. This means that, in the unmarked cases, the topic is either object of a transitive verb or subject of some other verb. There are, however, a variety of mechanisms by which the Teribe speaker may put something else first and thereby make that element the topic of the clause.

In the discussion below, section 1.1 describes the kinds of grammatical forms that may serve as clause topics. Section 1.2 describes the various processes by which a speaker may put a particular element in topic position.

1.1 Topical elements

All topics are nominal elements. They may be demonstratives, pronouns, nominalized clauses, or any other type of noun phrase.

1.1.1 Demonstratives. Out of a set of four demonstratives (Koontz and Anderson 1977), three may serve as topics of clauses: *e* 'that, nonspecific',[2] *cwe* 'that, specific', and *ëre* 'this, specific', As topics, *e*, as in example 1, and *cwe*, as in example 2, are anaphoric, referring back to someone or something already mentioned. *Ëre*, as in example 3, is cataphoric, referring forward to someone or something to be mentioned subsequently.

> (1) ***E bu tuv.***
> **that=nonspecific** lie ground on
> 'That one is sick in bed.' (No concept of exclusiveness is involved.)
> (2) ***Cwe boy dret to?***
> **that=specific** wife none tag-question
> 'That one (as opposed to some others) hasn't got a wife?'
> (3) *Ëre wos bamgo guing e pa zhëbo toc guing.*
> (4) *Pa shiti toc, pa cöchi toc, pa vaca toc dbo shco e shco ga era pa boy crono enijã.*
> (3') **this-specific** do-imp before until that=nonspecific you=topic things exist until
> (4') you=topic dog exist, you=topic pig exist, you=topic cow exist apart at that=nonspecific at depen contrast you-topic wife get-compl then-future[3]
> (3") 'This specific thing do first: get things first.'
> (4") 'When you have a dog and a pig and a cow of your own, then and only then may you take a wife.'

1.1.2 Pronouns. There are four sets of nondemonstrative pronouns: topic pronouns, freestanding possessives, specialized pronouns, and nontopic pronouns. Topic pronouns are used to refer to the topic when the pronoun itself is in topic position, as in examples 5-9. Freestanding possessive pronouns are used when the thing possessed (not the possessor) is topic, as in example 10. Of the three specialized pronouns, *op* 'reflexive', as in example 8, and *eng* 'reciprocal', as in example 9, refer back to whatever was topic of the clause, while *om* 'paragraph topic' refers back to the topic of the paragraph (1.2.4). Nontopic pronouns serve wherever else a pronoun is needed. Most commonly, they serve as possessive pronouns, as in example 5, as objects of embedded clauses, as in example 6, or as heads of postpositional phrases, as in example 7. The pronoun forms are shown in table 1; bound person suffixes are described later.

		Topic	Nontopic	Freestanding possessives	Bound subject*
Singular:	1st	ta	bor	botoya	-t
	2nd	pa	bop	bopoya	-p
	3rd	∅	ba	ba îya	-ya
Plural:	1st excl.	tawa	borwa	borwatoya	-(r)wa
	1st incl.	shi	mi	mishîya	-y
	2nd	pãy	bomi	bomipoya	-mi
	3rd	∅	ba	ba îya	-ya

Table 1: Pronoun Forms
   *section 1.2.1

(5) *Ta to bor mequë îc.*
   I=topic go **my=nontopic** mother see=incompl
   'I am going to see my mother.'
(6) *Ta to ba îc.*
   I=topic go **her=nontopic** see=incompl
   'I am going to see her.'
(7) *Ta to bop toc.*
   I=topic go **you=nontopic** with
   'I am going with you.'
(8) *Tawa op dë zhëme.*
   we=excl=topic reflexive care-for-incompl not-stative
   'We don't take care of ourselves.'
(9) *Pãy eng quimtozo.*
   you=pl=topic reciprocal help-imp
   'Help each other.'
(10) *Bopoya zröra crobö döe.*
   of=yours=sg kill-compl-they few only
   'Of yours (your soldiers) only a few were killed.'

1.1.3 Nominalized clauses. Following are examples of nominalized clauses that serve as topics of other clauses.

In example 11, the clause is nominalized by the clitic -*ga* 'subject nominal'.[4] This clitic occurs only on transitive clauses and adds the idea of 'the one(s) who' or 'the thing(s) that' to the verb on which it occurs.

(11) *Cäga za-**ga** e dbo shco.*
      (head cut-**subj=nominal** that apart at
      'Those who cut off heads were a separate group.'

In examples 12 and 13, the clauses that serve as topics are
nominalized by *-c* 'object nominal'. This clitic occurs only on transitive
clauses and the resulting form refers to an object or person that has
been affected by something. In example 12, the speaker's corn has
been affected by being planted. Since the topic of this particular clause
is the corn and not the speaker, the nontopic pronoun is used to refer
to the speaker. In example 13, a skull has been affected by being
placed in a particular spot. (The particle *ri* 'known' identifies a nominal
element that has previously been introduced within the discourse.)

(12) *Bor ëp dga-**c** ri be bu prue.*
      my corn plant-**obj=nominal** known remain be=lying good
      'My corn that has been planted is doing well.'
(13) *No cäga va-**c** be bu rasho quinggo.*
      human head put-**obj=nominal** remain be=lying sand on=top=of
      'A human skull had been placed on top of the sand.'

1.1.4 Other types of noun phrases. Following are examples of some
other types of noun phrases that serve as clause topics.
      The noun phrase in example 14 consists of a possessive (nontopic)
pronoun and a head noun. As in example 12, the nontopic pronoun is
chosen because the topic is the ocelots rather than their owner.

(14) ***Bor dbongwa** vër ev ame.* (**my ocelot**
      put=incompl-I that-at no=more
      'My ocelots I put there no more.'

In addition to the pronoun and the head noun, a noun phrase may
have a modifying phrase. The following example has a postpositional
phrase meaning 'of the house'.

(15) *Ga bor dbongwa **u shco so** e ta quimtë ara e shco.*
      depen[5] my ocelot **house in inhabitant=of** that I=topic
      help=incompl much that at
      'My ocelots of the house (housecats) help me a lot there.'

Relative clauses also occur in noun phrases:

(16) *Dwřo **söva** cwe ba cong.*
medicine **bring=incompl-he** give=incompl-he him to
'The medicine that he has brought he gives to him.'

1.2 Devices for clause topicalization

When a Teribe speaker puts a particular clause element in clause-
initial position, he is actually accomplishing two tasks at once: he is
making that element the topic of the clause, and he is preventing
everything else from being topic. He may have one or several reasons
for not wanting other elements to be topicalized. The three reasons
suggested below all have implications for cohesive relationships, and
the first and third also have implications for the content organization of
a text. These further implications are not, however, followed up in this
paper.

The first reason the speaker may not want to topicalize an element
is that it is only enablement information and not important in its own
right. **Enablement** information is information that is included primarily
so that events subsequently related will make sense to the hearer
(Schank ms). A hearer can only accept a statement as coherent within
a text if he has previously been informed of all the necessary
prerequisites or if he can assume them easily. For instance, he can
accept the idea that John flew to the moon last week only if he knows
that John is an astronaut and has access to the kind of rocket that
could get him to the moon. However, if the rocket itself is not
important to the story, the Teribe speaker may want to retain John as
topic and keep the rocket in a nontopic position.

The second reason the speaker may not want to put a reference to
someone or something in the topic position is that the clause under
consideration is the first one in which that participant has been
mentioned. In Teribe, as in some other languages, it is considered bad
form to make a participant the topic without having previously
introduced him in a nontopic role. Of course, neither the speaker (**I**)
nor the hearer (**you**) needs introducing, and discourse-initially someone
or something must be made topic without previous introduction, but
speakers take pains to keep this from happening elsewhere.

The third reason suggested here is that many discourses seem to
have elements that function in overall discourse roles. For instance,
one participant may be cast in the overall role of initiator and another
in the role of responder, and these relationships may influence
topicalization even on the clause level (Wise and Lowe 1972).

The following devices are used to control topicalization at the
clause level: (1) unmarked word order, (2) fronting the subject of a
transitive verb, (3) fronting postnuclear elements, (4) reprise, (5)

thematic partitioning, (6) topicalized modifiers of nouns, and (7) topics in quoted material.

1.2.1 Unmarked word order. In clauses with unmarked word order, the nuclear elements precede the peripheral elements. One nominal element precedes the predicate and is clause topic. The predicate may be a transitive verb, an intransitive verb, a motion verb, an existential verb, a nominal complement, or an adjectival complement.

Only in the case of a transitive clause is there a choice of word order, a choice between subject and object in clause-initial position. In all other clauses, the subject precedes the predicate and, in the case of unmarked clauses, is therefore the topic. That it really is a topic is indicated by the choice of topic pronoun when a pronoun is needed as subject of the clause. In marked clauses, which are discussed later, some other element precedes the subject and is topic of the clause.

The following examples show **intransitive** clauses with unmarked topics. In example 17, the topic is the speaker. In example 18, the topic is Juan, and in example 19, the third person topic pronoun, which has a zero representation, refers back to a previously established third person topic.

(17) *Ta parcono.*
      I=topic work-compl
      'I worked.'
(18) *Juan parcono.*
      Juan work-compl
      'Juan worked.'
(19) *∅ parcono.*
      he=topic work-compl
      'He worked.'

Some verbs of speech and thought are intransitive and have the clause order subject-verb-indirect object. They refer to the manner of speaking or thinking. The content of what is said or thought follows this nucleus and is connected to it by *ga* 'dependent'. By using this type of verb, the speaker must make the participant who speaks the topic of the clause. He may at the same time introduce a new participant by casting that person in the nontopic position of indirect object, as in example 20.

(20) *Ga ∅ tĩē ba boy cong ga —Esi. Shi toe.*
      depen he=topic speak=incompl his wife to depen—hurry.
      we=incl=topic go-stative

'He spoke to his wife, "Hurry! Let's go!" '

(21) *Tëtë wotřïc ca[6]—Řõe, bor wawa ãsca wřēnot ëmdë.*
      grandma think=incompl depen—truth-stative my child-little
      in=place=of find-complete-I almost
      'Grandma thought, "It's true! I've found someone who can
      almost replace my daughter." '

Example 22 shows a **motion** clause with an unmarked topic.

(22) *Ta to bor mequë shwo.*
      I=topic go=incompl my mother where
      'I am going to where my mother is.'

Example 23 shows two consecutive **existential** clauses with
unmarked topics. As is the case with most existential verbs, the verb
used in each of these clauses indicates the position of the subject as
well as its existence.

(23) *Cwozirwa ři buc u shco zhëme, Ø buc cro shco polae.*
      child-little known be-lying house in not, he=topic be=lying
      jungle in far=away
      'The child didn't lie in the house; he lay in the jungle far
      away.'

Example 24 shows a clause with a **nominal** complement. Again, the
topic is unmarked.

(24) *Cwe bor boy.*
      that=specific my wife
      'That one is my wife.'

The following examples show clauses with **adjectival** complements
and unmarked topics. Adjectives may occur without existential verbs,
as in example 25, or with them, as in example 26. The clitic -*e*, which
occurs in example 26, means 'stative' and always occurs on the final
element of a clause that defines a resultant state rather than an action.

(25) *Cvong quësbang.*
      canoe big
      'The canoe is big.'

(26) *Tawa dena shco ga mär řöng eni. Ouïshco ga tawa řöng pru-
      e.*
      we=excl=topic long=ago at depen be=protected=incompl thus.
      therefore depen we=excl=topic be=plural good-stative

'Long ago we were protected in that way. Therefore we were doing fine.'

When the last element in a stative clause is a addition of the verb, -e 'stative' apparently changes the verb into an adjective. This is suggested both by the stative meaning of the new form and by the fact that the form loses the word stress typical of verbs and acquires the stress typical of most adjectives, in which the stress falls on the syllable immediately preceding the -e. Example 27 shows an intransitive verb that describes an action, and example 28 shows the same verb, now changed into an adjective by the addition of the clitic -e. The stress on the form has changed to that typical of adjectives, and the meaning has changed to indicate a resultant state rather than an action. (Stress on the verb or adjective is indicated by an acute accent.)

(27) *Juan shróno ëre shco.*
      Juan arrive=here-compl-this at
      'Juan arrived here.'
(28) *Juan shronó-e.*
      Juan arrive=here=compl-**stative**
      'Juan is one who has arrived.'

As mentioned previously, **transitive** clauses have two possible word orders for the nuclear elements; these are subject-object-verb (SOV) and object-verb-subject (OVS). SOV is a marked order and is discussed in section 1.2.2. The unmarked order is OVS, and the object, appearing first in the unmarked clause, is the clause topic.[7]

Transitive verbs that appear in the OVS construction are inflected for aspect and person. This contrasts with all other classes of verbs, which are inflected only for aspect. When the subject is third person, a nominal subject (followed by *rë* 'subject') sometimes follows the verb, as in example 31, but when the subject is first or second person, only the bound subject pronoun (table 1) occurs. (Some aspects of the verb distinguish between -*wa* 'we, exclusive, unmarked' and -*rwa* 'all of us, excluding you'; in other aspects, there is no distinction and -*rwa* is always used.)

(29) *Shwong cwoshcworo-t.*
      clothes wash-compl-I[8]
      'I washed clothes.'
(30) *Shwong cwoshcwar-a.*
      clothes wash-compl-she
      'She washed clothes.'

(31) *Shwong cwoshcwar-a María* rë.
clothes wash-compl-she María subject
'María washed clothes.'

The following example illustrates the use of the OVS order to
present enablement information in a nontopic position. It comes from a
text by a young girl, who tells about her mother being sick. The mother
is topic of nearly every clause in the text, whether she is subject or
object of the verb, and other people are mentioned only as they are
needed to explain how her mother is cared for. In this example, the girl
mentions her father in order to explain how her mother gets downriver
to the doctor, casting him in the nontopic position of subject of an
OVS clause.

(32) *E irgo ga ∅ ör bu grave obi.*
(33) *E ga ∅ shira bor data rë ga ∅ to söra.*
(32') that after depen she=topic went be=lying ill again
(33') that depen she=topic take=out-compl-he **my father subj** depen
she=topic go take-compl-he
(32") **'Later she became ill again.'**
(33") 'So being taken out by my father, she was taken (downriver).'

As already mentioned, some speech verbs are intransitive and
precede the quoted material. Others, however, are transitive and follow
the quoted material. The transitive clause has the form object-verb-
subject-indirect object, in which the quoted material is the object of the
verb. Since the subject of such a verb is never clause initial, it is never
clause topic. By using this type of verb, the speaker can allow a
participant to speak without making him clause topic. If he wishes to
make the participant topic, he uses both the preceding intransitive verb
and the following transitive verb.

The following example comes from the story of a snake which has
transformed itself into a man. The snake-man is topic of the first
sentence, appearing clause initial before the intransitive verb *trē*
'speak'. Because the discourse role of the second character, a lady, is
that of responder rather than initiator, the speaker wants to avoid
making her topic of the second sentence. Therefore he does not use an
intransitive clause before the quotation. Instead he ties the parts of the
conversation together with the perception verb *cuva* 'it (his speech)
was heard.'[9]

(34) *Ga e t̄rē ga —Bop cwozirwa cwe twos bor cong— r̆e trabga r̈i
cong.*

(35) *Cuva ga –Jörö– r̈e.*

(34') depen that**speak=incompl** depen   —your   child-little   that=
specific   give-imp   me   to—**say=incompl-he**   respected=person
known to

(35') hear-incompl-she depen   —okay—**say=incompl-she**

(34") 'That one spoke, "Your daughter, give her to me," he said to
the lady.'

(35") 'When it was heard, "Okay," she said.'

Perception verbs, like some speech verbs, are a special type of
transitive verb. The two most common perception verbs are *ic* 'see'
and *cuc* 'hear'. When the object of such a verb is a noun phrase, the
normal OVS construction is used:

(36) *Pa ïna bop me rë.*
you=topic see-compl-she your mother subj
'You were seen by your mother.'

When, however, one of these verbs takes a sentence or a paragraph
as a complement, the complement is moved to the end of the clause
and preceded by the connective *ga* 'dependent'. In such a
construction, the person who does the perceiving (the subject of the
matrix clause) is still not in topic position and is not topic. This is
another way by which the speaker may maintain discourse roles in the
surface structure: he may have the responder see or hear things caused
by the initiator.

The form *ïva ga* 'he saw that' is often used by Teribe speakers to
introduce a scene within a story as seen from a particular participant's
viewpoint. What he sees is always a still scene rather than an action.
In other words, he both sees something in a particular state and
deduces why it is in that state, but he is never reported as seeing an
event take place. When an action verb like *sharivara* 'he made' is
used, the speaker means that the observer has deduced that the
participant referred to by 'he' made it, not that he saw him make it. In
the example below, for instance, the participant who has performed the
action is not even present when the resulting scene is observed by
another participant. It is as if the overall discourse were a moving
picture, which the speaker occasionally stops to interject a still shot,
and that still shot is the scene as perceived by an observing participant.
Having reported what that person saw, the speaker turns on the
moving picture again and goes on to report the actions that follow.

The following example comes from the folktale about the snake-man
who marries a Teribe girl. When their first baby arrives, he informs the
girl's mother that she may not see the baby. Since the mother does not

know that he is really a snake, she cannot understand why he should say such a thing. In the end she goes to see the baby and its mother, her daughter. She sees that something has happened to them and deduces that her daughter's husband is responsible. *Íva ba ter r̈i ga* 'his grandmother saw that' introduces the strange scene.

(37) **Íva ba ter r̈i ga sharivara bey ötong worbo ba pr̈ocso go vno, jem jem r̈i xm yno, cäga vno.**

(38) *Guenivo prarbo ra buc dgur.*

(37') **see-incompl-she** his grandmother known depen make-compl-he half went-removed-compl around their waist on human, go=up=inceptive to=up=inceptive known human, head human

(38'ʃ) but tail contrast be=lying snake

(37") 'His grandmother saw that he had made them half different: from the waist up they were human; their heads were human.'

(38") 'But from the waist down, they just had snake tails.'

1.2.2 Fronting the subject of a transitive verb. As mentioned in the last section, there is a second possible word order for transitive clauses: subject-object-verb (SOV). Verbs that appear in this construction are inflected only for aspect, since the freestanding subject carries the semantic load of person identification. The particle *rë* 'subject' does not occur in this construction.

SOV is a marked order. In contrast with the unmarked OVS order, SOV makes the subject topic of the clause. This construction serves three functions. Its first function is to present enablement information. Its second function is to introduce, in the noninitial position of object, a new participant or prop, which will subsequently become topic. When the SOV order signals enablement information, it may or may not introduce a potential topic at the same time. In other words, sometimes the person or thing needed as enablement information at one point becomes a topic at a subsequent point, but this is not always so.

The third possible function of the SOV order is to establish a paragraph topic. As is further discussed in section 2, paragraph topics must appear clause initial in the first clause of the paragraph, with some exceptions that are described there. When the SOV order is used to accomplish this purpose, neither enablement information nor participant introduction is involved, as these considerations have already been handled in previous clauses.

The clause in the following example illustrates only the first function, which is the presentation of enablement information; its object never assumes the role of topic. The example comes from a travelogue in which the speaker and his wife go first to a museum, then to a dock on the Panama Canal, then by boat to a different dock on the canal, then to a zoo, then back to the museum and home again. The only means of transportation that merits being topic is the boat; it is treated as a topic because the boat ride was one of the highlights of the day. The cars and buses used for other portions of the trip are all mentioned in subordinate ways. One such way is the use of clauses with SOV order, as shown in example 39. In this way, without making an unimportant bus into a clause topic, the speaker is able to let the hearer know that they got from the museum to the boat dock. He and his wife remain topic, but at the same time, information is added that enables the hearer to accept the speaker's next statement as logical. Had they been unable to catch a bus, it would have made no sense to say, "We being carried arrived at another place."

(39) *Tawa bus crono.*
(40) *Tawa söva ärong shto crina ob̈ë shco.*
(39') we=excl=topic bus take-comp
(40') we=excl=topic carry-incompl-it arrive=there-compl place one other at
(39") 'We caught a bus.'
(40") 'We being carried arrived at another place.'

The following passage illustrates all three functions of the SOV word order. It comes from a procedural discourse in which the speaker is describing how he raises corn. He says that after the seeds have sprouted he goes to see how they are doing. If he finds that mice or birds are eating the young plants, he takes his pet ocelots out and leaves them to catch the mice or birds. Taking his ocelots to the field is presented as enablement information in example 41; if the hearer did not know that they were there, he would find the following clauses incomprehensible. The same clause, by introducing the ocelots, makes them available as a potential topic. Several sentences later, the speaker digresses from his account of raising corn and spends a paragraph talking about how important his ocelots are and how well he cares for them. The first sentence of this paragraph, which is example 43, has the SOV word order. This time its function is to put the subject of the verb, the ocelots, in clause-initial position and establish them as paragraph topic. The indications that this is a marked order are reinforced by the fact that the object of the verb retains its topic pronoun. The object of the verb is still clause topic, even though the subject has become paragraph topic.[10] (Clauses within a sentence are separated by a slash mark /.)

(41) *Ga ĩn ga uwe zhëbo rë ga / era ta bor dbongwa u shco so söc*
      är e shco, / ∅ pöc mvã vër e shco zhëbo ba uwaga r̈i e zröva
      bor cong wr̈o.

(42) *Ga eni ga ĩn är prara cocshröng prara ga / ba zröga ba*
      uwaga r̈i zröra r̈öng bor dbongwa u shco so r̈i rë.

(43) *Ga bor dbongwa u shco so e ta quimtë ara e shco.*

(41') depen see=incompl-I depen eat=incompl-it something subj
      depen / contrast I-topic ocelot house in inhabitant=of
      carry=incompl arrive=there that at, / two three put=incompl-I
      that at something it eat-subj=nominal known that kill=incompl-
      they me for in=order=to

(42') depen thus depen see=incompl-I arrive=there once early once
      depen / it kill-subj=nominal it eat-subj=nominal known kill-
      compl-they be=pl my ocelots house in inhabitant=of known
      subj

(43') depen **my ocelot house in inhabitant=of** that I=topic
      help=incompl much that at

(41") 'When I see that something is eating it, I take my ocelots of
      the house (house cats) there; I put two or three of them there
      in order to kill whatever is eating it for me.'

(42") 'Thus, when I go to see it early one morning, I see that my
      ocelots have been killing whatever has been killing it and
      eating it.'

(43") 'My ocelots, they help me a lot there.'

1.2.3 Fronting postnuclear elements. Since peripheral elements normally
follow the clause nucleus, moving them to the front of the clause is
another way to create a marked topic. By fronting such an element, the
speaker avoids unnecessary changes of topic between clauses. Example
45, for instance, comes from a text in which the speaker is the only
major participant. Keeping himself topic of nearly every clause helps to
create cohesion within the discourse.

Example 44 shows a benefactive phrase in its normal position
following the clause nucleus. The unmarked topic of the clause is the
book, which is object of a transitive verb.

(44) *Bop quibocwo twos bor cong.*
      your book give-imp **me to**
      'Give your book to me.'

In contrast, example 45 shows a benefactive phrase that is taken
out of a text and that has been fronted. The topic of the clause is the
head of the benefactive phrase, and the pronoun *bor* 'me, nontopic' has
been replaced by *ta* 'I, topic'.

(45) *Ta cong quibocwo twara bor shiv rë cwara.*
   I=topic to book give-compl-he my older=brother one
   'To me, my older brother gave a book.'

While the function of the above pattern is to topicalize the head of a postnuclear clause, fronting can occasionally accomplish another function as well: it can indicate that a previous topic is giving way to a new topic, at least temporarily. The following example comes from the text about the girl's mother who was ill. To this point, the mother has been topic of nearly every clause. Now the girl wants to talk about some injections the doctor sent home with her mother to be given to her there. Rather than abruptly introducing the injections in topic position, she fronts the benefactive phrase 'to her' and then introduces the injections as object of the verb but not the clause topic. She uses the nontopic pronoun *ba* 'her' to warn of the coming switch in topic. Then in the following clause, the injections appear in topic position.

(46) *Ba cong shcö itivara doctor rë ga / Ø crara quëgong wïe.*
   her to thorn send-complete-he doctor subj depen /**they=topic**
   receive-compl-she up=there around
   'To her injections were sent by the doctor, and she received them up there.'

1.2.4 Reprise. Reprise, or left dislocation, is another kind of marked topicalization that occurs in Teribe. Grimes defines this construction as a noun phrase that is put at the beginning of a clause, but echoed at its normal place in the clause by a pronoun (Grimes 1975:342). In Teribe, a distinction must be made between noun phrases that would be clause initial even without reprise and those that would not be.

Noun phrases that would be clause initial even without the reprise marker are echoed in their normal place by *e* 'that, nonspecific', as in example 43, or rarely by *cwe* 'that, specific', as in example 34. Both examples are repeated below. This construction is used to establish certain kinds of topics.

In example 43, reprise indicates the establishment of a paragraph topic, which is a digression from the main purpose of the discourse. The speaker has been talking about raising corn; now he temporarily changes the subject and spends a paragraph talking about his ocelots.

(43) *Ga bor dbongwa u shco so e ta quimtë ara e shco.*
   depen **my ocelot house in** inhabitant=of **that=nonspecific** I=topic
   help=incompl much that at
   'My ocelots, they help me a lot there.'

Examples 34 and 47 involve the establishment of a previously unintroduced participant as topic. The speaker places him in topic position and then, referring to him as *e* 'that one' or *cwe* 'that specific one', goes on to say something about him. Such an abrupt establishment of a participant as topic is acceptable in example 34 because the clause occurs in a speech by another participant and involves exophoric reference to someone who is within the scene of the story but who has not previously been introduced to the hearer (1.2.7). It is acceptable in example 47 because the sentence involved is discourse initial and because a father really needs no introduction, as it can be assumed that everyone has had one. The speaker merely needs to let the hearer know that his topic is his father (2.1).

(34)   *Ga e tr̈ē ga–Bop cwozirwa cwe twos bor cong–r̈e trabga r̈i cong.*
       depen that   speak=incompl   depen—**your child-little**
       that=specific   give-imp   me   to— say=incompl-he
       respected=person known to
       'That one spoke, "Your daughter, give her to me," he said to the lady.'

(47)   *Dena shco, ta chirawa obi ga /bor data e dwr̈o cro shco mivdë arae.*
       long=ago in,   I=topic   small   still   depen   **/my father**
       that=nonspecific medicine jungle in know=incompl much-stative
       'Long ago, when I was still a child, my father, he knew a lot about herb medicine.'

Within a paragraph, reprise establishes a new clause-level topic. The following example is from the paragraph about the ocelots. The clause topics change frequently, but they all have to do with the theme of the paragraph, which is the benefit the ocelots are. Each change of topic is marked by the reprise pattern.

(48)   *Ga bor dbongwa e zhëm ga / bor ëp e uwe senwa rë e cwësi rë dret bor shirvo.*

(49)   *Zhë e crër e shco zhëme.*

(50)   *Bor pac e to jeno eni.*

(51)   *Cuzong ga bor dbongwa e wovdër ara dër ara.*

(48') depen **my ocelot that=nonspecific** not depen **/my corn
       that=nonspecific** eat=incompl-they bird subj that=nonspecific
       mouse subj my crop

(49') **what that=nonspecific** get=incompl-I that=nonspecific at non-
       stative

(50') **my work that=nonspecific** go be=lost-compl thus
(51') since depen **my ocelot that=nonspecific** want=incompl-I
care=for=incompl-I much
(48") 'My ocelots, if it weren't for them, my corn, it would all be
eaten up by birds and mice.'
(49") 'What I would harvest there, it would be nothing.'
(50") 'My work, it would all be lost that way.'
(51") 'Since that is so, as for my ocelots, I love them and care for
them very much.'

On the other hand, noun phrases that would not be clause initial if
they were not part of a reprise pattern are echoed in their normal place
by *om* 'paragraph topic pronoun'. In the following example, *om* occurs
as object in an SOV construction and refers back to the paragraph
topic, which has now been fronted to clause-initial position.

(52) *Trabgaga shquë so ̈ri tawa* **om** *cowë cös.*
respected=people night inhabitant=of known we=excl=topic
paragraph=topic call=incompl *cös*
'The people of the night, we call them "*cös*".'

Both *e* and *om* may occur in the same clause. This is apparently the
result of ordered rules: first a nontopic element, such as the object in
an SOV construction, is fronted to topic position; and then it is fronted
again and the marker *e* left to mark its place in reprise.

(53) *Wäïë obïë e ta* **om** *barwë zhëm.*
woman other **that=nonspecific** I=topic **paragraph=topic**
bother=incompl not
'Other women, them I don't bother at all.'

1.2.5 Thematic partitioning. Thematic partitioning, or pseudoclefting, is
a special kind of topicalization by which the content of a clause is
broken into two parts, which have a question and answer relationship.
The construction is an inverted equative one, with the question and
answer parts simply juxtaposed. The answer part, as is indicated by the
particle *rë* 'subject', is subject, but contrary to the normal order in
equative clauses, it occurs following the predicate. The question part,
which occurs clause initial and serves as predicate, is always a
nominalized clause (Grimes 1975:338-41).

One use for this construction seems to be to allow a smooth
transition between topics. When the clause begins, the initial element is
topic; when the clause ends, the answer part is ready to be established
or reestablished as topic in the next sentence.

The following example comes from a story about a young woman who often goes down to the river alone. When her brothers go down to see what she is doing, they find her with a spirit who is teaching her to sing. An embedded paragraph follows, the topic of which is the spirit. Part way through the paragraph (shown in examples 54-59), the woman becomes a local topic (as indicated by the reprise pattern) and the hearer is told that her hair has been braided. The last clause in the paragraph, which is the thematically partitioned one, smoothly switches the hearer's attention back from the braided hair to the spirit. Such an overt reference to the paragraph topic right at the end of the paragraph is very common in Teribe discourse.

(54) **Domer** *zhang crara quësbang ba so shco jūni, cvorcwo pang rëng, cvorcwo eje.*

(55) *Zhang cvorcwo rëng ba sov.*

(56) **Warë** *e tsirquera söc tö shco.*

(57) *∅ Caczong wac zhuc, cäczong progro myã ri waydë.*

(58) *Cäczong beno jong zhuc.*

(59) *E waga ava rë.*

(54') **man** be=standing one big her close at like-this, tongue be=hanging long, tongue long

(55') be=standing tongue long her close-to

(56') **woman that=nonspecific** seated be=sitting ground on

(57') she=topic hair do-obj=nominal hair number three known do-perfective

(58') she=topic hair remain-compl be=permanent braid

(59') that=nonspecific do-subj=nominal spirit subj

(54") 'There was a big man (really a spirit) standing close to her like this, and he had a long tongue.'

(55") 'He was standing with his long tongue close to her.'

(56") 'The woman, she was seated on the ground.'

(57") 'Concerning her, her hair had been braided.'

(58") 'Concerning her, her hair was braided.'

(59") 'The spirit was the one who did it.'

1.2.6 Topicalized modifiers of nouns. In the unmarked case, the head of a clause-initial noun phrase is topic of the clause. For instance, in example 14, which is repeated below, the ocelots are head of the noun phrase *bor dbongwa* 'my ocelots' and topic of the clause.

(14) **Bor dbongwa** *vër ev ame.*
    my ocelot put=incompl-I that-at no=more
    'My ocelots I put there no more.'

It is possible, however, for the speaker to make the modifier of the head serve as clause topic. When he does so, he changes nontopic pronouns like *bor* 'me, my' to topic pronouns like *ta* 'I'.

Frequently such a topicalized modifier is semantically the possessor of the nominal element immediately following it, whether that element is object of a transitive verb, as in example 60, or subject of some other predicate, as in examples 61 and 62. Once the modifier has been made topic, the construction must be translated not by 'my ocelots', for example, but by 'concerning me, my ocelots'. Topicalizing a modifier often serves a function quite similar to the fronting of a postnuclear element: it avoids unnecessary changes of topic between clauses and helps to create cohesion within the discourse. It says, in effect, that a certain participant is topic of the discussion whether he is subject of a verb, object of a verb, or simply the possessor of something.

> (60) *María cä zorop.*
> **María** head cut-compl-you 'Concerning María, you cut her hair.'
> (61) *Ta dbongwa prue.*
> **I=topic** ocelot good-stative
> 'Concerning me, my ocelots are good.'
> (62) *Ta cä wotřïc zhëbo owa.*
> **I=topic** head think=incompl thing bad
> 'Concerning me, my head thinks bad things.'

At times, this construction serves to introduce a possessed item, which subsequently becomes topic of a clause. In example 63, the speaker, who possesses three horses, is the topic. Then in the following clauses, the horses themselves serve as clause topics.

> (63) *Prara ta caballo teng dogřo myã, /Ø teng owa zhëme.*
> (64) *Öto mogřo cop ara ga / bor caballo e teng.*
> (63') once **I=topic** horse pertain number three, /**they=topic** pertain bad not-stative
> (64') went-removed month-pl amount much depen /**my horse** that pertain)
> (63″) 'Once I had three horses; they were beautiful horses.'
> (64″) 'For many months, my horses were here.'

The object of a nominalized clause, which takes the form of a modifier, may also serve as topic of the matrix clause in which the nominalized clause is embedded. Example 65 shows an unmarked construction in which the nominalized clause is the subject of the matrix clause, and the head of the nominalized clause (*zröga* 'one who killed') is topic. Example 66, on the other hand, shows a marked construction in which the object of the nominalized clause (the speaker) is the topic of the matrix clause. This clause is thematically partitioned, and its purpose is thus to provide a smooth transition from a previous topic ('I') to a later topic (the snake).

> (65) *Ba zröga ři to parquë, řö re?*
> him **kill-subj=nominal** known go work=incompl truth question
> 'The one who killed it went to work, right?'
> (66) *Ta uwaga dgur dë.*
> **I=topic** eat-subj=nominal snake subj
> 'Concerning me, a snake was what bit me.'

1.2.7 Topics in quoted material. Conversations in discourse also play a role in topicalization procedures since they provide another means of introducing potential topics.

When one participant in a story speaks to another, he often makes exophoric references; that is, he refers to something that is part of the situation in which he finds himself but which has not previously been mentioned to the hearer. Such a reference is exophoric as far as the participant speaking is concerned; for the narrator of the story, it is a technique for introducing a new participant. For instance, in the story of the snake-man, he tells the lady, "Your daughter, give her to me" (example 33). Although the hearer has not previously been informed that the lady has a daughter, he is willing to assume that the man sees a daughter and therefore asks for her. Having assumed that she needs no formal introduction, the hearer is also willing to allow her to appear as topic of the quoted clause the first time she is mentioned.

Once a participant has been introduced as topic within a quotation, he is available to become topic of nonquoted material. This is what happens in the story of the snake-man. Examples 34 and 35 are repeated here and followed by one more sentence, example 67, in which the daughter is topic of the nonquoted clause.

> (34) *Ga e tře ga–Bop cwozirwa cwe twos bor cong–ře trabga ři cong.*
> (35) *Cuva ga–Jöřö–ře.*
> (67) *∅ Twara ba cong.*
> (34') depen that speak=incompl depen—your child-little
> that=specific give-imp me to—say=incompl-he
> respected=person known to

(35') hear=incompl-she depen —okay— say=incompl-she
(37') she=topic give-compl-she him to
(34") 'That one spoke, "Your daughter, give her to me," he said to
      the lady.'
(35") 'When it was heard, "Okay," she said.'
(67") 'She was given to him.'

2 Paragraph topics

The paragraph in Teribe is a referential unit that refers to an idea, a
scene, or a series of events that fall together into a single semantic
unit. A trip, for instance, can often be described within the limits of a
paragraph. A mother's illness, an unusual scene, or the value of
owning ocelots can be the subject of a paragraph, as can each of the
major steps in raising corn or building a house. Whatever the subject,
the paragraph is a unit with a single semantic theme and consequently
a single paragraph-level topic. There are no characteristic syntactic
patterns that identify paragraphs beyond those that identify topics.

Paragraphs, furthermore, can either be part of the main line of
development within a discourse, with each following the last in
chronological or logical order, or be embedded one within the other,
with the embedded paragraphs giving explanatory background
information, which makes the unembedded paragraphs more
understandable. An embedded paragraph typically has a topic different
from the topic of the paragraph in which it is embedded.

Because of the variety of material that may be encoded in a
paragraph and the variety of relationships that may exist between
paragraphs, the most reliable criterion for regarding a section of a
discourse as a paragraph is unity of paragraph-level topic within that
unit. Section 2.2 describes how a paragraph topic is maintained within
a unit.

Generally speaking, consecutive paragraphs have different topics,
and paragraph divisions can be determined by the change of paragraph-
level topic. Occasionally, however, two consecutive paragraphs have
the same topic. When this is so, the hearer must consider other minor
clues in determining the division between semantic units. The nature of
these clues is partially dependent on the discourse genre involved. In
narratives, time and setting changes often provide clues to paragraph
divisions, since the unity of a series of events is often coextensive with
a unit of time or a single location. In procedural discourses, the
divisions between major steps in a process are indicated by prenuclear
clauses that specify the completion of the previous step. Other
discourses suggest divisions in other ways. These signals serve either
to reinforce a paragraph break indicated by a topic change or to help

the hearer determine the paragraph break when no topic change occurs.

Since paragraphs are composed of sentences and sentences of clauses, establishing and maintaining paragraph-level topics in Teribe is largely a matter of manipulating the various options for topicalization on the clause level.

2.1 Establishing a paragraph topic.

The first participant mentioned in a paragraph is the paragraph topic. There must be an overt reference to the topic unless there is no change of topic from the previous paragraph. From among the clause topicalization options available to him, the speaker chooses the one that will make the participant he wants as topic the first participant he mentions in the paragraph. He may choose an unmarked word order, in which the topic is object of a transitive verb or subject of some other verb, or one of the marked orders, such as (1) the SOV transitive construction, (2) a fronted postnuclear element, (3) a reprise, or (4) a topicalized modifier.

The word *participant* is an important one in the above definition of paragraph topic, especially when the paragraph in question is discourse initial. This is because sometimes, in the process of establishing time or location, the speaker mentions people who are not really participants in the story. Not until he mentions someone or something that has an actual part in the discourse has he established a paragraph topic. If the clause that follows the setting clause overtly refers to a participant, it is quite likely that this participant, rather than the person referred to in the setting clause, is the paragraph topic. This conclusion is confirmed if, in the following clauses, the person mentioned in the setting clause is not referred to again.

Example 47, which is repeated here, illustrates this. It begins a discourse about how the speaker's father used to heal people with herbs. In establishing the time setting of the discourse, the speaker mentions himself, but he does not appear as a participant in the following events. The first actual participant he mentions is his father, who is the overt topic of the clause following the setting clause, and therefore the paragraph topic. Two topicalization options, SOV and reprise, are combined here in order to put the father in both clause and paragraph topic position. Discourse initial, of course, a participant may be topic without previous introduction, and this one probably needs no introduction anyway since the hearer can assume that everyone has had a father. In addition, the reprise pattern helps to make the topicalization less abrupt by meaning in this instance, 'As for my father, well he'.

(47) *Denashco, ta chirawa obi ga / **bor data e** dwïo cro shco mivdë*
arae.
long=ago in, I=topic small still depen / **my father that-
nonspecific** medicine jungle in know=incompl much-stative
'Long ago, when I was still a child, my father, he knew a lot
about herb medicine.'

It is also important to note that the reference to a new paragraph
topic must be overt. This is because a special prenuclear anaphoric
linking clause is often used to tie two paragraphs together. This link
never has the topic (subject or object of the verb) expressed overtly,
even when the topic is first or second person. Instead, it is understood
that its topic is the same as the topic of the previous paragraph. A
prenuclear clause that has no overt topic, therefore, refers back to the
preceding paragraph; and a prenuclear or nuclear clause that has an
overt topic establishes a new paragraph topic. Example 68 shows the
first sentence of a paragraph in which the topic (*cwozirwa* 'the girl') is
established overtly in a prenuclear setting clause. Example 69 shows
the first sentence of another paragraph. This time, the prenuclear
clause is an anaphoric link with no overt topic and the new paragraph
topic (*ba bov ïi* 'his wife') is established in the nuclear clause.

(68) *Damat scho ga **cwozirwa** zhang chirawa ga caczong eje,*
caczong tira zhëme, caczong quësbange.
before at depen **child-little** be=standing small depen hair long,
hair little not, hair big
'Before, when the girl was small, she had had abundant, long
hair.'

(69) *Ga era söc söc söc ötong moc pöc mogro myã ga **ba boy ïi***
zhang craso zhëme, cwozirwa toc.
depen contrast be=sitting be=sitting be=sitting went-removed-
compl month two month-pl three depen **his wife known**
be=standing just=one not, child-little exist
'After (he) had been there two or three months, his wife was
expecting a child.'

When a paragraph is episode[11] or discourse initial, the paragraph
topic is occasionally lifted out of the clause of which it is topic and
placed before a prenuclear time clause. Example 70 begins a new
episode within a discourse, and the paragraph topic, which is marked
as reprise (*ba cjorcwo dgara ïi e* 'the seeds that he had planted, they'),
has been fronted to precede the time setting clause (*dïo dïu ga* 'at
noon'). This construction suggests the possibility that the episode
should be considered as a fourth level of topicalization, but there is not

enough evidence at this point to determine whether or not this is necessary.

(70) *Eni ga era* **ba cjorcwo dgara** *r̈i e dr̈o dr̈u ga wen eni r̈õe.*
     thus depen contrast **his seed plant-compl-he known that** sun top
     depen appear=incompl thus truth-stative
     'Thus, the seeds that he had planted, they at noon really did
     sprout.'

2.2 Maintaining a paragraph topic

Once a paragraph topic is established, the manner in which it is maintained as topic depends on whether the paragraph has one major participant or several.

If a paragraph has a single major participant, the speaker makes every effort to keep that participant topic of every clause. This is relatively easy to do since every action either affects that participant or is performed by him. The following paragraph comes from the account of the girl's mother who was ill. The mother is topic of every clause except those in which the injections are made topic in order to highlight them.

(71) *E irgo ga/ Ø ör bu grave obi.*
(72) *E ga Ø shira bor data rë ga/ Ø to söra.*
(73) *Ga Ø ör bu dau ga / irgo ga Ø vone.*
(74) *Ø Quimtë Coc rë ga / Ø von ga / Ø shrono; ba cong shcö itivara
      doctor rë ga/ Ø crara quëgong wr̈e; Ø crara pir ga/ Ø cong
      dwr̈o twara obi, pastilla e ga shcö obi.*
(75) *E ga eri ga Ø vone.*
(71') that after depen / **she=topic** went be=lying ill again
(72') that depen **she=topic** take=out-compl-he my father subj depen /
       she=topic go take-compl-he
(73') depen **she=topic** went be=lying downriver depen / after depen
       she=topic better-stative
(74') **she=topic** help=incompl-he God subj depen / **she=topic** better
       depen / **she=topic** shrono, **her** to thorn send-compl-he doctor
       subj depen / they=topic receive-compl-she up=there around,
       they=topic receive-compl-she all depen / **she=topic** to medicine
       give-compl-he again, pill that depen thorn again
(75') that depen today depen **she=topic** better-stative
(71') 'Later she became ill again.'
(72'') 'So being taken out by my father, she was taken (downriver).'

(73″) 'And being down there, later she was better.'
(74″) 'God helping her, she was better and she came back; to her
       injections were sent by the doctor, and she received them up
       there; having received them all, she went back and she was
       given more medicine, pills, and more injections.'
(75″) 'Because of that, today she is better.'

If, on the other hand, the paragraph involves several participants,
the speaker does not attempt to keep the paragraph topic in clause-
initial position. He uses the SOV order for enablement information,
and elsewhere, unless he has a special reason for a marked order, he
simply uses the unmarked order.

Third person participants are referred to overtly as little as possible.
When there are several participants involved, the hearer must often
depend on clues such as established cultural roles (a man chops
firewood and a woman cooks) or on established patterns within the
discourse in question (the spirit chases the woman, and she runs).
When overt reference to a participant is necessary in order to avoid
confusion, he may be referred to by (1) a noun phrase ('the man'), (2)
embedded descriptive clauses ('the one who was running'), or (3)
kinship terms ('his wife'). When kinship terms are used, all the
participants in the paragraph are described as they relate to the topic of
the paragraph.[12] Very frequently the paragraph closes with some form
of overt reference to the paragraph topic.

The following example comes from the discourse about the father
who healed people with herbs. This is a customary discourse,
describing a series of events that occurred many times. The paragraph
topic is the speaker's father, who is overtly referred to twice as *bor
data* 'my father'. There is one other major participant, the sick person,
who is introduced as *no* 'person, people' in example 76 and overtly
referred to again in example 78 as *cavo* 'the sick person'. The healer is
topic of four clauses: twice as subject in an SOV construction, once as
object in an OVS construction, and once as subject of a motion verb.
The sick person is topic of three clauses, always as object in an OVS
construction. A variety of other items are topics of other clauses, but
in spite of the many clause-level topics, there is no doubt that the main
idea of the paragraph is herbal healing and the paragraph topic is the
speaker's father.

(47)   *Dena shco, ta chirawa obi ga / **bor data** e dwïo cro shco
       mivdë arae.*
(76)   *E **bor data** e no dwïomnec.*

(77) *Cä bang* cong *bugwo bang* cong, *cŕicono jong* cong ga/ *∅ wŕēc oba twe ba dwŕomnec wŕo.*

(78) *Ga ∅ dwŕomneva, / ∅ īva jegue, /∅ är cavo bu cone ga /∅ īva e shco.*

(79) *Orcwo ve ba go ga/ dwŕo söva cwe ba cong, / ∅ dwŕomneva zhang e shco.*

(47') long=ago in, I=topic small still depen/ **my father that** medicine jungle in know=incompl much-stative

(76') that **my father that** people heal

(77') **head pain** for, **abdomen pain** for, **hot-get-compl be=permanent** for depen / **he=topic** look=for=incompl they=impersonal come them heal in=order=to

(78') depen **they=topic** heal=incompl-he, / **they=topic** see=incompl-he set=out-stative, / **he=topic** arrive=there sick=person be=lying where depen / **he=topic** see=incompl-he that at

(79') **hand** put=incompl-he him on depen / **medicine bring=incompl-he** give=incompl-he him to, / **he=topic** heal=incompl-he be=standing that at

(47'') 'Long ago, when I was still a child, my father, he knew a lot about herb medicine.'

(76'') 'My father, he healed people.'

(77'') 'For headache, for stomachache, for fever, they looked for him to come and cure them.'

(78'') 'So he healed them; he went to see them; going to where the sick person lay, he saw him there.'

(79'') 'Laying his hand on him, he gave him the medicine that he had brought, and he healed him there.'

After further description of the healing ceremony, the speaker closes the paragraph with an overt reference to the paragraph topic in a summary statement.

(80) *Eni, bor data e parquë eni ba pevo toc, nasoga obŕë toc.*
thus, **my father that** work=incompl thus his people with, Teribe-group with
'Thus my father worked in this way with his people, with the other Teribes.'

Notes

1 Teribe is a member of the Chibchan language family (Reverte 1967:136; Levinsohn 1975:5). It is spoken by 750 to 1000 people in the province of Bocas del Toro in northwestern Panama along the Teribe, San San, and Changuinola Rivers. The texts used in the preparation of this paper were recorded by the author and Joanne Anderson Ostendorph during field trips to Bocas del Toro between 1972 and 1976.

The field trips were undertaken under the auspices of the Summer Institute of Linguistics and the National Institute of Culture (Dirección del Patrimonio Histórico) of the Republic of Panama. Many of the texts were transcribed by Mauricio Aguilar, a Teribe speaker, and his help in this and many other areas of language study is gratefully acknowledged. Thanks are also in order to Manuel Aguilar and other Teribe speakers who have assisted us. A concordance based on 100 pages of Teribe text has proved beneficial. It was produced at the University of Oklahoma under the Project for Computer Support of Linguistic Field Work and was supported in part by National Science Foundation Grant GS-1605. Further research for this paper was done during a workshop held in Bogotá, Colombia, at the University of the Andes by Joseph E. Grimes of Cornell University and the Summer Institute of Linguistics. I wish to thank Dr. Grimes for his assistance in this research project.

2 The Teribe alphabet is based on the Spanish one and has the following orthographic symbols: *a, e, i, o, u, ä, ë, ö, ã, ẽ, ĩ, õ, ũ, b, c/qu, ch, d, g/gu, j, l, m, n, ñ, ng, p, r, ř, s, sh, t, w, y, z, zh*. These are pronounced as in Spanish with the following exceptions: *ä* represents a vowel lower than *a*, *ë* represents a vowel midway between *i* and *e*, *ö* represents a vowel midway between *u* and *o*, the tilde on a vowel indicates that it is nasalized, *ng* represents a velar nasal, *ř* represents a retroflexed flap, and *sh* and *zh* represent, respectively, voiceless and voiced alveopalatal fricatives. The following morphophonemic rules apply to the data in this paper:

$$\ddot{e}ya \rightarrow e;\ roya \rightarrow ra;\ c/qu \rightarrow \emptyset\ / \left\{{n \atop \ddot{e}}\right\}-;\ \ddot{e} \rightarrow \left\{{a \atop o}\right\}/-C_o\left\{{a \atop o}\right\}(\text{right to left});$$

$$n +y \rightarrow \tilde{n};\left\{{C_a \atop V_a}\right\} \rightarrow \emptyset\ /-\left\{{C_a \atop V_a}\right\}.$$

3 The abbreviations of category labels used in glosses are compl completive, depen dependent, excl exclusive, imp imperative, incl inclusive, incompl incompletive, obj object, pl plural, sg singular, subj subject, 1st first, 2nd second, and 3rd third.

4 It is possible that further study will determine that 'subject nominal' would be better defined as 'agentive nominal' and 'object nominal' as 'patient nominal'.

5 *Ga* 'dependent' is homophonous with *-ga* 'subject nominal'.

6 Following a word ending in *c, ga* becomes *ca*.

7 In order to reflect the fact that the object of the transitive verb is topic, the English translation sometimes employs a passive construction, but this is not really a part of the meaning of the Teribe form.

8 The morpheme meaning 'completive' has three allomorphs: (1) *-ro* before subject markers on transitive verbs, (2) *-ong* on some intransitive verbs that take patients and on some motion verbs, and (3) *-no* elsewhere.

9 For further discussion of quotation margins in Teribe, see Koontz 1978.

10 Further study is needed to determine why, in an SOV construction that presents enablement information, the object does not seem to be topic, while in an SOV construction that establishes a paragraph topic, the object functions as clause topic.

11 An episode is a semantic unit larger than a paragraph, still incompletely understood. An episode consists of one or more paragraphs, and a discourse consists of one or more episodes.

12 For a fuller discussion of clues to participant identification, see Koontz 1978.

References

Grimes, Joseph E. 1975. *The Thread of Discourse*. The Hague: Mouton.

Koontz, Carol. 1978. "Características del Diálogo en el Discurso Narrativo Teribe." *Lenguas de Panamá* 5:29-61. Panamá: Instituto Lingüístico de Verano.

—— and Joanne Anderson. 1977. "Connectives in Teribe." In *Discourse Grammar, Part 2*, ed. by R.E. Longacre. S.I.L. Publication 52. Dallas: Summer Institute of Linguistics.

Levinsohn, Stephen H. 1975. "El Bokotá, el Guaymí y el Teribe, Respecto al Proto-Chibcha." *Lenguas de Panamá* 2:4-18. Panamá: Instituto Lingüístico de Verano.

Reverte, José M. 1967. *Los Indios Teribes de Panamá*. Panamá.

Schank, Roger C. MS. "Understanding Paragraphs."

Wise, Mary Ruth and Ivan Lowe. 1972. "Permutation Groups in Discourse." *Georgetown Languages and Linguistics: Working Papers* 4:12-34.

Topicalization in Nambiquara

Ivan Lowe

Fronting and left dislocation, the two most common topicalization processes in Nambiquara, not only topicalize an element in a clause but also begin topic spans which are entire sequences of clauses with the same overall topic. A topic span begun by left dislocation can embed within it a topic span begun by fronting, but not vice versa. Topic spans typically end with a conjunction that announces the beginning of the next topic span, but an embedded topic span can also end with the return of the embedding topic. A different set of conjunctions precedes topic spans begun by fronting from those begun by left dislocation.

Pseudofronting gives a fronted element that is topic of a whole clause span but not a constituent of the first clause, even though the surface result looks like that of fronting. Topics are typically given information and besides the usual devices of mention in previous context to make sure that an element is given, additional devices available in Nambiquara are collective verification and part-to-whole relationships with previously mentioned items.

This paper deals with marked topicalization in Nambiquara.[1] Topicalization needs to be considered in both its surface and its functional aspects; that is, both the surface devices that are used to topicalize and the effects that topicalization has on the meaning of the discourse merit study.[2]

An element in a Nambiquara clause can be topicalized by fronting or by left dislocation. Other topicalization processes exist but are not considered in this paper. Having arrived at the topicalized surface forms, the question remains, What does the topic do to the meaning structure both of the clause that it is in and of the discourse that the clause is in? This is the functional aspect of topicalization.

What is a clause about? is the question that is answered by the topic of the clause and that unifies all the diverse surface topicalization processes such as fronting and left dislocation.[3] Pursuing the same question, we can extend the idea of topic to a span of discourse greater than that of clause and ask, "Do there exist spans of consecutive clauses for which it is meaningful to ask the question, What is this clause span about?" If this question has an affirmative answer, we call what the span is about the *span topic* or topic of the span, and the span itself we call *topic span*. The concept of a topic span is indispensable for the understanding of complete Nambiquara texts but could not have been reached with a strictly clause-bound approach to topicalization.

In this paper, I show that both left dislocation and fronting define topic spans in Nambiquara, which I call left dislocation spans and fronting spans respectively. Furthermore, left dislocation spans can embed fronting spans within them, but never vice versa.

Clearly, in order to establish a topic span, we need to be able to recognize where it begins and where it ends. It is shown that both left dislocation and fronting begin spans. These two kinds of span end, however, in different ways. A left dislocation span ends immediately before another left dislocation span begins; that is, such a span runs right up to the next left dislocation span. Or a left dislocation span can end immediately before a clause with an informationally new time setting.

However, because a fronting span can be embedded within a left dislocation span, the ways that a fronting span can end are much more diverse. When a fronting span is not embedded in a larger span, it can run right up to the beginning of the next topic span whether the latter is a left dislocation span, as in examples 1 and 2, or another fronting span. On the other hand, when a fronting span is embedded in a larger span defined by left dislocation, its end can be indicated by an explicit return to the already defined left dislocation topic. In this case, the first nominal in the first clause after the fronting span has lexical cohesion with the old left dislocation topic, and this tells us that return to that topic has occurred.

The idea of a span topic can be made more precise as follows.[4] If left dislocation or fronting defines a span with topic T, and J is any clause within this span, then it should be possible to read J as 'concerning T, J'. The actual surface form in discourse is obtained from this by deleting the topic 'concerning T'. In other words, if the idea of a topic span is valid, then every clause within the span with topic T should pass this criterion as a test, and no clause in another span should pass it. The existence of such a hypothetical form finds confirmation in example 3, where the actual surface form of a clause shows a left dislocated topic followed by a fronted topic, and then the rest of the clause.

The question of how the topic system relates to the information distribution system[5] has been discussed by Halliday (1967) and more recently by Gundel (1974). The latter sets out to show that topic is always given information. Every marked topic[6] in the Nambiquara data has been checked for this, and it has been found that with the reasonable extensions made in sections 1 and 2 of the idea of 'given', all these topics confirm Gundel's proposal.

This paper, therefore, first deals in sections 1 and 2 with fronting and left dislocation and how the topic spans defined by these two processes relate to each other. In this discussion I carefully define the ends as well as the beginnings of the spans and also examine each marked topic to see whether it is given or new information. Section 3 then deals with how topicalization is used in special ways to indicate titles and climaxes of myths.

1 Fronting and pseudofronting

1.1 Fronting

Fronting of a nominal clause constituent in Nambiquara topicalizes that constituent. Nambiquara clauses spoken in isolation characteristically have constituent orders TS(O)V or LS(O)V; therefore, fronting takes a nominal constituent that is not leftmost, i.e., S or O in these isolation orders, and moves it to the leftmost position, i.e., the first position in the clause.

The fronted constituent is in every case what the clause is about. In each of the following examples I show that this is the case by giving an adequate amount of the context of the clause under study.

Except for story titles (sec. 3), the fronted element so topicalized is always given information. Various surface devices in the text show this. In some of the examples, the verb carries the collective verification set of suffixes, which have a meaning component 'information in this clause is known to both speaker and hearer'.[7] In others, the fronted element is a pronoun which is given information; in others again, the fronted element has been mentioned earlier in the story.

The fronted clause is always preceded in discourse by a conjunction which connects it logically to what has preceded. The conjunctions that can precede a fronted clause are[8] -$kxai^2nān^2tu^3$ 'conditional', -$kxa^2hax^3ta^3nān^2ti^3$ 'concessional', and $xyān^1ta^1$ 'adversative'. These conjunctions are more often used between clauses and only occasionally between larger units, thus pointing to the tendency for fronted clause spans to be short. In contrast, the left dislocated clauses dealt with in section 2 must be preceded by one of a totally different set of conjunctions that are used mainly between larger units.

In the following five examples of fronting, the first three are from first person texts, the last two from myths. The subject is fronted in examples 1 to 4 and the object in example 5. The fronted element is always given information. In examples 1 and 2 it is the pronoun 'I', in example 3 its given status is shown by the collective verification suffixes on the verb, and in examples 4 and 5 its given status is shown by anaphoric reference suffixes on the fronted element. The end of the topic span is indicated by a topic change conjunction in examples 1, 2, and 4 and by an explicit return to the topic of the embedding span in example 3.

In all the examples in this paper, the data are presented in three subsections. Immediately following the number of an example, the Nambiquara is given, clause by clause, each clause being numbered by a lower case letter in square brackets so that consecutive letters of the alphabet indicate consecutive clauses in running text. Following the number of the example marked with a single prime, such as (1'), is the corresponding word by word gloss, and then following the number of the example with a double prime, such as (1''), is the free translation. When essential context precedes the example clauses, or follows them, or both, it is given within parentheses in the free translation.

In example 1, the preceding context talks about some people who are about to go off on a journey. The speaker then adds, "As for me, I am staying behind." The implication is, "As for them, they'll probably go off on a trip, but as for me, I'll not go." He thus begins to talk about himself and what he will do. The topicalized clause [a] has constituent order SLV rather than the unmarked order LSV. Its topic is the fronted pronoun subject 'I', which is always given information. The span ends after one more clause at the conjunction $jut^1ta^3la^3$ $na^1ha^2kxai^3$ 'major topic change', which introduces a new topic span.

(1) [a] $Nain^1kxa^2hax^3ta^3nãn^2ti^3$ $txai^2li^2$ $yon^3nãn^2ta^3$ $sxa^3na^1tũ^1$.
(1') [a] even-though-they as-for-me behind I-will-stay
(1'') '[a] Even though they go off on a journey, as for me I am staying behind. ([b] So you will come back and meet me here. [c] Major topic changer, as for my house, . . .)'

In example 2, the preceding context talks about some people who are working in the fields. The speaker then begins to talk about himself and what he is going to do: "As for me, I'll stay behind," i.e., not join the others in their work on the fields. The topicalized clause has constituent order SLV rather than the unmarked order LSV, the topic being the fronted subject pronoun 'I', which is always given information. Like example 1, the span ends immediately preceding the conjunction *jut¹ta³la³ na¹ha²kxai³* 'major topic change'. Unlike example 1, however, this span in example 2 extends over several pages of text.

(2)　(c) *Nain¹kxai²nãn²tu̇³ txai²nãn²tu̇³ yon³nãn²ta³ sxa³na¹tũ¹.*
(2')　[c] since-they-do as-for-me behind I-will-stay
(2")　'([a] Now they are working in the fields. [b] They are cutting the fields.) [c] Since they are, as for me, I will stay behind. [d] I will go off hunting on another trail. . . . Major topic changer, . . .)'

In example 3, the subject, 'rain', is fronted to give the constituent order STV in clause [c]. This clause, then, tells us about the rain, that it usually falls nonstop at this time of the year.

In clause [a], which is two clauses before this fronted clause, the marked topic 'house' is introduced by left dislocation. This, as we see in example 14, defines a left dislocation span that embeds the span with topic 'rain'. The clause [b] that immediately precedes the clause having 'rain' as topic is "We are getting rained upon," and this has no nominal constituent, the verb 'to be rained upon' being a state verb whose surface form bears no resemblance to the lexical noun root 'rain'.

This fronted span with topic 'rain' ends in an unusual way: by return to the major topic, 'house', of the embedding span as follows.

The final clause [e] in the free translation 'thus my task, I will calmly work at,' shows us that the speaker has finished talking about 'rain' and has returned to talking about 'work on the house'. The beginning of this clause, therefore, indicates the end of the topic span on 'rain', which began with the fronted clause [c].

(3)　[c] *Xyãn¹ta¹　a¹jut³ta³la³ wẽ³hai²nãn²tu̇³*
　　　hĩ¹ta³te²la³ ãn³six³wi¹wi¹hxai²te¹ti²nhe³.
(3')　[c] but my-situation the-rain right-this-time-of-the-year usually-falls-nonstop-collective-verification)
(3")　'([a] Concerning houses, the work on my house isn't finished. [b] We are getting rained upon.) [c] But in this matter, the rain usually comes down nonstop this time of the year, as we all know. [d] But now it is not doing that any more. [e] Thus my task, I will calmly work at it.'

The next two examples, 4 and 5, have to do with fronting to topicalize participants in myths. Fronting of a participant in a clause within the body of a myth defines a topic span all of whose clauses say something about the topicalized participant. The topic or fronted element is given information since it carries the ending $n\bar{u}^1ta^2kxai^3lu^2$, which in a myth marks a constituent that refers anaphorically to some preceding part of the context.

However, a fronted clause that is the first clause of a story is the verbal title of the story, and reports not the first event of the story but the most significant event. Verbal titles have a topic, which is new information. Such clauses are treated in detail in section 3.

In example 4, the subject, 'mother', is fronted so that the constituent order STV departs from the unmarked order TSV. Thus 'mother' is the topic of this clause and remains the topic for the whole of the following span given until the switch conjunction signals a topic change. The fronted clause in this example is not a title but reports the first event in the sequence.

(4) [a] $\bar{A}^2h\tilde{a}x^3k\tilde{a}^3nu^2n\bar{u}^1ta^2kxai^3 \; kx\tilde{a}^3na^3ha^2ta^3a^2$
$t\tilde{a}^2te^3lhx\tilde{a}^3 \; xai^3t\tilde{a}u^3\tilde{a}n^2t\grave{u}^3$

(4') [a] mother-anaphoric-reference the-morrow in-order-to-defecate while-going

(4") '[a] Then the mother, on the morrow, while going out to relieve herself, ([b] saw cutter ants bearing manioc leaves. And she said in wonder, "Look! Cutter ants have cut up manioc leaves and are coming." Switch conjunction then indicates topic change.)'

In example 5, the object constituent, 'child', is fronted[9] from the unmarked clause order SOV. Thus 'child' is the topic of this clause and remains the topic for the whole of the following context given. This fronted clause is not the first clause in the story, so it is not a title, but rather reports the first event in a long sequence.

(5) [a] $Te^3nah^1lxi^1$ [b]$w\tilde{e}^3sa^3n\bar{u}^1ta^2kxai^3lu^2$
$w\tilde{e}^3sa^3n\bar{u}^1t\tilde{a}^2 \; \tilde{a}^2w\tilde{\imath}^3nu^2su^2 \quad e^2kxai^3lu^2$
$t\tilde{e}^3sx\tilde{a}^3 \; xai^3ta^1hxai^2h\tilde{e}^1ra^2.$

(5') [a] this-is-how [b] child the-child's father this-one took-and went

(5") '[a] This is how. [b] Concerning the child, the child's father led him. ([c] And the father went in front and the child came along behind. And. . . .)'

1.2 Fronting near the beginning of a text

All fronted topics treated so far have been given information, and we expect every fronted topic to be given information. We have seen in section 1.1 that the use of pronouns, collective verification, and mention in preceding context are ways of indicating that information is given. However, if the fronted clause is the first clause in the discourse that has a marked topic, then one way to make sure that the topic is given information is to have an introductory stretch of discourse where the topic referent can be introduced before it is topicalized. This introductory section is essentially a device for introducing the referent that is to be made the marked topic later and for making a few incidental remarks about it. Such a section has its own topic, which is usually, but not necessarily, coreferential with what will be the marked topic. Immediately after the introductory section comes the clause with a topic marked by fronting, and this clause can be regarded as initiating the first main argument of the text.

The following two examples, 6 and 7, both commence with a section which introduces and gives past time information on the items 'house rafters' and 'manioc shoots', respectively. The fronted elements in the clauses designated [c], both of which have marked topics, refer back anaphorically to the previously mentioned items, introducing them as marked topics for the text span to follow, which tells the hearer what the speaker intends to do with these items.

The first clauses of the introductory sections of examples 6 and 7 introduce their own unmarked topics in different ways. Example 6 introduces 'house rafters' in clause [a] with a verb in collective verification, but the nominal itself has no verification suffix. Example 7, on the other hand, introduces 'manioc shoots' in clause [a] with collective verification suffixes on the nominal itself, showing it clearly to be given information. On the other hand, the verb itself is suffixed for individual verification, so it is new information. It could be argued, but less convincingly in my opinion, that the topic for the introductory sections was the time setting itself, i.e., ' this morning' and 'today', respectively, for examples 6 and 7. This possible indeterminacy does not affect the topic of the main argument, which is selected unambiguously by the fronted element in the first clause having marked topic.

Thus in example 6, the first constituent, 'these my rafters therefore', of clause [c] refers back anaphorically to 'house rafters' of clause [a] and is the fronted topic for the whole of clause [c].

(6) [a] $Kx\tilde{a}^3na^3ha^2ta^3na^2$ $sxi^2ha^2ni^3ta^2$
$yo^3te^3lhx\tilde{a}^3$ $xai^3na^1ten^1tu^3wa^2$.
[b] $Xyan^1ta^1$ $yo^3a^1ra^2$. $A^2yut^3ta^2$ $yo^3\tilde{a}^1a^1ra^2$
[c] $Na^1ta^3ni^3tai^2na^2sa^2kxai^2lu^2$ $kx\tilde{a}^3na^3ha^2tai^2n\tilde{a}n^2ta^3$
$h\tilde{a}i^1x\tilde{a}^3na^1a^1kax^3t\mathring{u}^3$ $sa^2so^1xi^2sx\tilde{a}^3$ $h\tilde{a}i^1sx\tilde{a}^3$ $sa^2tait^3ta^2$
$jut^1tai^2na^2$ so^1li^3 $na^1t\tilde{u}^1x\tilde{a}^1$ $na^1h\tilde{e}^2ra^2$.

(6') [a] this-morning house-rafters in-order-to-cut I-went-collective-verification. [b] but I-cut-them. valley-I-cut-left. [c] these-my-rafters-therefore tommorrow I'll-leave I-gather just tie-up this-only I-future I-intend

(6") '[a] This morning I went to cut rafters for the house. [b] And I actually cut them too. I cut them and left them in the valley. [c] These my rafters, therefore, I'll leave them tomorrow—that is to say, all I intend to do is to gather them and tie them up.'

In example 7, the first constituent, 'these my shoots therefore', of clause [c] refers back anaphorically to 'manioc shoots' of clause [a]. 'These my shoots therefore' is the fronted topic of clause [c].

(7) [a] $Hi^1na^2su^2$ $wa^3lin^3sun^3ti^2$ $\overset{?}{i}{}^3a^1ra^2$
      [b] $xyan^1ta^1$ $su^3ha^1li^1$ ot^3sxa^3 $a^3si^1na^1ra^2$
      [c] $na^1ta^3su^3ai^2na^2sa^2kxai^3lu^2$ $kxa^3na^3ha^2$-
           $tai^2nan^2ta^3$ $te^2yax^1ne^2$ $\overset{?}{i}{}^3a^1tu^1xa^1$ $na^1he^2ra^2$.
(7') [a] today manioc-shoot-we've-seen I-planted. [b] but some-shoots left-over we-left. [c] these-my-shoots-therefore tomorrow in-the-same-way I-plant-intend I-subjective)
(7") '[a] Today I planted manioc shoots, [b] but we left with some shoots still unplanted. [c] These my shoots, I intend to plant tomorrow.'

However, after an item has been introduced in a first clause, the argument concerning it, which follows, need not necessarily start with a fronted anaphoric element. After a first clause introduction, the item can be referred to by zero in the following clause. When zero anaphora is used, however, there must be time continuity between the first and second clauses so that if, for instance, the first clause deals with a future time event so must the second. Thus in example 8 the item 'bamboo' introduced in the first clause is referred to by zero in the second clause rather than by a fronted anaphoric element. The clauses [a] and [b] form a short span with unmarked topic 'bamboo'. The span is embedded in a larger span with topic 'baskets', which was introduced by fronting, and immediately after clause [b] there is a return to the topic of the embedding span. Unlike the topic in examples 6 and 7, the topic 'bamboo' of example 8 never gets fronted. Both the verb 'see' of clause [a] and 'show' of clause [b] of example 8 refer to future events, so the time continuity requirement is satisfied. This is in contrast to the time orientation shifts in examples 6 and 7 where the events in the introduction are past events but the events in the argument that follows are future events.

(8) [a] *Ax³lu³kwhi³la² e³kxain¹to³jut³tait³ta³li²*
ĩ²na¹hxã³nhi² na¹hẽ²ra² [b] *jã¹xne³sxã³*
xwã²nãu³ũ¹sain¹na³na¹ [c] *na¹kxai² nãn²tu³*
(8') [a] bamboo that-they-talked-about I-see-desiderative I-
subjective [b] and-so if-they show-me [c] then-I'll . . . .
(8") '[a] I want to see the bamboo they talked about. [b] If they
show it to me [c] (then I'll weave baskets. . . .)'

1.3 Pseudofronting

Sometimes a clause has what looks like a fronted element, yet this
element does not fit into the clause in any definable role at all. In other
words, it is not possible to match it to a well-formed unfronted clause.
I call this pseudofronting because, although the result sounds
superficially like a fronted clause, in fact an extraneous element has
been added to the front of the clause.

Pseudofronting, however, functions in the same way as fronting
because this extraneous element, like the fronted element in a regularly
fronted clause, is the topic for the whole clause span beginning with
the first clause.

Thus in example 9, the word *hi³a²* 'poles' at the very beginning of
the first clause is a pseudofronted element. A literal translation of the
first clause by itself, 'poles, we were staying at the Fox headwaters',
makes poor sense at best, and it is impossible to assign a role to 'poles'
in that clause. However, if we take the next clause as well, then 'poles'
fits very well as what is being talked about for the span consisting of
both clauses. 'Poles' is given information, having been mentioned
previously in the text. The topic span so defined is just two clauses
long. A new span, preceded by *xyãn¹ta¹* 'adversative' and introducing
the next topic, follows immediately.

(9) [a] *Xne³kxai²nãn²tu³ hi³a² yax³wa³la³ne³ki³a²*
ã³xyau³sain¹na²hẽ³ra² [b] *ya³sai¹nha²kxai³*
"*hi³a² ĩ³hax³ja³sah¹lxi³hẽ¹ri¹,*" *nai¹na¹hẽ²ra².*
(9') [a] thus poles headwaters-called-Fox we-were-staying-at [b] at-
that-time poles let's-make-a-bridge I-to-them
(9") '[a] Thus, concerning the poles, we were staying at the Fox
headwaters, [b] and I said to them, "Let's build a bridge with
these poles." '

2 Left dislocation

Left dislocation also topicalizes a Nambiquara clause. This section
shows how left dislocation topicalizes, how left dislocation topic spans
are set up, and how such spans can have topic spans that are defined
by fronting embedded within them.

I define the surface process of left dislocation in Nambiquara as that of adding to the beginning of a clause a nominal constituent with a close lexical relationship to a nominal already inside the clause, without deleting that old nominal. Although this looks very different from the original definition given by Ross (1967), which involved leaving a pronoun in the clause in place of the dislocated element, I shall show how similar the final results of the two processes are.

First, however, is presented an example of how it works in Nambiquara. Were the Nambiquara process exactly reproducible in English, we might have something like 'work on my house, my house is not being built', where the nominal 'work on my house' with a close lexical relationship to the in-clause nominal 'my house' is added at the front of the original clause 'my house is not being built'. The corresponding Nambiquara form is $Txa^2sxi^2hyut^3tai^2na^2$ hai^3txi^3 $sxi^2hai^2nan^2tu^3$ $ton^3nu^3xn^3ti^2nhe^3$. (work-on-my-house negative this-house construct-negative-collective-verification) 'Concerning the work on my house, my house is not being built.'

Let us now look more closely at the lexical relationship between the dislocated element and its in-clause counterpart. This is sometimes a part-to-whole relationship and sometimes an activity-to-associated-item relationship.

As illustrations of the part-to-whole relationship, example 10 presents dislocated element 'work on the fields', which bears a part-to-whole relationship to its in-clause counterpart 'manioc shoots', and example 11 has dislocated element 'the open country', which bears the same relationship to its in-clause counterpart, 'the piece at the back of the little woods'—this being clear to a hearer who knows the layout of the village being talked about.

As an illustration of the activity-to-associated-item relationship, in example 12 dislocated element 'work on wood' is an activity associated with item 'wood', which is its in-clause counterpart. In general, the dislocated element describes an activity, while its in-clause counterpart mentions some item that is involved in that activity. Example 13 shows the same relationship between dislocated element and its in-clause counterpart. Example 14 also shows the same relationship, but the order of the two elements has been reversed in surface structure, with dislocation of the item rather than the activity.

What I call left dislocation in Nambiquara differs in surface detail from the sense in which the term was introduced by Ross, but the final result is similar in the two cases. In the original usage, a constituent was fronted, but a pronoun was left in place of the former constituent in the clause, as in Gundel's example for English, "As for the proposal, Archie rejected it," which is related to "Archie rejected the proposal'' by left dislocation. Thus there is referential identity between the dislocated element and its in-clause counterpart in English. In Nambiquara left dislocation, as I have defined it, the relationship between the dislocated and in-clause elements is not one of referential identity but rather one of the two mentioned in the preceding paragraphs, either part-to-whole or activity-to-associated-item.

Left dislocation spans can have fronting spans embedded within them, but the converse is not true. This does not lay down any limits on the number of clauses that either of these kinds of topic span can have. Although fronting spans typically tend to be just a few clauses long and left dislocation spans much longer, there are, in fact, examples of fronting spans that extend over most of a long text. There are also examples of a left dislocation span exactly one clause long (see ex. 12).

All the following examples, 10 to 14, show how left dislocation topicalizes and defines a topic span. The last examples, 13 and 14, also show fronting spans embedded within left dislocation spans and how a fronting span so embedded can end.

Different examples illustrate different lexical relationships between the dislocated element and its in-clause counterpart.

The topic is always given information, but this is rather subtle in two of the examples, 11 and 12. In example 11 the topic, 'open country', is given because it is a referential part of the topic, 'all the land where we live', which was announced in the very first clause of the text by the speaker. In example 12 the topic, 'work on wood', is given information because a lexically related activity, 'house construction', has been discussed before in the same text. On the other hand, the left dislocated elements in examples 10, 11, and 14 are shown to be given information by the common device of suffixing the verb in the clause for collective verification, just as was done in example 3 on fronting.

As regards surface markers, the left dislocation span is always immediately preceded by one of three conjunctions: $jut^1ta^3la^3$ $na^1ha^2kxai^3$ 'major topic change', $na^1ha^2kxai^3$ 'similarly', or $haun^2xwan^3ta^3$ 'eventually'. These do not include any of the conjunctions that introduce the topic span for fronting, and the first two of these conjunctions always connect large units in discourse.

The last word in the left dislocated constituent is almost always suffixed with either $-tu^3$ 'incomplete' or $-sa^1$ 'cataphoric', which tell the hearer to expect more information on the topic just announced.

In example 10, left dislocation in the first clause defines a topic 'work on the fields' with a topic span extending over the two clauses given. The left dislocated element has a whole-to-part relationship with its in-clause counterpart. Collective verification suffixes on the verb show the topic to be given information. The topic span ends with the end of the story.

(10) [a] *Jut¹ta³la³-na¹ha³kxai³ hai³syut³tai²nān²tǔ³ wa³lin³su³ai²nān²tǔ³ ā³nī¹xn³nha²khi³ xne³kix³jau³su³ to³kix³tait¹ti²ti³.*
[b] *Xyān¹ta¹ su³ka³na³ku² ī³hxa³kix³tait¹ti²ti³.*

(10') [a] major-topic-change work-on-fields these-manioc-shoots want-badly-to-plant our-thoughts we-collective-verification. [b] but a-few-shoots we-have-planted-collective-verification)

(l0") '[a] Concerning work on the fields, we've been saying we very badly want to plant these manioc shoots. [b] However, we have planted a few shoots as everyone knows!' (End of story.)

Example 11 comes out of a discourse in which an Indian is discussing the imminent coming of some surveyors who will measure his land, some of which may be taken away from him. He is spelling out what parts of the land he is willing to give up and what parts he wants to keep at any price. In the immediately preceding context he has been discussing the land 'near the village', and now he passes on to discuss the 'open country'.

(11) [a] *Na¹ha²kxai³ ha³lo²ai²na²sa¹ yu³sa³txi²ta³lo³kxa³tī³nha² xyan¹txi²hax³ti³tī³nha² ha³lo²a² ā³ten³sa²tī³nāu¹la³ sa³ha²kxai³ xne³sa³nha²wa².*

(11') [a] similarly open-country the-piece-at-the-back-of-the-woods the-piece-over-yonder place I-want to-me me-subjective

(11") '[a] In the same way, concerning the open country, I want the piece of land over yonder at the back of the woods.'

The following example, 12, again illustrates left dislocation with a whole-to-part relationship between the dislocated element and the in-clause element. It differs, however, from the other examples of this section in two important respects.

First, it illustrates how the topic can be given information without having been mentioned explicitly in the preceding context, provided that the context mentions something else that is in a part-to-whole relationship with the element to be topicalized. Thus in this example, the topic, 'work on wood', has not been explicitly mentioned in the previous context, nor is the verb suffixed for collective verification. However, in the previous context 'house construction' has been discussed, and 'house construction' includes work on getting wood for the house, which is the topic of the dislocated clause.

Second, it illustrates a topic span that is unusually short for one defined by left dislocation—only one clause long. Right after the end of the topicalized clause is the conjunction $jut^1ta^3la^3$ $na^1ha^2kxai^3$, which always announces a new topic.

(12) [c] $Hāun^2xwān^3ta^3$ $hi^3yut^3tai^2nān^2tử^3$
       $hi^3nān^2ta^3$ $ã^3sa^2so^1hxĩ^3na^1xã^1$
       $ye^1xna^2ha^1wa^2$ [d] $jut^1ta^3la^3$ $na^1ha^2kxai^3$

(12') [c] eventually work-on-wood wood I-will-probably-get I-to-you
       [d] major-topic-change

(12'') '. . . ([a] Tomorrow I'm thinking of nailing up the house. [b]
       But if I get hungry I'll go hunting and get some food. . . .)
       Then [c] eventually concerning work on the wood for the
       house, I'll probably get some wood, I'm saying to you.
       (Change of topic. . . .)'

The following two examples, 13 and 14, illustrate how a span introduced by left dislocation can embed within it a span introduced by fronting. Both examples illustrate left dislocation topicalization with a whole-to-part relationship between the dislocated element and the in-clause counterpart. Note that in example 14 the order of these elements is the reverse of the normal. The topic is known to be given information because of collective verification suffixes on the verb.

In example 13, the left dislocated topic of clause [a], 'work on my house only', is the overall topic for clauses [a], [b], and [c]. Then a further left dislocated clause [d] gives 'house' as overall topic for clauses [d] and [e]. Clause [f] starts with a new setting 'some time later in the year' as topic and 'weather drying out' as comment, while clause [g] takes the comment of clause [f] and makes that its topic. Finally, clause [h] has fronted topic 'house' which is a return to the topic defined by left dislocation of clause [d].

(13) [a] $Hāun^2xwān^3ta^3$ $txa^2sxi^2hyut^3tai^2na^2$ so^1li^3
       hai^3txi^3 $sxi^2hai^2nān^2tử^3$ $ton^3nũ^3xn^3ti^2nhe^3$.

(13') [a] eventually work-on-my-house only negative this-house
       construct-negative-collective-verification

(13'') '[a] Concerning work on my house, my house is not being
       built. [b] I don't want a big house, [c] just a smallish one so
       that I can keep dry do I intend to build. [d] But concerning
       the house, if only I'd got some thatch some time ago. [e] But
       now the weather is so unreliable. [f] Some time later in the
       year, the weather usually dries out. [g] It's about to happen
       now, I believe. [h] And so concerning the house at present,
       I'm not worried.'

In example 14, I give the whole span, [a] to [g], of the topic, 'houses', which is defined by left dislocation in clause [a]. The span thus includes the span consisting of clauses [c] and [d], defined by fronting the span topic, 'rain'. The 'rain' span ends with clause [d] since the first nominal in clause [e] is 'my task', which refers anaphorically to 'work on the house' and thus brings us back to the left dislocated topic 'houses'. The topic span defined by left dislocation in clause [a] ends at the new time setting 'now' given at the beginning of clause [h], and this clause and following clauses go on to talk about a completely new topic.

(14) [a] $Jut^1ta^3la^3$-$na^1ha^2kxai^3$ $sxi^2hai^2n\bar{a}n^2t\dot{u}^3$
    $txa^2sxi^2hyut^3tai^2n\bar{a}n^2t\dot{u}^3$ $ta^3lu^2ni^2kxi^2nh\bar{u}^1xn^3ti^2nhe^3$.

(14') [a] major-topic-change houses the-work-on-my-house not- yet-
    finished-collective-verification

(14'') '[a] Major topic change. Concerning houses, the work on my house isn't finished yet. ([b] We are getting rained on. [c] But in this matter, the rain usually comes down nonstop this time of the year. [d] Now it doesn't. [e] Thus my task on the house I'll calmly work away at, [f] and when I finish the house, I'll leave it. [g] But this sickness has disabled me, so I have nothing to say. [h] But now the people who have gone off to hunt the anteater. . . .)'

3 Topicalization in myths

In myths, topicalization is used in two ways in which it is not normally used in nonmythical texts: in verbal titles and in indicating a climax.

Verbal titles are given as follows. The first nominal in a story is its topic. If the first nominal appears in an equative clause, then the subject of this clause is the topic; temporals and locatives are not counted as nominals in this reckoning. If the first nominal is in an active clause whose time reference is later than the first event of the story, then this clause constitutes a verbal title and the topic of the story is the topic of this clause. If, in addition, the title clause is transitive and the story topic is its object, then this object has to be fronted to topicalize it.

In example 15, the object element, 'the orphans', is fronted out of the unmarked clause order TSOV. Since this is the first clause of the text, 'the orphans' are the topic of the story. They are the main participants throughout the story, and this story is referred to by all Nambiquaras as 'the story about the orphans'. Note that this clause does not report the first event of the story. The event of the devil's eating up the Nambiquara is a very significant event in the story, but it occurs far into the body of the story.

(15) $Sai^3ki^3n\tilde{a}^3x\tilde{a}^2$ $kx\tilde{a}^3nh\tilde{i}^1n\tilde{u}^1tai^2na^2$ $six^3wh\tilde{i}n^1jah^3la^2$ $ho^3hxa^3ta^1hxai^2h\tilde{e}^1ra^2$ $te^3nah^1lxi^1$.

(15') the-orphans long-time-ago the-devil ate-them-all-up this-is-how . . .

The story titles that are fronted clauses are transitive clauses with fronted objects reporting significant events of the story. Intransitive clause titles reporting significant events like 'the old woman shed her skin' are not fronted. Other possible titles are equative clauses asserting the existence of the main character, like 'there was once an anteater'. These also are not fronted.

Retopicalization of the principal character by fronting is one of the ways of indicating climax in myths. What is different in this use of topicalization is that the principal character is already being talked about in the part of the text just before topicalization occurs, but right at the point of climax he is topicalized for a very short span.

In example 16, the context is that Woodpecker Man, who is the principal character of the story, has previously been told that he must on no account open a certain box called the darkness box. His curiosity, however, gets the better of him, and he decides to open the box, whereupon darkness descends upon him. The clause that is topicalized reports Woodpecker Man just at the point when he is about to open the box. The subject is fronted, thus clearly showing the Woodpecker Man to be the topic; that is, he is the one to whom our attention is directed. The constituent order in this clause is STOV, the subject being followed by the time element 'at the time when he was about to be turned into a woodpecker (bird)'. The topic is given information because he was introduced in the first clause of the story.

Immediately after the fronted clause describing the climax, the topic changes to 'darkness'; in fact, the topic span at the climax is just one clause long.

(16) $Xne^3jau^3t\mathring{u}^3$ $ut^2jah^3lo^2n\tilde{u}^1ta^2kxai^3$ $ut^2tai^2na^2$ $te^2ut^1tai^2na^2$
$wen^1te^3lhx\tilde{a}^3$ $jut^3tu^1tai^2na^2$ $kx\tilde{a}^3na^3t\tilde{e}^3n\tilde{u}^1ta^2kxai^3lu^2$
$kx\tilde{a}^3na^3hi^2$ $xne^3jut^3jut^1tu^1tai^2na^2$
$\tilde{a}^2\tilde{e}^1n\tilde{u}^1ta^2kxai^3lu^1$ $sa^2n\tilde{e}^3tha^2na^1t\tilde{u}^1x\tilde{u}^3$ $xne^3te^2an^1tux^3ti^1$
$hax^3y\tilde{a}u^3kw\tilde{a}i^3$ $xne^3te^3x\tilde{a}^2$ $kx\tilde{a}^3na^3ti^2tu^3wa^2$
$kx\tilde{a}^3na^3khaix^3ne^3ju^3kxai^3$ $kx\tilde{a}^3na^3ti^2tu^3wa^2$
$j\tilde{a}^1xne^3ti^3$ $ti^1a^2kxai^3lu^1$ $kx\tilde{a}^3na^3ye^1ta^1hxai^2h\tilde{e}^1ra^1$.

(16') with-these-thoughts the-Woodpecker-Man woodpecker this-one about-to-be-turned-into at-that-time the-darkness-box darkness matters-concerning the-box resolved-to-open-and-did just-when-he-did darkness-falling-ideophone that's-how it-gets-

dark-as-we-all-know with-extreme-darkness it-gets-dark-as-we-all-know
in-just-that-way it-got-dark-on-the-woodpecker

> (16") 'And with these thoughts, the Woodpecker Man, just at the
> time when he was about to be turned into a woodpecker bird,
> resolved to open the box that had to do with darkness and did
> so. At that very moment when he did, wham! we all know
> that's how it gets dark. It gets dark with a really thick
> darkness. Well, that was exactly what happened to the
> woodpecker.'

Notes

1 Nambiquara was classified by McQuown and Greenberg (1960) as in the Ge-Pano-Carib phylum of languages. There are approximately two hundred speakers of Nambiquara in northwestern Mato Grosso, Brazil. The number of dialect groups remains uncertain at present. The data for this paper comprise over 1000 pages of text gathered on field trips between 1960 and 1976 in accordance with contracts between the Summer Institute of Linguistics and the Museu Nacional do Rio de Janeiro and more recently between the Institute and the Fundação Nacional do Índio. The present paper was written under the auspices of the Summer Institute of Linguistics at a 1976 field workshop held at Porto Velho, Rondônia, Brazil, under the direction of Joseph E. Grimes. The author is indebted to the indigenous communities in the Nambiquara villages of Serra Azul and Camararé for help in learning to speak the language and in the explanation of the meanings of texts and to Joseph E. Grimes and Robert A. Dooley for many helpful discussions and comments in the development of this paper.

2 Kroeker (1975) discusses another aspect of the topicalization problem in Nambiquara.

3 At the level of clause, various authors, notably Halliday (1967) and Gundel (1974), have presented the idea of topic or theme as "what the clause is about." Thus Halliday (1967) defines the theme of a clause as "what is being talked about" or "point of departure for the message" and the rheme as "what is said about the theme." Gundel's topic is essentially the same as Halliday's theme except for her reservations, which are summarized in note 5.

4 This can be regarded as an extension applicable to higher-level spans of Gundel's proposal for clauses that all clauses have the left dislocated topicalized form as their underlying form and that the surface forms with unmarked topic are derived from these by topic deletion.

5 Halliday (1967) also introduces another system: that of information focus with the options *given* and *new*, where *given* is what is recoverable from the preceding discourse and *new* is not. On the other hand, Gundel (1974), using the terms *topic* and *comment* to correspond to Halliday's *theme* and *rheme*, sets out to show that *topic* is no different from *given* and *comment* from *new*. Thus if Gundel is right, there is only one system to deal with here, not two.

6 By *marked topic* is meant any topic defined by fronting or left dislocation.

7 All present and past verb forms in Nambiquara are obligatorily suffixed for verification, which can be either individual or collective. Individual verification means that all the information in the clause containing the verb is known only to the speaker with an exception to be noted below, while collective verification means

that all the information in the clause is known to both speaker and hearer and hence is given information. Nominals, temporals, and locationals can also be independently suffixed for collective verification. When a nominal, temporal, or locational is suffixed for collective verification, however, the verb is not information known to the hearer unless it is also suffixed for collective verification. Thus for a clause with the verb suffixed for individual verification and a nominal suffixed for collective verification, the nominal is information known to both speaker and hearer, but the verb is information known only to the speaker. This is the exception mentioned at the beginning of the paragraph.

8 The phonemes of Nambiquara are /p/, /t/, /k/, /d/ (implosive alveolar stop), /x/ (glottal stop), /j/ (alveopalatal affricate), /n/ (with six allophones: [m] after nasalized vowel glide /au/, [bm] after oral vowel glide /au/, [gŋ] preceding a velar stop and following an oral vowel, [ŋ] preceding a velar stop and following a nasalized vowel, [dn] on all other occasions following oral vowels, and [n] on all other occasions following nasalized vowels), /N/ (voiceless nasal), /r/ (only in the final syllable of the independent verb), /l/ ([ř] after front vowels, [l] after all other vowels), /s/, /h/, /w/, and /y/. Vowels occur in oral and nasalized series (written with a tilde ṽ): /i/, /e/, /a/, /o/, /u/ and two vowel glides /ai/ and /au/. Both series of vowels also occur laryngealized, indicated by ['] over the vowel letter, i.e. v̓. There are three tones in Nambiquara indicated by raised numbers [1] [2] [3] at the end of every syllable. [1] is a down glide; [2] is an upglide; and [3] is a low-level tone.

9 This is indeed a case of fronting and not of left dislocation as might be thought. The endings -kxai[3]lu[2] on the first occurrence of 'child' and on 'father' show that these are both clause-level constituents, so that 'child' is object on its first occurrence and 'child's father' is subject so that the constituent order is OSV so there has been a fronting from the unmarked order SOV.

References

Gundell, Jeanette M. 1974. "The Role of Topic and Comment in Linguistic Theory." Ph.D. dissertation: University of Texas.

Halliday, Michael A.K. 1967. "Notes on Transitivity and Theme in English." Part 2. *Journal of Linguistics* 3:199-244.

Kroeker, Menno H. 1975. "Thematic Linkage in Nambiquara Narrative." In *The Thread of Discourse*, ed. by Joseph E. Grimes. The Hague, Mouton.

Lowe, Ivan. 1972. "On the Relation of Formal to Sememic Matrices with Illustrations from Nambiquara." *Foundations of Language* 8:360-90.

McQuown, Norman and Joseph Greenberg. 1960. "Aboriginal Languages of Latin America," ed. by Sol Tax. *Current Anthropology* 1:431-36.

Ross, John R. 1967. "Constraints on Variables in Syntax." Ph.D. dissertation: M.I.T.

Topicalization and Constituency in Coreguaje Narrative

Frances Gralow

In Coreguaje narrative discourse the speaker's method of identifying and referring to topics throughout the text is used to segment the text into paragraphs and episodes. Topicalization and participant reference patterns also help distinguish such elements of the story as introduction, complication, resolution, peak, and conclusion.

The first section of this paper enumerates the ways a speaker may choose to establish global and local topics and how he may change from one topic to another. Then the second section shows the relationship of topic status to paragraphs along with an explanation of what a Coreguaje paragraph is, including a description of the different types of links and conjunctions used in paragraphing. The third section shows how Coreguaje discourse is broken into its constituent parts, mainly using participant reference and the particle -bi. The paper concludes with a brief section on the peak of the discourse.

1 Topic

Coreguaje[1] discourse employs two types of topic: global and local. Word order is one way of pointing out topic. The normal word order for Coreguaje clauses is time, location, instrument or manner, verb phrase, subject, indirect object, and direct object. The first four examples[2] illustrate various combinations of constituents in their normal order.

(1) *Úcua-aso-mн reбaн reba-huaᶦ-o-re chaᶦiraᶦca.*
[caused=to=drink-rep-masc+sing]$_{verb}$ [he]$_{subj}$ [that-creat-fem-obl]$_{iobj}$ [medicine]$_{dobj}$

149

'He reportedly gave her medicine to drink.'[3]

(2) *Chijaʹiro ñami sнo-ra chii-mo chнʹн.*
[tomorrow before=dawn]$_{time}$ [toast-fut want-fem+sing]$_{vp}$ [I]$_{subj}$
'Tomorrow before dawn I will want to toast cassava.'

(3) *Jobogacho-na jнo-aso-тн rebaн anillogahua.*
[middle=finger-on]$_{loc}$ [put=on+comp-rep-masc+sing]$_{verb}$ [he]$_{subj}$
[ring]$_{dobj}$
'He reportedly put the ring on his middle finger.'

(4) *Bararн-ji tota ūha-si-na-ʹ-me.*
[shovel-with]$_{instr}$ [pounded leave-comp-plur+nom-stat-plur]$_{vp}$
'They pounded it with a shovel and left it.'

Subject, indirect object, and direct object can all be moved to
positions before the verb—one at a time, in pairs, or all three at once,
though the latter is very infrequent. In so doing, the speaker makes
these items topic—local, global, or both. The actual order in which
constituents appear in a clause is variable according to the degree of
prominence assigned to each by the speaker. The item in a clause
closest to the beginning is given the most prominence.

There are four processes affecting Coreguaje noun phrases that may
be used to identify global and local topics: fronting, left dislocation,
splitting, and reiteration. Later in this paper I describe still other uses
for these processes in narrative discourse.

In order to understand how these processes work, one must
understand Coreguaje noun phrases. A noun phrase can take many
forms, the simplest being a pronoun or a noun.

(5) *chнʹн* 'I'
(6) *oco* 'water'
(7) *bōsн-н* (youth-masc+sing+nom) 'the young man'
(8) *bнca-jaʹco* (poss-mother) 'his/her/their mother'

Often, however, noun phrases are complex, involving nominalized
adjectives or verb phrases, or combinations of various elements in
apposition. Adjectives are very limited in number, however, so
nominalized verb phrases are used with much greater frequency. The
two examples that follow are noun phrases using a nominalized
adjective and a noun in apposition.

(9) *bōsн-huaʹ-н ñame-huaʹ-н*
youth-creat-masc+sing+nom lazy-creat-masc+sing+nom
'the youth, the lazy one'[4]

(10) *нja-н tao*
big-masc+sing+nom eagle
'the big one, the eagle'

The next two examples contain nominalized verb phrases in apposition with other elements.

(11) *rебaн campesino cho'ojeн-'te huanisõ-si-'-cн*
he peasant younger=brother-obl kill-comp-stat-masc+sing+nom
'he, the peasant, the one who killed the younger brother'[5]
(12) *rebana campesino bãi chosa'aro ba'i-si-na, cннcнпа ja'me'ba'i-si-na*
they peasant people Florencia be-comp-plur+nom we+excl with be-comp-plur+nom
'they, the peasants, those who were in Florencia, those who were with us'

Noun phrases may contain both nominalized adjectives and nominalized verb phrases:

(13) *rебaн Rafael gu'a-cн huē'hue-н*
he Rafael is=bad-masc+sing+nom crazy-masc+sing+nom
'he, Rafael, the one who is bad, the crazy one'[6]
(14) *bнca-ja'co ai-hua'-o rнa cннo-hua'-o ba'i-si-'-co*
poss-mother old-creat-fem+sing+nom very poor-creat-fem+sing+nom be-comp-stat-fem+sing+nom
'his mother, the old woman, the one who had been very poor'

When a local or global topic is introduced in a section of a text, the noun phrase referring to that topic must be either fronted or left dislocated. In *fronting*, the entire noun phrase is moved to a position ahead of the verb in the clause in which it occurs. The exact order in which the preverbal elements occur depends on how much prominence the speaker wishes to give to each item, as stated above. Conjunctions are usually first in the clause.

(15) *Cã'a ta'ni rebaн gu'eн Agustín cññн-aso-тн.*
[that but]conj [he grandfather Agustín]subj [moved-rep-masc+sing]verb
'However, he, my grandfather Agustín, reportedly moved.'
(16) *Rebaн ūjн icheja ra-si-'-cн-a'-тн reba-hua'-o-re.*
[he husband]subj [here]loc [bring-comp-stat-masc+sing+nom-stat-masc+sing]verb [that-creat-fem+sing+nom-obl]dobj
'He, her husband, brought her here.'

(17) *Huau-'te rнa ja'cha-cн bani-aso-mн rebaн.*
[brother=in=law-obl]$_{dobj}$ [much disobey-temp=ovlp+masc+sing
was-rep-masc+sing]$_{vp}$ [he]$_{subj}$
'His brother-in-law he used to really disobey.'

Though it is not very common to find two local topics on the same
level in the same sentence in natural language, it is possible in
Coreguaje. This is shown by fronting two noun phrases to a position to
the left of the verb. Or, one may be fronted and the other left
dislocated. In every case, the fronted items exist and are known to the
hearer. One of these local topics may also be the global topic. There is
no way of knowing from an isolated sentence whether the fronted
elements are global or simply local topics. The criteria for global topic
identification are discussed later.

(18) *Maja-a'cho rebau-'te be'ru-co bani-aso-mo.*
[his-older=sister]$_{subj}$, local topic [him-obl]$_{dobj}$, global topic
[angry-temp=ovlp+fem+sing was-rep-fem+sing]$_{vp}$
'His older sister used to be angry with him.'

(19) *Rebana iracusa jo'e rebau-'te ŭju-re soi-si-na-'-me.*
[they whites]$_{subj}$, local topic [again][him-obl husband-obl]$_{dobj}$,
local topic [call-comp-plur+nom-stat-plur]$_{verb}$
'They, the whites, again called him, the husband.'

(20) *Reba-hua'-o-re rebana sabanacā rea-aso-me.*
[that-creat-fem+sing+nom-obl]$_{dobj}$, global topic [they]$_{subj}$, local
topic [sheet]$_{instr}$ [wrapped-rep-plur]$_{verb}$
'Her, they reportedly wrapped in a sheet.'

(21) *Huāsocabuā rŭjo-re ma īsi-aso-mн.*
huansoco=fruits]$_{dobj}$, local topic [wife-obl]$_{iobj}$, local topic
[took=up gave-rep-masc+sing]$_{vp}$
'He reportedly carried up **huansoco** fruit and gave it to his
wife.'

In *left dislocation* of a noun phrase, the noun phrase is fronted to ı
position somewhere to the left of the verb, while a pronoun or other
term equally or less specific than the left dislocated element, having the
same referent, is left in its place.

(22) *Chura chu'u chio-na sai-mo chн'н.*
[now]$_{time}$ [I]$_{subj}$ [field-to]$_{loc}$ [is=going-fem+sing]$_{verb}$ [I]$_{subj}$
'Me, I'm going to the field now.'

(23) *Miércoles sai-si-'-cн chн'н Puerto Diego-na cāi-ja-'-mн chн'н.*
[Wednesday go-comp-stat-masc+sing+nom I]$_{subj}$ [Puerto Diego-
at]$_{loc}$ [sleep-int-stat-masc+sing]$_{verb}$ [I]$_{subj}$

'As for me, the one who will have gone on Wednesday, I plan
to sleep at Puerto Diego.'

(24) *Abe-ɣɯmɯ* **rebaɯ Rafael** *soni-aso-mɯ* **rebaɯ** *rebana-re.*

[before-time]ₜᵢₘₑ [**he Rafael**]ₛᵤᵦⱼ [called-rep-masc+sing]ᵥₑᵣᵦ [**he**]ₛᵤᵦⱼ
[them-obl]_dobj

'Rafael, he reportedly called them earlier.'

(25) *Chura ta'ni reba-hua'i ra-si'e, co'sa hua'i huai-si'e sẽjo-aso-me*
hua'i rebana.

[now   but]_conj   [that-fish   bring-comp+nom   risen   fish   kill-
comp+nom]_dobj [discard-rep-plur]ᵥₑᵣᵦ [**fish**]_dobj [they]ₛᵤᵦⱼ
'The fish that the flood had killed and brought, they reportedly
threw it away.'

Splitting is a process in which a noun phrase consisting of two or
more elements in apposition is split by something else. If the noun
phrase has been fronted or left dislocated to a position left of the verb,
the last part of it occurs at the very end of the clause.

(26) **Rebana campesino bãi** *meta bani-aso-me* **chosa'aro ba'i-si-na,**
chɯcɯna ja'me ba'i-si-na.

[**they   peasant   people**]ₛᵤᵦⱼ   [came=downriver   were-rep-plur]ᵥₚ
[**Florencia   be-comp-plur+nom   us+excl   with   be-comp-**
plur+nom]ₛᵤᵦⱼ
'They, the peasants, came downriver and were there, the ones
who were in Florencia, the ones who were with us.'

(27) *Ãña-re ɯja-ɯ-'te gua-si-na-'-me hɯɯ'e-na* **hɯãcɯhɯɯ-'te.**

[snake-obl   big-masc+sing+nom-obl]_dobj   [bring=in-comp-
plur+nom-stat-plur]ᵥₑᵣᵦ [house-into]_loc [**species=of=snake-obl**]_dobj
'They brought the snake, the big one, into the house, the equis
snake.'

Occasionally splitting occurs at the end of a paragraph where the
topic has already been established for the paragraph and there is,
therefore, no need for fronting or left dislocation of the noun phrase. In
that case, the noun phrase referring to the topic is split by another
noun phrase or some other constituent such as a time word.

(28) *Chɯ'rihua-na teo-sõ-aso-mɯ* **rebaɯ-'te** *rebaɯ* **guasa-ma-'-cɯ-ni.**

[nape=of=neck-on]_loc   [cut-ints+comp-rep-masc+sing]ᵥₑᵣᵦ [**him-**
obl]_dobj [he]ₛᵤᵦⱼ [**think-not-stat-masc+sing+nom-obl**]_dobj
'He reportedly cut him up on the back of the neck, him who
was not thinking (because he was drunk).'

(29) *Rна be'ru-aso-mo* **reбаи- 'te** *majaa'cho* **bōsи-и- 'te** *ñame-и- 'te.*
[much got=angry-rep-fem+sing]$_{vp}$ [him-obl]$_{dobj}$ [his-
older=sister]$_{subj}$ [youth-masc+sing+nom-obl lazy-
masc+sing+nom-obl]$_{dobj}$
'His older sister used to get really angry with him, the lazy
youth.'

If two or more noun phrases have been fronted or left dislocated,
one of them may be *reiterated* before the verb, using a pronoun, one
element of the noun phrase, or another coreferent term. Reiteration
differs but slightly from splitting: only one element is split off from the
rest of the noun phrase, and it must occur directly before the verb. If
there are two noun phrases and nothing else before the verb, only the
first noun phrase may be reiterated. If there are three noun phrases,
the second may be reiterated. However, if there is a time word, a
location word, or an adverb between the noun phrases and the verb,
then any one of the noun phrases may be reiterated. The same phrase,
which is reiterated, also may be split.

(30) **Reбаи** *campesino hua'ti ba-cн-ni* **reбаи** *cho'o-aso-тн* **reбаи.**
[he]$_{subj}$ [peasant knife have-masc+sing+nom-obl]$_{dobj}$ [he]$_{subj}$ [did-
rep-masc+sing)$_{verb}$ [he]$_{subj}$
'Him, he did it to the peasant who had a knife.'
(31) **Rufino-ni** *Ramón gahин-na* **reбаи- 'te** *rӣso hӣeasō-ra chini-aso-
тн.*
[Rufino-obl]$_{dobj}$ [Ramón]$_{subj}$ [neck-on]$_{loc}$ [him-obl]$_{dobj}$ [choke kill-
fut wanted-rep-masc+sing]$_{vp}$
'Rufino, Ramón grabbed him around the neck wanting to kill
him.'
(32) **Cā'a-ja'ñe** *ba'i-ja-и-ni* *тн'н* **тн-che'и-re** *be'ru-co ba'i-si-'-co-
a'-mo.*
[that-way be-int-masc+sing+nom-obl]$_{dobj}$ [you]$_{subj}$ [your-
younger=brother-obl]$_{dobj}$ [get=angry-temp=ovlp be-comp-stat-
fem+sing+nom-stat-fem+sing]$_{vp}$
'With the one who was going to be that way, with your
younger brother, you were always getting angry.'[7]

As is apparent from some of the examples above, the four
processes can be used in combination with each other, with up to four
processes being applied to the same clause. Splitting, however, usually
occurs only when at least one noun phrase is fronted or left dislocated.
Reiteration can occur only when at least two noun phrases are fronted
or left dislocated or when there is some other constituent after the
noun phrase and before the verb. Fronting is the only process that can

occur twice or more in the same clause. In the following example, all processes apply: left dislocation of the subject, fronting of object, reiterated subject, and splitting of subject:

(33) *Rebaи cati-chejña-re* **campesino** *cu'e-aso-mн* **rebaи cho'ojeи-'te huanisõ-si-'-cи.**
[he]ₛᵤᵦⱼ, ₗd [hide-places-obl]ₒᵦⱼ, fᵣₜ [**peasant**]ₛᵤᵦⱼ, ᵣₑᵢₜ [looked=for-rep-masc+sing]ᵥₑᵣᵦ [**he younger=brother-obl kill-comp-stat-masc+sing+nom**]ₛᵤᵦⱼ, ₛₚₗₜ
'He, the peasant, he looked for places to hide, the one who had killed the younger brother.'

Left dislocation of object, fronting of subject, and splitting of object:

(34) *Rebana-re jamuchai cũcu huẽasõ-aso-mн* **rebana-re bãi.**
[**them-obl**]dobj [dog]ₛᵤᵦⱼ [bit killed-rep-masc+sing]ᵥₚ [**them-obl people**]dobj
'The dog reportedly bit and killed those people.'

Fronting of object, left dislocation of subject, and splitting of object:

(35) **Campesino-'te** *rebaи mini su'a bõna tõa-aso-mн rebaи* **rubи ñu'i-cи-ni caca-cи.**
[**peasant-obl**]dobj [he]ₛᵤᵦⱼ [picked=up threw turned=around dropped-rep-masc+sing]ᵥₚ [he]ₛᵤᵦⱼ [**nothing stand-masc+sing+nom-obl enter-masc+sing+nom**]dobj
'The peasant he reportedly picked up threw, turned him around, and dropped him, him who was standing there doing nothing but entering.'

Fronting of subject, fronting of indirect object, and fronting of direct object:

(36) *Rна chнo-hua'-o beore chнcнna-'te chн'o rao-aso-mo.*
[very poor-creat-fem+sing]ₛᵤᵦⱼ [all us+excl-obl]ᵢₒᵦⱼ [word]dobj [caused=to=come-rep-fem+sing]ᵥₑᵣᵦ
'The very poor creature sent word to all of us.'

All the possible combinations of two processes have been observed in text, but five combinations of three processes have not been observed to date: (1) subject fronting with object fronting and subject splitting; (2) subject fronting with object left dislocation and subject splitting; (3) subject fronting with object left dislocation and subject reiteration; (4) subject fronting with object left dislocation and object reiteration; and (5) subject left dislocation with object fronting and object reiteration.

Global topic is signaled by one or more of a number of devices. Normally the global topic is the first person or thing mentioned in a story. Thereafter the topic character is almost always referred to with the pronoun {rebaн}, which for simplicity I gloss as 'he'.[8] When the topic character is referred to without using rebaн, it signals an episode break as discussed under nonpronominal reference. Other important characters may also be referred to with this pronoun, but in that case it is usually followed by a noun or nominalized form for clarification, as in rebana jñataqui bāi 'they, the Inga people'. The only time a minor character may be referred to with rebaн is when that character is the local topic.

When characters are referred to by kinship terms, the relationship expressed is their relationship to the topic character, usually the global topic. In one text the global topic is a youth who is lazy. He is most often referred to as rebaн 'he'. The other characters are referred to as hиaн 'brother-in-law', majaa'cho 'his older sister', and bиcaja'co 'his mother'.[9] At one point in the story the husband of the youth's sister temporarily becomes the global topic and is referred to with rebaн. The lazy youth is then called hиaн 'brother-in-law' in that section and his sister is called rūjo 'wife', both in relation to the new topic. I do not see any strong reasons in the content of the story that would require a change of global topic at this point. Since this is the only text I have where the global topic seems to change temporarily, I do not know if this is just a poorly formed text or a phenomenon that is simply infrequent in occurrence.

Another way of pointing out the global topic is by splitting the noun phrase that refers to the topic at the end of the introductory background information of the story, at the paragraph boundary. This topic noun phrase is made up of three, four, or five simple but coreferential elements, no two of which are the same. If any or all of the elements have the enclitic -bi, however, the noun phrase in this position refers to the antagonist rather than the global topic, or protagonist. The use of -bi is discussed later in this paper.

There is a story about a man named Rafael, who has built a canoe and is looking for people to help him launch it. The introductory section tells about all the people asked and how some refused. Then he finally gets some people to help him. At that point he says, 'Let's drink beer and launch the canoe.' In this sentence he is referred to as chohu-tē'tosi'cи 'the one who carved the canoe', rebaн 'he', Rafael, gu'acи 'the one who is bad', and huē'hиeн 'the crazy one'. The last four elements occur after the verb. After this sentence, the participants begin to drink and launch the canoe. Eventually they get drunk and the whole thing turns into a brawl.

There are two things foreshadowed in the sentence with the split topic. One is the introduction of the beer, which takes the enclitic -*bi*. This is important to the story because the fight would not have developed without it. The second foreshadowing in this sentence is when Rafael is referred to as 'the one who is bad, the crazy one'. This is information known to anyone who lives in the area where the story is told, but it explains what Rafael does later, for which he is arrested.

In a story about a snake in the house, the introductory section tells how the occupants of the house had gone hunting and returned and gone to bed. After they had been asleep a while, the dogs began to bark. The dogs brought a large poisonous snake into the house. The snake, which is the global topic and the object of the verb, is introduced in this sentence as *aña-re* 'the snake', *njan-'te* 'the big one', and *huảcнhин-'te* 'the equis (species of poisonous snake)'. Only the last element, *huảcнhин-'te*, occurs after the verb. The fact that the snake was big, poisonous, and in the house is all that is needed to set up a situation for the rest of the story.

In another story about a fight, there is introductory information that gets a few characters on stage and mentions that one of them is drunk. He becomes angry and tries to choke someone else. That person hits him back and a fight starts. The main character, the global topic, arrives and is attacked by someone who was already there. At this point the story of the fight is narrowed down to these two. In the sentence in which the global topic character is attacked, he is referred to by these elements as *campesino-'te* 'the peasant', *rubн ñu'icн-ni* 'the one who was standing there doing nothing', and *cacacн* 'the entering one'. The second two elements are after the verb. The fact that the attack was unprovoked, as expressed by *rubн ñu'icнni* after the verb, is important because the peasant gets so angry he ends up killing the assailant.

In the story about the lazy youth, the introductory section tells about his promising to go to the field the next time someone else does, but he never goes. At the end of this section he is referred to as *rebaн-'te* 'him', *bōsнн-'te* 'the youth', and *ñameн-'te* 'the lazy one'. All information contained in these three references is old information. Here the youth is the object of the sentence and all three elements occur after the verb, but the subject occurs after *rebaн-'te*, thereby splitting the noun phrase that refers to the youth, and so making him the global topic at the end of the introduction.

Reiteration of a subject or object, so that one element of the noun phrase referring to a topic immediately precedes the verb, is a process not fully understood yet. It appears to bear no relation to establishing topic status.

When a local topic is introduced, either fronting or left dislocation is used. Fronting is more common because left dislocation is reserved for more important events.

For example, in the text about the fight between the peasant and the nonpeasant, left dislocation introduces the global topic (which in this case is not mentioned at the beginning of the text), and then it is used again at the point where he is attacked by the character who is the local topic. Then it is used to point out that the victim, who is the global topic, has a knife. After he uses the knife on his attacker and kills him, the older brother of the dead man goes after the peasant with a gun. Thus a new episode begins and left dislocation is used again to refer to the peasant.

In the story of the lazy youth, left dislocation is used in the first sentence following the introductory background material. This sentence describes the global topic character's reaction to the situation described in the introduction. The next two times left dislocation is used in this story are after lapses of time, one lapse of two days and the other of five days. In both of these instances the fact that he is still in the tree is emphasized. After the two days, he is covered with sap, which causes feathers to grow on his body. After five days, when his family goes out to see him again, he has turned into an eagle.

The last use of left dislocation in the lazy youth story is where the global topic character gives the reason for the way things have developed and then says his farewell to his sister. Thus we have the beginning of the end.

In the story of Rafael and the canoe left dislocation is used at the beginning of the text, at the beginning of the drinking, and at the beginning of the fighting. A young man is attacked by Rafael during the course of the fight. Left dislocation is used at the point where Rafael attacks him and again where the victim complains to the police resulting in Rafael's arrest.

2 Paragraphs

Once a topic has been established by fronting or left dislocation it remains the topic until a new item is topicalized at that level. When a topic is changed, a different element is fronted to become the new topic. Usually there is also a recapitulative dependent verb link or connector with a change of subject marker **-to**, **-ru**, or **-na**. A recapitulative link is a dependent verb clause in which a verb from the preceding sentence is repeated or paraphrased and which precedes the independent clause of the sentence where it occurs. A link can, when in combination with other devices, signal a paragraph break. Connectors function as links in a less specific way by linking the new section to an indeterminate something that went before. They are formed in a similar way to the recapitulative links, but more general terms are used, such as the verb *cho'o* 'do'.

Topic changes coincide with paragraph breaks. Thus a paragraph is defined as a section in a text in which the local topic remains the same. Each paragraph relates one incident, which may be made up of one event or a few closely related events.

For example, in the story of Rafael, who built the canoe, the first paragraph after the introduction has 'canoe launchers' fronted as the local topic and tells how Rafael tried to find some. Each person or group he invites to help him represents a separate event.

The second paragraph begins with a dependent verb link *cu'e-cи-na* 'looking for', repeating the verb of the preceding sentence and including the change of subject suffix *-na*. Rafael himself is the topic, established by left dislocation in the independent clause, and his invitation to those who agree to launch the canoe is described.

The third paragraph begins with the dependent verb link *cā'a chi-te-na* 'having said that', again using a change of subject suffix *-na* and repeating the verb of the previous sentence. The canoe launchers, here referred to as *rebana* 'they', are again the local topic, this time by left dislocation.

Paragraph four is the first paragraph of a new, larger section. These sections I call episodes. There is a turn of events that is signaled differently from paragraph breaks. In this case the first paragraph of the episode begins with *go'i, cā'a cho'o-to* 'after they returned, at the time they did that', using the suffix *-to*, which includes change of subject. Here in apposition with the dependent verb link *go'i* there is a connector *cā'a cho'o-to*, which links this second episode to all that was said previously. This first sentence of the paragraph and episode has *Rafael* fronted as topic and is a paragraph in itself. Also in this sentence the global topic, *Rafael*, is referred to only by name, not with the usual pronoun *rebaн*, thereby further setting off this section from the previous section. In the next sentences this story changes from a canoe-launching story into the account of a fight.

Other connectors used to begin the first paragraph of an episode besides *cā'a cho'o-to* are *abe-rчmч* 'earlier', *ūgua-rчmч* 'about that time', *cā'a ta'ni* 'however (lit., that but)', and *cā'a-je-cи-na* 'because of that'. Occasionally the last two connectors mentioned may be used on a lower level within an episode, but most commonly they are used to begin one. A general summary statement, which is a separate complete sentence, may be used in addition to or instead of one of the above connectors. It is difficult to say whether this sentence ends an episode or begins the next one. It forms part of the boundary between them, which I call the transition. An example of a summary statement would be *Cā'a-ja'ñe rebana cho'o-aso-me*. (that-way they did-rep-plur) 'That's reportedly the way they acted.'

Within a paragraph there may also be other dependent verb links. It is clear that there is no paragraph break because the local topic does not change. The purpose of these links is to show progression in the action of the story. They are not used when a sentence is merely amplifying what was said in the preceding sentence.

There are three ways to form recapitulative links: the verb is nominalized, it has the general time suffix *-гнтн*, or it has one of the dependent verb suffixes. The dependent verb suffixes are shown in the following chart.

	Temporal		Contingency	
Subject:	Same	Different	Same	Different
Sequence	∅	-rena	-ni	-ru
Overlap	-ju	-juna	-ni	-to

The above are only representative forms. Complete paradigms are given in Cook in this volume.

The temporal suffixes are not incompatible with a causal relationship, though they do not assert causality. In other words, the action or state expressed by the independent verb can be thought of, except when that verb is *ba'i* 'be', as the result of the action or state expressed by the dependent verb. Another distinction is whether the action of the dependent verb was completed prior to the beginning of the action of the independent verb (sequence) or whether there is partial or complete overlap in time between the two (overlap). The third distinction is whether the subject of the verb of the dependent link is different from the subject of the independent verb of the sentence. Except for the sequential same subject suffix, all of these have further distinctions of gender and number. The following example illustrates the use of the temporal overlap suffix for different subject.

(37) *Āu ūse-ju-na i-hua'-na chī-hua'-na ba'i-che gu'a-cн-'-тн.*
food **refuse=to=give-ovlp+plur-dsubj** this creat-plur+nom child-creat-plur+nom live-nom is=bad-masc+sing+nom-stat-masc+sing
'Since these children refuse to share their food, life is bad for them.'

The contingency suffixes, while still distinguishing time sequence and overlap like the temporal suffixes, convey a more vague relation to time. The emphasis here is on contingency: 'if' or 'when'. Whereas -*ru* denotes an action that takes place prior to that of the main verb as the basis of the contingency, -*to* simply means 'within the same time span' in a general sense. The dependent verb using -*to* can in practice refer to something previous to the main verb, but that fact is taken as irrelevant to what the speaker is saying. Some verbs, such as *rai* 'come' and *sai* 'go', are not normally treated as denoting an action that is completed at a specific point in time, which would allow for this seeming discrepancy. For that same reason, the verbs 'come' and 'go' are not used with the auxiliary verb *bi'ni* 'finish'. The contingency suffix -*ni* for same subject does not distinguish at all between sequential and overlapping action. None of the contingency suffixes are inflected for gender or number. The following example illustrates the use of the same subject contingency suffix -*ni*:

(38)   *Mʉ'ʉ masi-ni que'se cho'o-ma'-ñe?*
       (you **know-if** how do-not-interr+plur)
       'If you know about it, how is it you are not doing anything?'

A dependent clause formed using these suffixes must either end with the verb or have *ta'ni* 'but, however' after the verb. Subject, object, and modifiers must all precede the dependent verb in the clause. Whenever there is linking, new information follows in the independent clause. The following are examples of some dependent clauses used as links:

(39)   *oco-bi tī'a-sō-cʉ-na*
       water-subj arrive-ints-ovlp+masc+sing-dsubj
       'as the water was arriving . . .'
(40)   *gaje-to*
       go+down-when
       'when he went down. . .
(41)   *reba-hua'-o-re ũha-ni*
       that-creat-fem+sing+nom-obl lay=down-when
       'when he laid her down'
(42)   *co-∅*
       buy-temp=seq
       'having bought it . . .' or 'after buying it . . .'

The general time suffix -*rʉmʉ* is less specific than -*to*. It provides the time setting for the action or state expressed by the independent verb in the same way any other time expression would do, such as *chura* 'now', *na'a bani* 'later', *chija'iro* 'tomorrow', or *iūmuguse* 'today'. *-rнmн* can occur on nouns, adjectives, or verbs. The following show only a few of its many uses:

(43) *йsнн-rнmн* (sun-time) 'dry season'
(44) *beo-rнmн* (not=be-time) 'the time when there was none'
(45) *rai-si-rнmн* (come-comp-time) 'the time after coming'
(46) *sai-ja-rнmн* (go-int-time) 'the time before going'
(47) *chī-rнmн* (child-time) 'childhood'
(48) *abe-rнmн* (before-time) 'earlier, a long time ago'

Aspect suffixes *-si* 'completive' and *-ja* 'intentive' can be used on a verb stem to denote that whatever is used with *-rнmн* has ended or has not yet begun relative to the action or state of the independent verb. There is no distinction between change of subject and same subject when this suffix is used. *-rнmн* can be used to form a general time setting for the independent clause without linking the sentence to anything previous.

The verb of the link can also be nominalized. This is another very general, absolute form of recapitulative link. There is no reference as to who performed the action expressed in the link or whether or not there is any subject change. The important thing is the action itself and its link with what comes after it. The suffixes used to nominalize verbs in links are *-che* and its completive counterpart *-si'e*. There is also an intentive nominalizer *-ja-che*, but to date it has not been observed as a dependent verb link. When *-che* is used, the action may have temporal overlap and may be thought of as a type of manner adverb. When *-si'e* is used, the action of the link has been completed before the action of the independent verb is commenced. Some examples of nominalized verbs used as links follow:

(49) *Rahин su-si-'-cн-a'-mн rebaн.* **Su-si'e** *que-cheja Getucha-na sa-si-'-cн-a'-mн.*
   disease   treat-comp-stat-masc+sing+nom-stat-masc+sing   he. **treat-comp+nom** that-place Getucha-to take-comp-stat-masc+sing+nom-stat-masc+sing he
   'He treated the disease. With reference to the treatment having been performed, he took her there to Getucha.' (The second 'he' is a different person from the first 'he'.)

(50) *Cā'a cheja āni, "I-jobo-na cāi-ja-goso-me mai," chii-si-'-cн-a'-mн chн'н huesн-cн chн'н. Cā'a-ja'ñe* **huesн-che** *garosaihин sa-si-na-'-me chнснна-'te.*
   that place ate this-village-at sleep-int-prob-plur we+incl say-comp-stat-masc+sing+nom-stat-masc+sing I not=know-

temp=ovlp+masc+sing I. that-way **not=know-nom** car take-
comp-plur+nom-stat-plur we+excl-obl
'After eating in that place, "We will probably sleep in this
village," I said, not knowing. With reference to not knowing,
they took us away in a car.'

3 Nonpronominal reference

Coreguaje employs various ways of referring to characters in a
story, depending on the importance of the character to the story. The
most common term used for reference is the pronoun {*rebʌн*} 'he'.[8] The
first reference to the topic character may be with or without this
pronoun, and the pronoun, if used, may be used alone or with
something else (see sec. 1 on noun phrases). Once he is introduced, the
global topic character is always referred to with *rebʌн*, either alone or
with something else, except at episode breaks.

At those points he is referred to by name, by a nominalized verb or
adjective phrase, or by a noun. These terms used at breaks to refer to
the topic character do not present new information, but repeat or
paraphrase information previously mentioned or the speaker believes
the hearer to be aware of already. At these points, where the character
is not referred to by *rebʌн*, there is no need to clarify his identity
because it is clear from the context. He is referred to in this way to
show where the episode break is. The nonpronominal reference to the
global topic occurs in a transitional sentence that begins the new
episode and links it to what went before.

Nonpronominal reference to the main character, or global topic, is
used to segment text into introduction, complication, solution, peak,
and conclusion. Except for peak (discussed in sec. 5), the boundaries
of these constituent parts coincide loosely with episode breaks.
Occasionally, however, the complication is divided into two episodes
and not all texts have conclusions. Since these constituents are
separated by episode breaks, all the criteria for distinguishing different
episodes also apply here.

One other use of nonpronominal reference is to distinguish
parenthetical remarks by the narrator from the body of the text. Some
conclusions consist of evaluations or comments by the narrator about
something in the text. These also can be classified as parenthetical
remarks using nonpronominal reference. Other conclusions are merely
final episodes and are separated by nonpronominal reference for that
reason.

In the story of Rafael, who built the canoe and was looking for
people to help him launch it, Rafael is introduced in the first sentence
of the text as *rebʌн Rafael*. Thereafter he is referred to by *rebʌн*
except at the point where the story changes from a canoe-launching

account to the story of a fight. At this point he is referred to only as *Rafael*.

In the story of the lazy youth who turns into an eagle, the topic character, after he is introduced, is referred to with *reбaн* in every case except two. The first instance is the sentence before he turns into an eagle, that is, the last sentence in which he is still human. Here he is referred to instead with a nominalized verb phrase *ñameн ba'isi'cн* 'he who was lazy'. The fact that he turned into an eagle is the whole point of the story—there would be no story without it. This sentence, which is a summary statement, is a transition between episode 2, the problem and attempts to solve it, and episode 3, the failure to resolve the problem.

The second instance is at the beginning of episode 4, the conclusion of the story. Here he is referred to as *нjaн tao, bāiн ba'isi'cн, ñameн* 'the big eagle, the one who used to be a person, the lazy one', with a noun, a nominalized verb phrase, and a nominalized adjective.

In the account of the dying woman there are five places where she is not referred to by *rebao* (or *rebahua'o*). The first such place is the end of some introductory background material, which tells how she was sick, went to a healer, and recovered. There she is referred to with a nominalized verb, *āisihua'o* 'she who had been eating'. This is the transition sentence which represents a turning point in the story and separates episode 1, which is the introduction, from episode 2, the problem. The next sentence begins the account of her relapse and eventual death plus some events immediately following her death.

The second instance of nonpronominal reference to the global topic in this text relates the state she was in when her family took her to a second practitioner, a healer and sorcerer. The act of taking her to this person is important to the story because it is suspected that what he did was what finally caused her death. She is referred to there by a series of nominalized verb phrases, such as *rнa sнchнsihua'o* 'the creature who had really gotten thin' and *hua'i jě'e beohua'o* 'the creature who did not have any meat on her', in the sentence before she is treated by the second healer. Thus begins episode 3, the attempted solution.

The next time she is not referred to with *rebao* is when she is beginning to die. Here she is called *cho'osō-gubahua'o* 'she who is about to die', using a nominalized verb phrase. Then she instructs her husband to tell all her relatives about her death. Since the narrator is a relative of the woman, she puts in a parenthetical remark, which states that they received word about the dying woman, referring to her inside the parentheses with *chнohua'o* 'the poor creature', a nominalized adjective.

Finally, in the conclusion of the story the woman is referred to with two nominalized verb phrases *āu jē'e āimahua'o* 'she who was not eating any food' and *hua'i jē'e beohua'o* 'the one who did not have any meat on her'. In this case the conclusion contains no more action, but is the narrator's comment on the story.

Other important characters in the story may also be referred to with *rebaн*, especially if they are the present local topic. More often than not, however, they are also referred to at the same time with another identifying term, such as name or a kinship term stating relationship to the global topic characacter. They can be referred to with *rebaн* alone only when it is clear from the context who they are. For example, in the account of a fight where one man stabs another, in the sentence where the stabbing is related, both men are referred to with *rebaн*. Previously, however, one of the men is described as *hua'ti bacн* 'the one who has a knife'. Therefore it follows indirectly that the one possessing the knife is the one who stabbed the other man.

The most common pattern for referring to an important character who is not the global topic is to introduce or reintroduce him as local topic with *rebaн* and possibly an identifying term and then to refer to him as *rebaн* until another local topic is introduced. For example, in the story of the dying woman her husband is most often introduced as *rebaн ūjн* 'he, the husband' in each paragraph of which he is the local topic and then referred back to with *rebaн* until the end of that paragraph. Minor characters, however, are always referred to by name, by kinship term stating their relationship to the topic character, or by some other identifying term or phrase. They are never referred to by *rebaн* unless they become a local topic. This is the case in the story of the dying woman, where the healer who was consulted first is the local topic for two sentences and is never mentioned again.

4 -*bi* 'counterexpectancy'

A device for signaling discontinuity in a story is the counterexpectancy enclitic -*bi*, which occurs on animate subjects of both transitive and intransitive verbs and on inanimate objects.[10] It signals an impending change of events that affects the outcome of the story significantly or surprisingly, or after the change has already occurred it can occur in a statement that gives the reason for that significant change. In most cases it makes the person or thing it is attached to into a sort of antagonist relative to the global topic as protagonist. Without this antagonist the plot would have little interest. When -*bi* is used, the outcome of the story is different from what might ordinarily be expected.[11] Usually -*bi* occurs at or near episode boundaries.

In the story of the dying woman, she is taken to a healer-sorcerer, who treats her and says she will get better. After she leaves, however, it is said that he *-bi* is probably thinking about her husband. (It is believed that sorcerers can do harm from a distance by merely thinking about it.) The woman does not get better, but dies. The rest of the text tells about her death and the events surrounding it. In the conclusion, it says that sorcerers *-bi* did that to her, implying that she would have been all right had it not been for them.

A text about a bad flood upriver describes all the destruction and loss of life and then tells how the crest began to go downriver to the narrator's place. He says there was a lot of water, but it did not flood badly as it had upriver. Then he says, 'God-*bi* knows about that', implying that God changed things so the narrator's place did not receive the damage that was expected.

In the story of the snake in the house, the snake is identified as the global topic and main character by the use of splitting at the end of the introductory section and by its being referred to after that by *reбaн*. It is ready to strike and someone kills it. The snake killer, introduced with *-bi*, turns the tide.

In one of the fight stories, the one who starts the fight is marked with *-bi* as he is introduced. He actually starts the fight within a few sentences of that point. He then leaves the scene and is not mentioned again.

The enclitic *-bi* can occur within a quotation. In that case it may be used either from the narrator's point of view, relating to the whole text, or merely from the point of view of the character who is speaking at the moment. There is no overt discrimination between the two cases.

An example of a quoted *-bi* that reflects the narrator's assessment of things is the text where Rafael tries to get his canoe launched. *-bi* occurs within a quotation on the inanimate object 'beer'. Rafael says, 'Let's drink beer-*bi* and launch the canoe.' It is the beer that turns the situation from a canoe-launching story into a fight story. The beer is also like an antagonist in relation to the global topic character, Rafael, in that it is because of what he does while drunk that he gets arrested in the end.

On the other hand, a quoted *-bi* that shows the point of view of a speaker in the text is one where a man has been trying to kill another man by shooting him, but keeps missing. A third person says, 'Give the gun to me-*bi*,' by which he implies, 'so I can do things differently'. The first man does not give him the gun and there is in fact no change in the way things are going, so the *-bi* has to be the character's in this case, not the narrator's.

5 Peak

Peak is the general term I use to refer to the section of a story where there is some climactic development. It is not clearly definable, nor is it clearly set off by specific linguistic phenomena, but in most texts there is a general area where some of the normal characteristics change. Paragraph breaks, linking, topicalization, and clear participant reference may be totally abnormal. The sentence may suddenly become extremely long or extremely short.

For example, in the story of the fight between the peasant and the nonpeasant, where the latter gets killed, there are two main parts to the story, each with its own peak. In the first part, the climax of the fight is all stated in one sentence, which is thirty-five words long as compared with the average sentence length of seven words. In the second part of the story, where Luciano, the older brother of the one who was killed, takes a gun to the peasant, first the paragraph breaks drop out and no clear topic is marked. Then at the most climactic part of the action the sentences become very short, having one to three words, with no dependent clauses and, therefore, no links, when normally there would be links because of progression in the action. Also in this section there is almost no explicit participant reference; the sentences are mainly made up of verbs, adverbs, and locatives.

Many times at the peak there is conversational exchange or monologue, which carries much of the information. In the example cited above, in which the first peak of the text is contained in a single sentence, that sentence includes a quoted conversational exchange between the two characters who are fighting. In the other fight story, there is a conversation between the victim and someone else, presumably the police, just before the conclusion of the story where Rafael, the global topic and malefactor, is arrested and taken away. This peak conversation is set off by a general summary statement immediately preceding and following the conversation. Within the conversation, however, the identity of local topics is not clear, and there is no linking.

In the story of the dying woman, the whole peak section, which begins with *cho'sõ-guha-hua'o* 'the one who is about to die', is a monologue of her dying words.

The text about the lazy youth who turns into an eagle also has conversation at its peak. Here the youth blames his sister for the way things have turned out and bids her farewell. At the same point, furthermore, the local topic is not clearly indicated as it is in other parts of the text.

Notes

1 Coreguaje is spoken by between five hundred and six hundred people of that same name. They live in seven or eight villages located on the Orteguaza River and its tributaries in the Intendencia de Caguetá in Colombia, South America. The present analysis is based on texts given by members of this language group who live in the village of Maticurú. Coreguaje is a member of the Western Tucanoan language family.

2 The Coreguaje transcription reflects a sound system of voiceless aspirated stops /p/, /t/, /k/ (written with c/ qu as in Spanish), voiceless unaspirated stops /b/, /d/ (rare), /g/, /'/ (glottal), fricatives /s/, /h/ (written with j as in Spanish), nasals /m/, /n/, /ñ/, /jñ/ (voiceless alveopalatal), alveolar tap /r/, semivowels /w/ (written hu as in Spanish) and /dy/ (written ch), vowels /a/, /e/, /i/, /o/, /u/, /ʉ/ (high central unrounded), and their nasalized counterparts written with ⁻. /ch/ and /ñ/ neutralize to /ñ/ when occurring in a suffix that is contiguous to a nasalized vowel. The symbol h is used between a u and another vowel to signify a syllable break as opposed to a diphthong.

3 Abbreviations used in examples in this paper are conj conjunction, comp completive aspect, cont contingency, creat creature, dsubj different subject, dobj direct object, excl exclusive, fem feminine, frt fronting, fut future, iobj indirect object, incl inclusive, int intentive aspect, interr interrogative, ints intensifier, ld left dislocation, lit literally, loc location, masc masculine, ncls noun class suffix, nom nominalizer, obj object, obl oblique case, ovlp overlap, plur plural, poss possessive, prob probably, reit reiteration, rep reported speech, seq sequential, sing singular, splt splitting, ssubj same subject, stat stative, subj subject, temp temporal, and vp verb phrase.

4 When hua' 'creature' is used on one element of a noun phrase, it must be used on all nouns or nominalized forms in that noun phrase except kinship terms. This suffix can be used to show emotional involvement of the speaker, such as pity or endearment. It is used extensively in a text about a dying woman, for example, and shows the narrator's feelings of pity for her. It can also be used without emotion to refer to an animal of unknown name, or to a group of different animals.

5 -'re and -'te are alternate forms of the same morpheme, which is an oblique case marker. The rules governing the choice of forms are not yet known. The other oblique marker -ni has a slightly different meaning from -re/-'te in that it is used on more specific or exclusive objects, and only on animate objects.

6 Animate nominalizers are masculine singular -ch, feminine singular -co, and plural -na. There is no distinction for plurals in Coreguaje. The gender-number suffixes for animate nouns are masculine -ʉ, feminine -o, and plural -na. The noun suffixes are used to nominalize adjectives as well. Gu'a is the stem of the verb 'be bad' and for that reason takes a verb suffix rather than an adjective/noun suffix.

7 The intentive suffix -ja takes the noun suffixes -ʉ, -o, and -na in this construction instead of the regular -ch, -co, and -na.

8 {rebaʉ} is used to refer to a person or persons not in view of the speaker. It is also used for animals and heavenly bodies. It is inflected for gender and number, but can be used for first, second, or third person. (It is not used for first person very frequently, but when it is, the reference is removed in time and space. In the case of second person, the speaker may be outside the house, for example, while the addressee is inside the house, making the latter invisible to the former). The inflected forms of {rebaʉ} are masculine singular rebaʉ, feminine singular rebao, and plural rebana. Inanimate objects important to the story can also be referred to anaphorically within a text using this pronoun. Some inanimate nouns have class suffixes. A class suffix is used in place of the gender-number suffix when referring to such a noun. For example, referring back to a specific canoe, cho-huʉ, one would

say *reba-huн*, meaning 'that canoe of which I spoke before'; in referring back to a tree, *sūqui-ñн*, one would say, *reba-ñн* 'that tree'. If an inanimate noun does not have a class suffix, the entire noun is used in place of the gender-number marker. For example, *cheja* 'place' does not have a class suffix, so to refer back to a specific place mentioned before one would say *reba-cheja* 'that place'. *Hua'ti* 'knife' would be referred back to using *reba-hua'ti* 'that knife'. Another suffix frequently used with *rebaн* for animate nouns is *-hua'* 'creature'. This suffix occurs before the gender-number suffix to give masculine singular *rebahua'н*, feminine singular *rebahua'o*, and plural *rebahua'na*. *Reba* used without inflection means 'that', referring to a whole situation. It is not to be confused with its homonym *reba* 'true, truly', which when modifying a verb precedes the verb and when modifying a noun occurs after the noun. *-reba* can also be used as a verb suffix, in which case it is an intensifier.

9 Some kinship terms have special prefixes to denote possession by third person singular or plural and others do not. *Ruaн* 'brother-in-law' and *rūjo* 'wife' have no such prefixes, possibly because they do not refer to blood relatives. *Ja'co* 'mother' and *ja'cн* 'father' take the possessive prefix *bнca-* 'his/her/their', and *a'cho* 'older sister' and *a'chн* 'older brother' take the possessive prefix *maja-* 'his/her/their'. The resultant forms are *bнcaja'co* 'his/her/their mother' and *majaa'cho* 'his/her/their older sister', etc.

10 The suffix *-bi* has an alternate form *-ji* used with some words in the same way that *-'te* is an alternate form of *-re*. The same set of words take both *-bi* and *-re*, and *-ji* and *-'te* are used on the same words.

11 The suffix *-bi/-ji* also has other uses besides the one discussed here. It is used on inanimate objects to denote instrument or means and on location words meaning 'place from which'. It can also be used to distinguish the subject of a sentence from the object or from a dependent verb when it is not otherwise clear. This is especially true when the subject is expressed by an animate nominalized verb that is identical with the temporal overlap form and that could otherwise be interpreted as being a dependent verb in the sentence, as in *Rнa mia-si-'-cн-a'-тн rнa mia-cн- ji*. (much shine-comp-stat-masc+sing+nom-stat-masc+sing much shine-masc+sing+nom-**subj**) 'The one who really shines (the moon) really shone.'

Repetition in Jamamadí Discourse

Barbara Campbell

In Jamamadí narrative discourse twenty-five to thirty-five percent of all clauses are repeated in exact, reduced, expanded, or paraphrased form. The key criterion for determining the functions of repetition is the distinction between both medial and final clauses that are repeated.

Repetition has three major functions: (1) medial clauses that repeat medial clauses draw attention to the process or progress of an action resulting in a change of location or state; (2) final or medial clauses that repeat final clauses establish, reinstate, and close a topic; and (3) the information in repeated clauses is ranked from more important to less important according to the various combinations of final and medial clauses that result whenever a clause is repeated.

0 Introduction

In Jamamadí[1] narrative discourse twenty-five to thirty-five percent of all clauses are repeated in exact, reduced, expanded, or paraphrased form. Depending on its form and place in the discourse, repetition has three major functions: (1) it indicates certain changes in location and state; (2) it establishes a topic; and (3) it defines the relative importance of certain information in respect to other information.

0.1 Discourse groupings

Certain groupings in Jamamadí discourse structure are needed for this discussion. A **paragraph** is a group of event clauses having unity of place. A change of setting necessitates a new paragraph. The boundaries of paragraphs are often indistinct. A **transition paragraph** often links two paragraphs. It contains only medial clauses with the motion verbs required to get from one setting to the other. Such information is difficult to assign to either the preceding or the following paragraph. If there is also to be a topic change in the next paragraph, an event in the previous paragraph (usually the last one) is repeated in the transition. An **episode** is one or more paragraphs and usually covers a day's happenings. It ends with a time phrase and a special kind of medial clause (see sec. 0.2). No transition paragraph occurs between episodes.

0.2 Independent final and medial clauses

It is necessary to distinguish between independent final and independent medial clauses. An independent final clause has final intonation (downglide) and may end a sentence. The downglide is represented by a period (.). The verb of the clause must contain a suffix from the verification system and usually contains a suffix from the perspective system. In the following example, a full gloss of *maro* is 'narrator is eyewitness of event in remote past'.[2] A full gloss of *ke* is 'this is a major event that took place in chronological sequence after the previously mentioned event'.

> *O-ko-ma-maro-ke.*
> I-motion-back-eyewitness-sequence
> 'I came back.'

An independent medial clause has medial intonation (upglide), represented by a comma (,). It does not end a sentence and lacks verification and perspective suffixes.

> *O-ko-ma,*
> I-motion-back
> 'I came back,'

An exception to this description of independent medial clauses regularly occurs at the end of an episode and occasionally in an episode introduction. A medial verb occurring episode-final lacks the verification and perspective suffixes, but has final intonation and ends the sentence and episode.

> *Amo-o-na.*
> slept-I-stem=closure
> 'I slept.'

On rare occasions this kind of medial clause with final intonation occurs in an episode introduction and indicates a lower ranking of importance of that episode relative to others in the same discourse (see sec. 3). In the following example, the episode topic is a fishing trip that was a complete failure. They had gone to shoot fish with arrows, but had not taken any arrows along.

> *Sako me oda disa-na-bone oda **toka**....Oda to-ka, sako me oda **disa-na**.*
> fish   plural   we   shot-stem=closure-purpose   we   **away-went**. ...we away-went, fish plural we **shot-stem=closure**
> 'In order to shoot fish we went [minor episode]....We went, we shot fish [minor episode].'

Throughout this paper an independent final clause is designated simply as **final** and an independent medial clause as **medial**.

0.3 Kinds of repetition

Four kinds of repetition are considered in this paper: exact, expanded, reduced, and paraphrased. **Exact** repetition is the repetition of a clause in identical form.

> *O-ko-ma, o-ko-ma,*
> I-motion-back, I-motion-back
> 'I came back, I came back,'

Expanded repetition in Jamamadí is the repetition of a clause with some new information added. Some given information may be omitted in the repetition, but the verb stem must be the same in both clauses.

> *Yama soki bidi-ya oda kobo-na-ma, **faya** oda kobo-na-ma,*
> thing dark small-location we arrived-stem=closure-back, **and=so** we arrived-stem=closure-back
> 'At dusk we arrived, thus we arrived,'

Reduced repetition is the repetition of a clause with some given information omitted and nothing new added.

> *Bade tao-o-ka-na-maro-ra. Bade tao-o-ka-na,*
> deer shot-I-instrument-stem=closure-eyewitness=past-nonsequential.
> deer shot-I instrument-stem=closure
> 'I shot the deer a long time ago. I shot the deer,'

Paraphrased repetition is repetition of a clause that results in one of the two clauses being lexically more specific than the other. Often a plan of action is given in a direct quotation followed by its confirmation in the second clause. Or the first clause may be a kind of title summary of an event with a specific event occurring in the paraphrase. Paraphrased clauses border on not being repetition at times, but function similarly to other kinds of repetition, so paraphrased repetition is included. The following example is a plan of action followed by its confirmation:

> *Aba bidi ai waka-na-mata-hi. Aba bidi-me oda waka-na-maro,*
> fish small plural we grabbed-stem=closure-must-imperative. fish
> small plural we grabbed-stem=closure-eyewitness
> '"Let's grab little fish." We grabbed little fish,'

A general-to-specific kind of paraphrase often contains ideophones, as in the following:

> *Taokana moni yana-ka-na-maro-m. Tayai, tayai, tayai, tayai, tayai*
> *yama na-maro-ke.*
> gun   sound   walked-instrument-stem=closure-past-identification.
> bang, bang, bang, bang, bang thing did-past-sequence
> 'The noise of a gun sounded. "Bang, bang, bang, bang, bang," it
> went.'

1 Changes of location, state, or episode

Repetition is used to draw attention to the process or progress of an action when such an action results in a change in location or state. This function of repetition is signaled by one medial clause being repeated in another medial clause. The form of the repetition may be exact, expanded, or reduced, but not paraphrased.

1.1 Continuation in location change

Continued progression towards or away from a spatial setting or goal is indicated by the repetition of a medial clause whose verb denotes motion. The following example at the beginning of an episode indicates progress towards a spatial setting (upstream) and objective (the tapirs, which were a long way upstream):

> *makobote awi me oda bosa-ka-na, oda to-ka-tima, oda to-ko-tima,*
> later tapir plural we at=dawn=went-with-stem=closure, we away-
> went,-upstream, we away-went-upstream

'later at dawn we went after the tapirs, we went upstream farther and farther,'

Within a paragraph such repetition can indicate continued progression towards a participant, as in the following:

sere rofi-o-na, wafa me kake, wafa me kake,
dart rolled-I-stem=closure, monkey plural-motion-near, monkey plural motion-near
'I rolled a dart, the monkeys approached closer and closer (to me),'

To indicate stages in the progress of a journey, transition paragraphs contain motion verbs that are repeated in medial clauses. The repetition, then, may be contiguous within the same transition paragraph or noncontiguous in different ones. In the following two transition paragraphs a paragraph about getting some nuts is omitted between them.

Kawi oda ka-nika, oda ka-ma,... mowi noko oda weye-na, oda ka-ma, oda ka-ma,
liquor we with-bought, we motion-back, ... Brazil=nut seed we carried-stem=closure, we motion-back, we motion-back
'We bought liquor, we started back,... we carried the Brazil nuts, we continued back for a long way,'

1.2 Change of state

To draw attention to some aspect of a change in state, medial clauses are repeated. Usually the action takes a great deal of time, effort, or skill to perform. In the following example, although it is not stated in the story, the participants have to chew a piece of wood in two to make a club since they do not have a knife:

awa oda baka-na-kosa, awa oda baka-na-kosa,
stick we broke-stem=closure-in=two, stick we broke-stem=closure-in=two
'we broke the stick with a great deal of effort,'

In the following example, an unusual amount of time and effort is also required to skin the jaguar with only a piece of a knife.

yima kote-ya yome atori oda ita, yome atori oda ita,
knife piece-instrument jaguar skin we skinned, jaguar skin we skinned
'with a piece of a knife we worked away at skinning the jaguar's hide,'

1.3 Episode termination

In the last paragraph of an episode, the expanded repetition of a medial clause signals termination of the episode. The new information added is usually an indication of time or a connective.

Oda amo-ka-na, **yama soki-ya** *oda amo-ka-na,*
we slept-dual-stem=closure, **thing dark-locative** we slept-dual-stem=closure
'The two of us slept, at night we slept,'

In the next pair, the added information is 'thus', and 'At dusk' is deleted.

Yama soki bidi-ya oda kobo-na-ma, **faya** *oda kobo-na-ma,*
thing dark small-locative we arrived-stem=closure-back, **and=so** we arrived-stem=closure-back
'At dusk we arrived, thus we arrived,'

2 Repetition in topical structure

Repetition of a clause in Jamamadí is one of the mechanisms used to establish a nominal element of a clause as topic, to reestablish it after parenthetical information, and to close it at appropriate intervals. Since a topic must be old information, the repetition of a clause is the mechanism used to make a prospective topic old information.

The repetition itself, however, does not designate who the topic actually is. Often the following signals cooccur with the repetition: fronted word order, gender agreement of the verb with the topic, an object enclitic, nonmention of the topic after its introduction, and any mention of body parts of the topic in unpossessed form. These signals identify a specific topic in the repeated clause, either the subject or object of the verb. When such signals occur, they designate a marked topic, usually for a span of one paragraph.[3] In the absence of such signals, the subject of the verb constitutes the unmarked topic of the paragraph.[4]

Some of the devices for signaling a marked topic are seen in the following example. Repetition of the first clause in the second establishes the topic. *Madoki* as topic is signaled by the fronted order of subject in clause two together with the object enclitic -*ra* on the object *wafa* 'monkey'. The last three clauses do not mention Madoki, but the object enclitic remains on the object. (Except on pronouns, when there would be ambiguity of case otherwise, the object enclitic occurs only in conjunction with a marked topic.) Gender agreement is

with Madoki throughout the paragraph, signaled by vowel changes in
verbal suffixes.

*Wafa di Madoki tabasi-**ne-mari**-m Some-ya. Some-ya **Madoki** wafa-
ra tabasi-**ne**, "Wafa o-doka-mati-ya," Fai **Madoki** wafa-**ra** tabasi-**ne**.
Wafa-**ra** tabasi-**nabe**. Wafa yoto-**ra** iba-**ne**,*
monkey the Madoki roasted-**stem=closure**-[masculine]-eyewitness-
[masculine]-new participant Someo-locative. **Madoki** monkey-**object**
roasted-**stem=closure-masculine.** "monkey I-burn=hair=off-must-
now," and-so **Madoki** monkey-**object** roasted-**stem=closure-
[masculine]**, monkey-**object** roasted **at night-[masculine]** monkey-
object roasted=in=fire-**stem=closure-[masculine,]**
'Madoki roasted the monkey at Someo. At Someo Madoki roasted
the monkey: "I'm going to burn the hair off the monkey" (Madoki
said), thus Madoki roasted the monkey, (he) roasted the monkey at
night, (he) roasted the monkey's intestines in the fire,'

Other signals such as place in the discourse distinguish whether a
topic is the topic of an episode, a paragraph, or a subsidiary level.
These levels can be thought of as the topical hierarchy of a discourse,
but they are closely related to the discourse groupings of episode and
paragraph:

episode topic

paragraph topic

subsidiary topic

An episode topic, for instance, continues until the next episode topic is
introduced. A paragraph topic contributes in some way to the
development of the episode topic and ends at the close of the
paragraph. A subsidiary topic is embedded within a paragraph topic.
Topics lower in the hierarchy than the three kinds just mentioned, such
as clause-level topic, are not considered here since they are not
established by repetition.

2.1 Establishing a topic

To establish a topic, three kinds of repetition may be used:
expanded, reduced, or paraphrased. (No unambigious examples of
exact repetition used in this way have been found). Paraphrased
repetition may repeat either a final or medial clause. When other kinds
of repetition are used, however, the clause to be repeated must be a

final clause. Paraphrased and reduced repetition are by far the most common kinds of repetition used for establishing topic. In the following example, a jaguar is established as the topic by reduced repetition. Both clauses are final, the second being in a coordinate relationship to the clause that follows it.

> *Yome oda-ra kiyoa-maro-ni. Yome oda-ra kiyoa-maro oda-ra waka-na-ne-mete yomahi.*
> jaguar us-object followed-eyewitness-comment. jaguar us-object followed-eyewitness us-object broken-stem=closure-subjunctive-past jaguar
> 'The jaguar followed us. The jaguar followed us and would have crushed us.'

Paraphrased repetition in the next example establishes 'wild pig' as topic.

> *Kobaya yana-ne-mari-maka. "Hosiho" kobaya ati-ne-mari-ka.*
> pig walked-stem=closure-eyewitness-identification-sequence. "oink" pig said-stem=closure-eyewitness-sequence
> 'The pig grunted. "Oink," the pig said.'

To establish a topic, the repeated clause does not have to be contiguous to the clause that is repeated. Parenthetical information may intervene. In the following example, 'I' is established as topic of the paragraph by reduced repetition of its prototype after a parenthetical clause in which 'we' is the subject:

> *Wafa tao-o-ka-sama-maro-m. Wafa me ati oda mita-ma. wafa tao-o-ka-na,*
> monkey   shot-I-instrument-downstream-eyewitness-identification. monkey plural voice **we** heard-back, monkey shot-I-instrument-stem=closure
> 'I shot the monkey coming downstream. We heard the monkeys' voices, I shot the monkey,'

2.2 Reinstatement and closing of a topic

The role of repetition in reinstating and changing a topic provides continuity to the topical structure. Noncontiguous repetition forms a boundary around parenthetical information. The repetition after such a parenthesis, secondary information, or subsidiary topic reestablishes attention on the higher-level topic. The paragraph topic of the following illustration is 'I', established previously. Two clauses within the paragraph, however, are not about 'me' but about 'the monkey', a subsidiary topic. To reinstate 'I' as the paragraph topic, the previous clause with 'I' as subject is repeated. In this case, the repetition also marks the end of that topic, the repetition becoming the first clause of a transition paragraph.

Wafa tao-o-ka-na, fai nafi-hari-marihi, wafa wataka-bote nafi-mari-ra. Wafa tao-o-ka-na,
monkey shot-**I**-instrument-stem=closure, and=so big-only=one-eyewitness, monkey fat-augmentative big-eyewitness-evaluation. monkey shot-**I**-instrument-stem=closure
'I shot the monkey, and so (he) is the only big one. The monkey is the biggest and fattest one. I shot the monkey,'

Another use of noncontiguous repetition is to maintain a topic while one or more subsidiary topics are brought into the same time span. In the following example, 'I' is the topic established previously. 'John' is then made a subsidiary topic by repetition and fronting signals. 'They' is also made a subsidiary topic by repetition and a special kind of fronting. Finally the last clause on which the higher-level topic 'I' was topic is repeated.

*Amo-o-na, bani me atori-ra **Yowaho** ite-mari-m. **Yowaho** kobaya atori-ra ita Yowaho, wafa me-ra **me** doka-na-maro-ke. Wafa me-ra **me** doka, makobote amo-o-na,*
slept-I-stem=closure, meat plural skin-object John skinned-eyewitness-identification. John pig skin-object skinned John, monkey-plural-object they burned=hair=off-did-eyewitness-sequence. monkey plural-object they burned=hair=off, later slept-I-stem=closure
'I slept, John skinned the animal's hide. John skinned the pig's hide. They burned the hair off the monkeys. They burned the hair off the monkeys, later I slept,'

A clause may be repeated to make a boundary around a fairly long parenthesis also.

Fai oda siba-ne, ... Kobaya oda siba-na,
and=so we searched-stem=closure-[masculine], ... pig we searched-stem=closure-[feminine]
'And so we searched,... We searched for the pig,'

These two clauses form a boundary around seven clauses in which a snake suddenly appears very close to the participants. The snake becomes a subsidiary topic. Because of the snake, the search for the pig is called off in the clause following the repetition of 'we searched for the pig'. The first clause relating the search for the pig has the marked topic 'pig', which had been previously established. The topic here is indicated by masculine gender agreement of the verb with 'pig' (masculine),[5] even with no mention of the pig in the clause. However, when 'we searched for the monkey' is repeated, 'we' is the unmarked topic since gender agreement is now with the subject 'we' (feminine) and *kobaya* 'pig' is restated in the clause.

2.3 Episode topic

In the introduction to an episode, the narrator specifies a topic for that episode. This topic is identified at the beginning of an episode by a noun standing alone with final intonation, followed by a repeated clause. This clause is either a paraphrase or a repetition of a final clause, as in section 2.1. The initial noun does not occur in all episodes, but usually does discourse initially. Often the repeated clause is a statement of the participant's purpose of a proposal followed by its confirmation. The episode topic may or may not be the topic of the introductory paragraph. If not, it usually becomes a topic in a subsequent paragraph. The topic of the following episode is 'deer'. To indicate this, *badehe* 'deer' stands alone with final intonation. *-he* on the end of this word is phonologically conditioned, but it occurs at the end of a pause group. This, then, is established as topic by the repetition of 'I shot the deer'. The story proper begins with breaking a trail and shooting two other animals, events that occurred before the shooting of the deer.

> *Badehe. Bade tao-o-ka-na-maro-ra. Bade tao-o-ka-na. Hawi oda ka-ka-na.*
> deer. deer shot-I-instrument-stem=closure-eyewitness-nonsequence. deer shot-I-instrument-stem=closure. trail we instrument-cut-stem=closure
> 'Deer! I shot the deer. I shot the deer. We broke a trail.'

Later the deer does become the topic of a paragraph, but without the usual repetition at the beginning, as the repetition at the beginning of the episode was sufficient introduction. The other signals of a marked topic do occur, namely, nonmention of the topic after its initial introduction, gender agreement of the verb with the topic, and the use of the unpossessed form in any mention of body parts of the deer. Occasionally the topic of an episode is dropped. The new topic is established by the usual repetition. In the following example, 'fish' is established as episode topic because of the initial noun title and the repeated clause. The next clause then contrasts the plan of action, 'fishing', with what actually happened, 'following pigs'. Pigs are then established as the new topic by repetition. 'Fish' is not mentioned again throughout the episode.

Aba madi. Aba me oda koro-na-ro-ni. Aba me oda koro-na, hiyama me oda kiyoa, aba me oda ati sawi-ra hiyama me oda kiyowa-ro-ra. Hiyama me oda kiyowa,

fish beings. fish plural we threw-stem=closure-eyewitness-comment. fish plural we threw-stem=closure, wild=pig plural we followed. fish plural we said go=with-but, pig plural we followed-eyewitness-but, pig plural we followed

'Fish: We went fishing. We went fishing, we followed the pigs, but we said we were going to go fishing. But we followed the pigs. We followed the pigs,'

An episode may be introduced by a noun title, which is to be established as the episode topic later. In the following example 'wild pigs' is introduced as a title, but before the pigs are established as topic, 'John' is established as the topic of a short paragraph with a marked topic. 'Wild pigs' are then established by repetition as topic both of the episode and of the second paragraph of the introduction.

Bani madi. Di Yowaho bani me-ra amo-ni-mata-maka. Yowaho bani me-ra amo-ni-nao, hiyama me oda kiyoa, me oda kiyoa-mara. Me amo-na-ni.

meat beings. the John meat plural-object slept-stem=closure-supposed-identification=and=event. John meat plural-object slept-stem=closure-verified. pig plural we followed, them we followed-eyewitness-but=did=we. they slept-stem=closure-comment

'Wild game: John put the pigs to sleep (by incantation). John put the pigs to sleep. We followed the pigs, we followed the pigs, but did we? They were asleep (implies we didn't have to follow them because they were asleep).'

Every episode has an episode topic or occasionally a series of such topics. Within a discourse the topic of a new episode is most often introduced and established by paraphrased repetition. A plan of action is stated in a direct quotation followed by its confirmation. The topic of the quotation becomes the new episode topic. In the following example, 'little fish' is the proposed new topic and confirmed in the second clause:

Aba bidi me ai waka-na-mata-hi. Aba bidi me oda waka-na-maro.

fish small plural we grab-stem=closure-must-imperative. fish small plural we grabbed-stem=closure-eyewitness

'"Let's grab at little fish." We grabbed little fish.'

3 Repetition to show importance

The importance the narrator gives to certain information furnishes clues about his purpose in telling the story. It is shown by his choice of final clauses for important information and medial clauses for less important. Final clauses, in particular, are used to build a story up to a climax of suspense and thus help to define its plot. In general, final clauses are used for major events and important information. Medial clauses are used for minor events, all processes, and most settings that are defined in relative terms by motion verbs.

Various combinations of final and medial clauses that occur whenever information is repeated are part of this same system. The entire content of a repeated clause can be ranked as more important or less important to the discourse as a whole according to whether or not the clause that is being repeated and its repeated counterpart are final or medial. These ranks are as follows:

more important
content

1. Final clause that repeats
   final clause
2. Medial clause that repeats
   final clause or vice versa
3. Final clause that repeats
   nothing
4. Medial clause that repeats
   medial clause
5. Medial clause that repeats
   nothing

less important
content

One consequence of this ranking is that medial clauses that repeat medial clauses are never more important than unrepeated final clauses.

This ranking results in a kind of hierarchy different from the topical one previously mentioned. The topical one is related to discourse groupings of episode and paragraph, as well as a lower subsidiary level. Importance ranking is related to topical structure in one respect in that the first two ranks of importance always establish topics. Repetition plays a role in both importance ranking and topical structure in that the topic is established by the repetition itself, while importance is determined by the medial or final status of the clauses involved in the repetition.

The events in the following jaguar story are ranked as to importance, as shown both by the numbers and the indentation. (F) indicates a final clause, and (M) a medial clause. Arrows are added for noncontiguous repetitions. Punctuation reflects the intonation. By reading only the statements in ranks 1 and 2, the main events of the story are given. These are also the clauses in which topics are established. These topics, then, are ranked as to importance in two categories. For instance, Arniso's unsuccessful attempt to kill the jaguar is presented as having less importance than the more successful attempts of the narrator.

The first five clauses are the introduction and a preview of the complication and first resolution of the story.

Further information about the plot structure can be seen from this ranking. The four final unrepeated clauses marked with rank 3 characterize the buildup of suspense before the jaguar is shot. By contrast, the events following the death of the jaguar are the dénouement and are mostly related in medial clauses indicating lesser importance.

Another characteristic this kind of ranking shows is that higher ranks occur at intervals in a text indicating peaks of important information in the paragraph structure. However, between these peaks there are no distinct paragraph boundaries.

1 Jaguar: The jaguar followed us (F). The jaguar followed us (F).
  3 and would have crushed us (F).
2 The jaguar followed us (M),
  3 With my only shell I shot the jaguar (F)
    5 I was coming back (M),
    5 I was walking through the jungle without a trail (M),
1 In my trail as a result of the jaguar a voice warned (F) "Raymond, jaguar!" Arniso said (F).
  3 The jaguar, running, was coming after (us), pad, pad, pad (F).
  3 "The jaguar is coming on our trail," Arniso said (F).
  3 I pulled the gun hammer back quickly (F).
  3 The jaguar came right up on me (F).
1 From close range in the mouth I shot (him) (F).
  3 for (his) teeth appeared to shatter out (F).
1 With my only shell I shot the jaguar (F).
1 If that shell had misfired, the jaguar would have eaten us (F).
  3 The jaguar was made to sit (F).
2 Arniso misfired his only shell—we had only one shell each in our guns (F). Arniso misfired at the jaguar (M)
  3 The gun finally went off and hit the jaguar in the stomach, bang (F).
    5 And so (the jaguar) sat there (M),
    4 We broke a stick (M), we broke a stick. We stepped on the stick

(M), and broke the stick (M),
   3 I killed the one sitting there (F).
   3 I hit (him) on the head (F)
 1 I killed (him) (F).
   3 When I hit him on the nose, (he) fell over (F).
     5 And so we tied the jaguar (M),
   3 "Should we carry it?" I said.
     4 And so we tied the jaguar (M),
   2 "You carry the jaguar first, over there I'll change" I said (F).
Arniso carried the jaguar (M),
     4 (He) started back with the jaguar (M),
       (He) started back with the jaguar (M),
     5 Arniso rested with the jaguar (M)
     5 And so (he) started out again with the jaguar (M),
     5 (He) kept returning (M),
     4 Later we were returning (M),
     5 Arniso was tuckered out by the jaguar (M), (so)
     5 I changed (with him) (M)
     5 I crossed (the stream) with the jaguar (M),
     5 We crossed the Curia (M),
   2 We were returning with (the jaguar) (M), we returned (F),
   3 Where we came back to (was) at Kaisama [dependent clause]
about that place, the Brazilians used to live there [dependent clause]
   2 At Kaisama we arrived (F). At Kaisama we arrived (M)
     5 We threw down the jaguar, (M)
   4 With a piece of a knife we skinned the jaguar (M), we skinned
the jaguar (M),
     4 or 5 We stretched the jaguar skin (M),
     5 When we finished stretching the jaguar skin [dependent clause],
we hung it up (M),
     4 We slept (M), we slept at night (M).

Another example of ranking by importance in a discourse is one in
which the narrator puts into the highest rank things he shoots that are
considered good eating and into a low rank things he shoots that are
not prized so much. Two monkeys and a wild pig are topicalized in
turn by a final clause repeating a final clause, putting them in the
highest rank of importance. Later he gets an anteater and three
monkeys of a different kind and tells about them using medial clauses
to repeat medial clauses, thereby putting them into a low rank of
importance.

Notes

1 Jamamadí is an Arawakan language spoken by an unknown number of people along the Purús River in the state of Amazonas, Brazil. The dialect under study consists of about one hundred speakers located above the town of Lábrea. Data were gathered during field trips from 1963 to 1976 under the auspices of the Summer Institute of Linguistics in accordance with a contract with the Museu Nacional of Rio de Janeiro and by permission of the Fundação National do Índio. I also wish to thank Joseph E. Grimes for his valuable advice given in a field workshop at Porto Velho, Rondônia, Brazil.

2 The phonemes of Jamamadí are vowels /a,e,i,o/, voiceless stops /t,k/, preglottalized voiced stops /b,d/, fricatives /f,s/, nasals /m,n,h/ (the latter frequently dropping from an unstressed syllable leaving only nasalization), resonants /w,r,y/. The phoneme /s/ is [ts] word initially; /f/ is [ɸ]; and /r/ is [l] initially and before front vocoids and [r] elsewhere. Vowels following nasals /m,n,h/ are nasalized. Stress alternates on every other syllable starting with the first. Sentence stress falls on the verb root and modifies the alternating stress pattern in some words.

3 Because such signals are a separate and complex system of their own, they are not discussed in detail in this paper. The information gained from these signals about who is the topic, however, is necessary to this discussion. Therefore, I have stated the topic where necessary without detailed explanation. The perspective suffix -*m* also has a major role in topic identification in that it identifies a new major participant. It has been discussed in an unpublished paper in the archives of the Fundação National do Índio in Brasília.

4 Whether the subject or the object of the verb is the unmarked topic is a debatable question. I have designated the subject because gender agreement in the verb is normally with the subject, changing only to designate the object when the object is a marked topic. Also, since the narratives studied are personal experiences, 'I' does have a prominent place in the discourse. Normal ordering of clauses is OSV, however, so that the initial position suggests that the object may be the unmarked topic.

5 Gender agreement in the verb is marked only for a masculine third person singular noun. All other forms (plurals, pronouns, and feminine nouns) are unmarked, i.e., take the feminine form.

Participants in Nambiquara Myths and Folktales

Margaret Lowe

The Nambiquara narrator introduces characters into a story in such a way as to distinguish the principal character, other major characters, and minor characters.

Principal characters are introduced in the title of a myth. Major characters are introduced either by a fronted topic in the form of a nominal phrase or by a description of their entry into the scene. Minor characters are introduced either by a simple motion verb or by a kinship term.

Any character can be dismissed from the narrative either by a complete change of scene or by a motion verb that takes him away from the scene.

Correct referents are established and maintained in narrative, whether they speak or act, by the judicious use of conjunctions and culturally expected sequences of action.

This paper describes ways in which Nambiquara[1] narrators introduce characters, how they keep the correct referents, and how the characters are dismissed from the story.

The characters divide into three categories, and the methods of introducing them vary accordingly. There is one principal character without whom there would be no story. There may be other major characters who influence the whole story or an important part of it. There may also be minor characters who are little more than props and exert minimal or no influence on the course of events in the story.

For Nambiquara myths principal *character* is a better term than *participant* or *actor* for the role described because the latter two imply that this person is the chief participator or actor in the story, and this is not necessarily so. The principal character says and does nothing at

187

all throughout some narratives, although he does most of the action in others. The criterion for choosing the principal character is not how much he is on stage, but whether there would be a story at all without him.

1 Text summaries

Abridged versions of three Nambiquara stories serve as the background from which most of the examples in this paper come. The principal characters in these stories are the anteater, the water boa's daughter, and a child.

Every Nambiquara Indian asked has declared that the first story is about the anteater, not about the man around whom most of the story revolves. In the structure of the story as well, the anteater is the principal character.

The beautiful water boa's daughter initiates the second story, though she is depicted only as sitting on the water boa's back and doing no speaking. She is a good example of a principal character who does almost nothing in the story.

In the third story a child is the principal character, but in this case he is also the main actor.

1.1 The anteater

Anteater was making arrows and using fine hawk feathers. A man came along and asked for hawk feathers so he too could make arrows. Anteater refused to give him any, but took him up a tree so he could get some hawk feathers of his own. Then anteater left the man up the tree and caused the tree to grow very tall so the man could not get down. A frog came up to the man who was by now hot and thirsty. Frog offered him a lift down on its back, but the man refused.

A monkey came up and offered the man a lift down. Although by this time the man thought he would soon die of hunger and thirst, he still refused help.

Then a vulture circled overhead and offered to fly the man down on its back. Since the man expected to die of heat and thirst up in the tree, the man got on the vulture's back and was flown to safety.

Then the vulture promised to give the man some poisonous narcotic tobacco to pay back the anteater. The man gave it to the anteater, who smoked it and went mad. They fitted a gourd on his head. Since then he has had a snout and has eaten only ants.

1.2 The water boa's daughter

A young man fell desperately in love with a very beautiful girl he saw. He was determined to win her. The obstacle was that her father was the water boa.

A dove came along and told the young man that if he was willing to follow his advice he would win the maiden. The man agreed, and he and the dove set off down a long dark tunnel. Eventually they came to a forest lake. The beautiful girl was sitting on the water boa's back in the middle of the lake. Dove told the man to go sit beside her. The man did so and a horse fly bit him, sucking his blood. Thus he paid the bride price and won his bride.

1.3 The child who made food

Father and son had an argument as to whether flutes could be heard playing. Finally the child got angry and told the father to take him into the jungle and leave him there. The father did so.

He returned home without the child, and the mother asked what had happened. Father returned to the jungle and found manioc growing for the first time, but no child.

2 Principal character

The principal character is introduced at the beginning of the narration by the title of the story. This title may be in the form of an existential clause or a summary of the main event of the story. In either case the title is not part of the main event line of the story, but rather precedes the first event.

An existential clause when used as a title always introduces the principal character and is the first clause of the narrative. It is distinguished from other clause types because it consists of a nominal followed by a verbal complex $ta^1hxai^2h\bar{e}^1ra^2$ 'as I was told' or $n\bar{u}^2nha^2$-wa^2 'I think I'm telling the story accurately'. (For an account of verb suffixes and the verbal verification system in Nambiquara see Lowe 1972).

Examples 1 to 4 are story titles expressed in existential clauses; 1 is the title of the anteater story and 4 the title of the story of the water boa's daughter.

(1) $Wa^3t\tilde{i}^3kah^3lxah^3lo^2su^2$ $ta^1hxai^2h\bar{e}^1ra^2$.
    anteater it-was-told
    'There was once an anteater.'
(2) $Kx\tilde{a}^3n\tilde{a}u^3ut^1tai^2na^2$ $\grave{a}x^3kax^3lu^3su^2$ $xyau^2xai^3n\bar{u}^2nha^2wa^2$.
    long-time-ago old-woman lived
    'A long time ago there lived an old woman.'

(3) $Ya^2na^1lha^3lho^2su^2\ ta^1hxai^2h\tilde{e}^1ra^2.$
jaguar it-was-told
'There was once a jaguar.'
(4) $Txi^3ha^2ta^3n\tilde{u}^1tai^2na^2\ \tilde{a}^2sa^3wi^3ha^3lxi^3su^2\ n\tilde{u}^2nha^2wa^2.$
water-boa's daughter was
'She was the water boa's daughter.'

The narratives of examples 5 to 7 begin with a title that summarizes the most important event in the story. The event itself is not fully described at the beginning of the story, but later in its proper time sequence in the event line.

(5) $W\tilde{e}^3sa^2\ yain^3txa^2\ xwen^1kxe^3su^2\ ta^1hxai^2h\tilde{e}^1ra^2.$
child food that-was-made it-was-told
'This is the story about the food the child made.'
(6) $Sai^3ki^3n\tilde{a}^3xa^2\ kx\tilde{a}^3nh\tilde{i}^1n\tilde{u}^1tai^2na^2\ six^3wh\bar{i}n^1jah^3la^2$
$ho^3hxat^3ta^1hxai^2h\tilde{e}^1ra^2.$
orphans long-ago the-devil ate-them-all-up-it-was-told
'About the orphans, a long time ago the devil ate them all up.'
(7) $Ax^3kax^3la^2\ ha^3yo^2xi^2ta^1hxai^2h\tilde{e}^1ra^2.$
old-woman shed-skin-it-was- told
'There was an old woman who shed her skin.'

Examples 2 and 7 are from different recordings of the same story; one has an existential clause title and the other a summary title.

3 Major characters

Apart from the principal character many myths have one or more other major characters. The influence of these may pervade the whole story as they influence the principal character, but grammatically they are handled differently.

For example, in the story of the child who made food, the father who argues with the child and precipitates the whole action is a major character. In the story of the anteater, a large part of the narrative is taken up with the account of the interaction between the man and the vulture, both major characters.

A major character can be introduced by a fronted topic in the form of a nominal phrase referring to him. This occurs as the first phrase in the stretch of narrative where he appears.

In example 8, $\tilde{a}^2n\tilde{u}^2su^2\ n\tilde{u}^3ta^2a^2sa^2kxai^2lu^1$ is the noun phrase referring to the man, but the clauses immediately following refer not to the man but to the anteater making arrows. Only after this has been described does the man come into the event line of the story. This is done by the use of the motion verb 'came'. The man came to the anteater and so entered the scene.

(8)   *Xnē³nū²la² ā²nū²su² nūn³te²a²sa²kxai²lu²*
      wa³tī³kah³lxa³lho²nū¹tā² ā²hau³ta² kāi³ye²yhu¹tax³we³ta²sa²kxai³
      tau²ta²we³ta²   kāi³ta¹hxai²hē¹ra²   te³na¹   ā²nū²su²
      nūn³te²a²sa²kxai³lu¹ wxā³nū²la².
      sequence man also-prominence anteater arrows the-feathers-he-
      was-making-with-regard-to   hawk's-feathers   he-was-making
      sequence man also-prominence came
      'So about the man, the anteater was making arrows out of hawk's feathers and the man came (up to him).'

Major characters may also be introduced by a description of their entrance on the scene. In example 9, which is from the anteater story, the vulture enters the story when he is described as circling above the man before he flies down to him.

(9)   *Nxe² xyau²tēn²su² wa²luh³xa² ta²a²kxai³lu²*
      xyau²kxi²te²a² ā²nā³ka³na² tī³nha¹ ā³sa¹xne³ki²la²
      yāi¹ nxe²xai³tit²tu²wa² jāx¹ye²ta¹hxai²hē¹ra² te²sē¹ra².
      and-so while-he-was-there vulture prominence the-man-who-
      was-staying above-(him) path circling ideophone it-flies that's-
      how-he-related-to-him as-I-understand-it
      'While the man was there, a vulture, vultures usually circle over the heads of people, that's what this vulture did to the man, as I understand it.'

Kinship terms may be used to introduce major or minor characters. Thus in the story of how the child made food both father and mother appear on the scene without any other introduction. Example 10 shows this in the case of the father who is shown to be a major character, not by his introduction but by the role he plays later in the narrative.

(10) *Wāix³la² wī³nu²kxai³lu² nē³ka²ta³nū²la²*
      xai³ta¹hxai²hē¹ra² xna²ha¹te¹ si³yo³nān²tù³
      ā²wē³sa²nū¹ta² ā²ki³lhax³nū¹ta²kxai³lu¹ xai³ta¹hxai²hē¹ra².
      child's father led-then went attention-switch behind-(him) son
      went
      'The child's father went on in front. Behind him the child went.'

4 Minor characters

Minor characters enter the narrative only once and have virtually no influence on the major characters or the course of events. For example, the frog and the monkey each offer to carry the man down the tree. But since they are so small, their offers are declined, and nothing more comes of their action—they are minor characters.

The mother of the child who made food has a conversation with her husband on the whereabouts of the child. She also sees leaf cutter ants with manioc leaves for the first time. The mother has no impact on the child or the story, however. She also is a minor character.

Minor characters may enter the text in one of two ways. They may enter as the subject of a motion verb taking them into the scene together with double identification of the character or else by a kinship term.

(11) $Nx\bar{e}^3sx\bar{a}^3\ xyau^2kxi^2t\bar{a}u^3\bar{a}n^1tux^3ti^1\ ta^2ki^2ha^2\ te^2a^2kxai^3lu^1$
$k\bar{a}^3lx\bar{\imath}n^3ta^2\ te^2a^2kxai^3lu^1\ xw\bar{a}^3ye^2ta^1hxai^2h\bar{e}^1r\bar{\imath}^1\ te^2s\bar{e}^1ra^2.$
then   while-he-(the   man)   monkey   prominence   monkey
prominence came as-I-understand-it
Then while the man was there, the monkey came to him, as I understand it.'

The monkey in example 11 enters the scene by means of the motion verb 'came', and the identification of the monkey is repeated the second time by a synonym.

(12) $A^3n\bar{u}^2la^2\ x\bar{\imath}^3x\bar{\imath}^2xna^2ha^1te^1\ \bar{a}^2h\bar{a}x^3ka^3n\bar{u}^2su^2\ te^2kxai^3lu^1\ \bar{\imath}h^1xn\bar{e}^3te^2$-
$sin^2ta^2ku^2\ w\bar{e}^3sin^3ti^2\ \bar{a}^2n\bar{u}^2su^2\ t\bar{e}^3sx\bar{a}^3\ x\bar{\imath}^3y\bar{a}^1xn^2nx\bar{a}n^3ta^2ku^2$
$nxe^3ta^1hxai^2h\bar{e}^1ra^2\ te^2s\bar{e}^1ra^2.$
(the father)-leaving and coming home-attention-switch the-
mother prominence what's-going-on it-was-told as-I-
understand-it
'On the father's arrival home, the mother said, "What's going on? Didn't you bring the child?'' as I understand it.'

In example 11 the child's mother is simply introduced by her kinship to the child. Every child presupposes a mother, and so the mother needs no further introduction.

5 Dismissal of characters

There is no distinction made between the dismissal of principal, major, or minor characters. Any character may be dropped from the scene of action in one of two ways. Either there is a total change of scene with the resultant dismissal of all characters in the scene, or else one character leaves the scene by the use of a suitable motion verb.

The most commonly used is the verb to leave or a verb that has as one of its components the root of the verb to leave.

Examples 12 and 13 show how a whole scene can be changed and a minor character, the child's mother, dismissed in the process. The text has been talking about the child's mother and what she saw. Then comes *xna²ha²te¹ ā²kxā³nxa²* 'scene change, some time previously'. In reply to the mother's question in 11 as to what happened, the scene reverts back to when the father and son started their journey into the jungle. The mother is not mentioned again.

(13)   *Xna²ha¹te¹, ā²kxā³nxa² ā²wī³na² ā²ki³lhax³la² è³ye²jàu³xa²*
       ī³yè³kxi²te³lhxā³ ta¹hxai²hē¹ra² xnē³txi¹ xīn¹kxai²nān² tù³ ....
       scene-change, some-time-back father son the-words-said he-
       said it-was-told listen, when-you-go ....
       'Now, some time back, the son had said to the father, "Listen,
       when you go ...."'

The other method of dismissing a participant, when the scene does not change, is to use a suitable motion verb, usually 'leave'. For example in 14 the anteater has taken the man up the tree. The anteater is effectively dismissed from the scene by the words 'The anteater left and came down.'

(14)   *Wa²tī³kah³ lxa³lho²te²u¹ta²kxai³lu² ā³sxā³ ka²nxi²ta¹hxai²hē¹ri¹.*
       the-anteater left came-down
       'The anteater left and came down.'

Similarly in example 15 of the same text the small monkey offered the man a ride down the tree on his back. The man refused because the monkey was too small, and so the monkey left. The monkey is thus dismissed from the story.

(15)   *Ā²nū²a²nū¹ta² xyau²kxi²jah¹lo²nū¹tā² wa²tī³kah³lxa³lha²*
       sa²xwe³kxi²jah¹lo²nū¹tā² wān³txi³kxai³lu¹
       kāi²nā²xna³i¹ ā³nhait¹sa²so¹xna²ha¹ha²kxai³ tē³sxā³
       a³hi²sa²kxa²yàn³ti³su² nxa²ha¹i¹ xne³ta¹hxai²hē¹ra²
       te²sē¹ra² xnē³sxā³ xyau³kxi²nhe².
       the-man the-one-who-was-there anteater one-who-had-been-put
       his-words you-are-not-big I-slip-off-you take lest-I-fall I-say-to-
       you-it-was-told as-I-understand-it thus leave-and
       Then said the one who was there, the one who had been put
       there by the anteater, "You are not big (enough). I don't want
       to slip off you and fall to the ground." And so he (the monkey)
       left.'

6 Tracing characters within the narrative

It is important not only to know how characters are introduced into a narrative and dismissed from it, but also to know who does what throughout. The problem is complicated by the fact that in Nambiquara there are no subject or object indicators on constituents of transitive clauses; neither is there a fixed order that determines which element is subject and which is object. Both SOV and OSV orders are permissible. Furthermore, many of the subject and object pronouns in a text are deleted.

Nambiquara has several methods for keeping track of characters in a narrative. First is the use of culturally expected sequences termed *scripts* or *dyads*, giving an expectation of who might normally do what. The sequence conjunction $n\tilde{u}^2la^2$ assures the hearer that the sequence is proceeding as expected, or else the adversative conjunction $xn\tilde{e}^3to^3ta^1$ alerts the hearer to the fact that the normal script is not being followed at that point.

Second is the use of conjunctions in dialogue to keep the references straight. The same adversative conjunctions can be used to signal change of speaker when the second contradicts the first. Or the attention-switch conjunction $xna^2ha^1te^1$ is used to signal change of speaker when no disagreement is involved and the second speaker accepts what the first has said and carries it forward.

Third is occasional restatement of an event with precise indication of who did what to keep the referential pattern up to date.

6.1 Scripts or dyads

A *script* in this context is a series of culturally predictable events (the idea came from an unpublished paper by Roger Schank). Once a script has been activated any member of the culture is able to predict the events occurring in it. A *dyad* is the simplest kind of script, in which only two events occur, such as offer and acceptance.

In Nambiquara the sequence conjunction $n\tilde{u}^2la^2$ assures the hearer that the expected sequence is taking place, as in example 16:

(16) $\bar{A}^2kox^1ko^1n\bar{u}^3xa^2$ $a^2ta^2la^2n\bar{u}^3n\bar{u}^1t\bar{a}^2$ $\bar{a}^2t\bar{i}^3nh\bar{a}^3la^2n\bar{u}^3n\bar{u}^1ta^2kxai^3lu^2$
      $\bar{u}^3h\bar{u}^1yhu^1ta^1hxai^2h\bar{e}^1ri^1$ $xn\tilde{e}^3te^2s\bar{e}^1la^2$ $n\bar{u}^2la^2$ $\bar{u}^3th\bar{u}^2nh\bar{u}^2la^2$
      $i^3ku^3li^2$ $ye^3ka^2n\bar{a}u^3ki^2$ $ku^3n\bar{u}^2la^2$ ....
      bad-tobacco devil's-tobacco poison-tobacco he-gave-him I'm-
      told sequence light sequence smoke once smoke-sequence
      '(The man) gave the bad devil's poison tobacco to him (the
      anteater) and he (anteater) lit (it) and smoked (it) and ....'

Here the man offers tobacco to the anteater, which is an expected action for a host toward a visitor. The anteater accepts—expected action—and he smokes it. The change in actor—from the man who offers to the anteater who receives—is indicated solely by the conjunction *nū²la²*, from which we conclude that the expected sequence has occurred. The tobacco is not the expected kind for a visitor, even though the behavior is expected; and from that discrepancy hangs the rest of the tale.

6.2 Conjunctions

When no predictable sequence is present, as often happens in dialogue or many other interactions between characters, the attention switch conjunction *xna²ha¹te¹* is used to signal change of speaker or actor. In the story of how the child made food we have the father and child walking single file down the trail, the father in front. Then after the attention-switch conjunction we are told about the child. (See example 10 above.)

In example 17 the man is speaking, but a quotation following *xna²ha¹te¹* is from the vulture. Similarly in example 18 the vulture's speech is followed by *xna²ha¹te¹*, and then the man's words.

(17) *Yả³lu²sa²ha²kxai³, wãn²sa²ha²hxai³ sa³nhai³*
nxe³ta¹hxai²hē¹ra² te²sē¹ra² xna²ha¹te¹
xne³ti¹ ta³lo³hēt³sē¹ri¹ . . . .
I'm-thirsty I'm-hot I-am closing-quote-margin as-I=understand-it attention-switch listen get-on-my-back . . . .
'(The man said to the vulture,) "I'm thirsty, I'm hot," he said. "Listen, get on my back," said (the vulture to the man).'

(18) *Hit³san¹ji¹ xne³ta¹hxai²hē¹ra² te²sē¹ra² xna²ha¹te¹*
ā²nū²a²hxi²sen²su² sa²xwe³kxi²sa²ha²kxai³lū¹.
are-you-angry closing-quote-margin as-I-understand-it attention-switch a-man put- me-up-here
'"Are you angry with me?" said (the vulture to the man). "A man put me up here," (said the man to the vulture).'

In the case of conversation, an adversative conjunction may be used instead of the usual attention switch. This indicates that there is disagreement in the reply of the second speaker. In example 19, a father speaks to his son. After an adversative conjunction the child's reply is given contradicting what has been said.

(19) *Xne³xna²ha¹te¹, xwai³lxa² wĩ³na² wãn³txi² kxai³lu¹*
hai³txi³ ain³kxi²nū²xna²ha¹jau³xa² e³kxi²to³-

hxān³nhai¹ ā³nāx³to³sa²xnān³nhai¹, xnē³to³ta¹
kwxa²nī¹lxi¹ wāi²la² yān³su² hān³su² hān³ nhai¹.
attention- switch child's father's words negative words-which-I-
understand-of-you   you-have-not-been-saying   I-hear-nothing
adversative nonsense flute sound is-sounding,
'Then the child's father said, "I don't understand what you
say. I hear nothing." But (the child answered), "Nonsense.
The flutes are playing."'

The adversative conjunction *xne³to³ta¹* indicates both that the
speaker has changed from the father to the child and that the expected
agreement of the script has not occurred. It is from this argument that
the story springs, because the child gets angry and goes off into the
jungle.

6.3 Restatements

In Nambiquara there is no overt way of marking subjects or
objects. A third way of indicating unambiguously which character does
which action is to restate the action in such a way as to clarify the
actions of at least one character. This clarification is made by the
addition of further information in the restatement. In example 20 we
have 'these children the jaguar found' as the initial statement. There is
no indication in the verb of that statement as to who did the finding,
nor is there any distinction between singular and plural. In the
restatement, however, we have 'these armadillo children house where
they lived'. This clearly indicates that it was the house of the armadillo
children, so we conclude that the jaguar found the children at their
house and not the other way round.

(20)   *Xnē³ta²a²sa²kxai³lu¹ ya²na¹lhah³lo²nū¹ta²kxai³la¹*
       a³ti²ta¹hxai²hē²ra² kxa²yuh³xa² wē³hax³li³nū¹tā²
       nū³na² ȧ³lxa²ta²nū¹ta² ā²wā³hax³li³nū¹tā² ā²xyau²-
       thī³na²sa²kxai²lu² ya¹na¹la²nū¹ta²kxai³lu²
       a³ya²ti²ta¹hxai²hē¹ra².
       these (armadillo children) jaguar found animal children
       armadillo this-armadillo children the house-where-they-lived a-
       jaguar found
       'These (the armadillos) the jaguar found. The jaguar found the
       house where the armadillo children lived.'

7 Restrictions on verbs

A verb that introduces a restriction on another verb can be used to clarify a situation. In example 21 we are told that the armadillo children took tough grass. Here there is no ambiguity; the tough grass cannot take the children so the subject of 'take' is known. The next verb is 'tie', and its subject will be the same as that of the last verb unless there is a conjunction telling us that there is a change of subject. So in this case it is clear that the children tied the jaguar. The verbs to take and to say are most commonly used to disambiguate in this way since the subject of each must normally be animate.

(21) $Nũ^2la^2 \ nũ^3nũ^1tã^2 \ ã^2wē^3hax^3li^3nũ^1tã^2 \ a^3lo^2xi^3$-
       $nho^2su^2 \ tĩ^3nho^2kxai^3lu^2 \ so^1xi^2tē^3na^1 \ ya^3na^1la^2nũ^1ta^2kxai^3lu^2$
       $taih^3kxi^2yah^3lxi^3ta^1hxai^2 \ hē^1ra^1.$
       sequence the-armadillo-children tough-grass fiber take-sequence
       jaguar tie-3rd-person-it-was-told
       'Then the armadillo children took some tough grass fiber and tied up the jaguar.'

Notes

1 Nambiquara was classified by McQuown and Greenberg (1960) as in the Ge-Pano-Carib phylum. There are approximately two hundred speakers of Nambiquara in Northwestern Mato Grosso, Brazil. The number of dialect groups remains uncertain at present. The data and information in this paper come from Ivan Lowe and are based on field work done between 1960 and 1976 in accordance with contracts between the Summer Institute of Linguistics and the Museu National do Rio de Janeiro and more recently between the Institute and the Fundação National do Índio. The present paper was written under the auspices of the Summer Institute of Linguistics at a 1976 field workshop held in Porto Velho, Rondônia, Brazil, under the direction of Joseph E. Grimes. The author is indebted to Grimes and Ivan Lowe for helpful discussions and comments in the development of this paper.
    The phonemes of Nambiquara are /p/, /t/, /k/, /d/ (implosive alveolar stop), /x/ (glottal stop), /j/ (alveolar affricate), /n/ (with six allophones: [m] after nasalized glide ãu, [bm] after oral vowel glide au, [gn] preceding a velar stop and following an oral vowel, [ŋ] preceding a velar stop and following a nasal vowel, [dn] on all other occasions following oral vowels, and [n] on all other occasions following nasalized vowels), /N/ (voiceless nasal), /r/ (only in the final syllable of the independent verb), /l/ ([ř] after front vowels), /s/, /h/, /w/, /y/. Vowels occur in oral and nasalized series (nasalization is written with a tilde ⁻): /i, e, a, o, u/, and two vowel glides /ai/ and /au/. Both series of vowels also occur laryngealized, indicated by a ʔ over the vowel letter. There are three tones in Nambiquara, indicated by raised numbers /¹, ², ³/ at the end of every syllable. ¹ is a down glide, ² is an up glide, and ³ is a low level tone.

References

Lowe, Ivan. 1972. "On the Relation of Formal to Sememic Matrices with Illustration from Nambiquara." *Foundations of Language* 8:360-90.

McQuown, Norman and Joseph Greenberg. 1960. "Aboriginal Languages of Latin America," ed. by Sol Tax. *Current Anthropology* 1.431-36.

Collateral Information

The Adversative Particle in Tucano Discourse

Birdie West

Pūricā, the adversative particle in Tucano, functions to suspend the movement of a story or change its direction. Sentences with *pūricā* are statements of counterexpectancy, contrary either to the expectations of the participant(s) in the story or to the expectations of the story's hearer.

The Tucano[1] particle *pūricā* 'but, however, contrary to expectations, contrary to what you may think' has to do with suspending the movement of a story or modifying its direction, much as a road block stops the flow of traffic and diverts it in another direction around the barricade.[2] Most of the instances of *pūricā* that I have observed come from a text about conflicts the narrator and his friends had with professional rubber hunters. These conflicts were verbal, so it is not surprising that 90% of the instances of *pūricā* in the texts[3] studied occur in direct quotations. The other 10% are instances where the narrator is explaining or describing something he feels to be contrary to his listeners' expectations.

Each of these points of conflict is critical to the development of the story and needs to be resolved in order for the story to move forward. It is in the resolution of the conflict that the story takes a new, or at least a modified, direction.

For example, in one small section of the long text about conflicts with rubber hunters *pūricā* occurs a number of times. In this section there is a rapid-fire exchange between the narrator and a rubber hunter with one assertion or proposal after another. *Pūricā* occurs in the assertions and proposals that are critical to the story and are points of conflict that need to be resolved. This exchange heightens the feeling of

201

conflict and tension in the story and causes the movement of the story to be suspended temporarily. The conflict is resolved when the rubber hunter and the narrator accept each other's proposals, and the story moves forward after this, but in a different way than the rubber hunter or even the narrator had expected.

Pūricā does not occur in sentences that are the main events of narrative discourse but in sentences that supply collateral information, that is, information about events that may or may not happen (Grimes 1975). Nearly half of the sentences (21) with *pūricā* are either imperative or in future tense. Sometimes the commands are carried out and sometimes not; some of the events predicted take place and some do not. The sentences with *pūricā* supply alternatives to the main events or anticipate events before they happen, thus causing the events that do happen to be presented more dramatically than they would have been without the collateral information.

The other sentences (26) are strong assertions. Most of these are positive: 18 positive statements as opposed to 8 negative statements. A few of the negative statements are given in disagreement with a previous statement, but most are negative assertions about real life situations. Many of these assertions are evaluative statements such as 'But I am not like other white men', 'But the girl sounds awful', 'But I'm good', or 'But I pay people well'. In the case of the latter two statements, the rubber hunter who made them did *not* pay the people, and it turned out to be a bad experience. The actual events stand out much more sharply because of the collateral information supplied by these strong assertions.

Pūricā occurs following simple noun phrases (nouns, pronouns, or locative words) when these act as the topic of a sentence. Sentence topic is marked by a clause constituent's being moved to the first position in the sentence. The normal word order of Tucano declarative sentences is subject-object-verb. So when the object is topic, it is moved to first position. Subject as topic is unmarked; that is, it stays in the same position. In the following example the object, *yн'н нacaro-re* 'what I wanted', is the topic of the sentence; it has been moved to a position before the subject:

Yн'н нacaro-re mн'н o'owe'e.
I what=I=wanted-oblique you don't=give
'You are not giving me what I wanted.'

Pūricā also occurs following dependent conditional clauses, demonstrative pronouns, and the verb *añu* 'be good'.[4] When *pūricā* follows either the demonstrative *te* 'those' or a dependent conditional clause, the resultant form serves as the topic of a sentence just like a noun phrase plus *pūricā*.

Pūricā may be followed by the enclitic *-re* 'oblique' when the noun phrase or dependent clause of which it is a part acts as the direct object, indirect object, time, or location constituent of the sentence.[5]

1 Noun phrase

Nouns and pronouns followed by *pūricā* are in contrast with previously mentioned nouns and pronouns: animate beings with animate beings, or inanimate objects with inanimate objects mentioned within the same sentence or the same paragraph. Often the contrastive items are in two adjoining sentences. When they are, the contrast is between the most recently mentioned noun or pronoun and those followed by *pūricā*. If the contrast is between nouns or pronouns within the same paragraph but not in adjacent sentences, the contrastive items are grammatically parallel but have other nouns or pronouns intervening. The contrast between the previously mentioned nouns and pronouns and the ones followed by *pūricā* underlines the conflict and the sense of being contrary to expectations.

Contrast between persons within the same sentence is seen in:

X—— *уӈ'гӊого butiaro na* **purica** *apema a'te di'tapӊ-re.*
X—— more=than very=much they *but* command=to=work this land-oblique
'But they command the people of this land to work much more than X——does.'

Na refers to the rubber hunters mentioned in the sentence immediately preceding in the text; *pūricā* sets it in contrast with X——. This is an instance of the narrator telling his audience something he feels is contrary to what they expect. The narrator is saying, in effect, 'You know that X—— commands people to work; well, contrary to what you might think to be true, the rubber hunters command people to work much more than X—— does.' *Na pūricā* as subject is the unmarked topic.

Pūricā also shows contrast between persons within the same paragraph but in different sentences. The following is another example of a strong assertion made by a narrator to his audience. The context is a story in which some children have turned into birds. Their calls are described. The boys' call is given first, with no value judgment. Then in the next sentence, with a value judgment that is presumably unexpected because none was attached to what the boys did, the narrator says:

Ña'aro co numio **pūricā** *bнsнwō.*
badly she female **but** she=sounded
'But the girl sounds awful' or 'Contrary to what you might expect
on the basis of how the boys sound, the girl sounds awful.'

Another example of *pūricā*, showing contrast involving persons
mentioned in different sentences, occurs in the text in which a rubber
hunter is trying to get the narrator to go rubber hunting with him. The
narrator relates the problems he has had with another rubber hunter.
The first one agrees and says:

Yн'н **pūricā** *āpi pecasн weronojo niwe'e.*
I **but** other white=man like I'm=not
'I, contrary to what you might think on the basis of the other
fellow, am not like other white men.'

This is an example of a strong assertion that is an evaluative statement
and that did not turn out to be true later in the text. This statement
helps to underscore the problems the narrator and his friends had with
this rubber hunter as well.
    Later on in this same text the narrator and his friends are discussing
the actions of this same rubber hunter. One of the group says that the
rubber hunter had wanted to give them a motor, but

Mari **pūricā** *nee o'otн'sawe'e.*
we **but** absolutely giving=not=pleasing
'As for us, however, his giving is not pleasing' or 'Contrary to the
expectation that his giving us the motor should please us, it
doesn't.'

The reason it does not please them is that the rubber hunter took back
the motor and is using it himself. This is a critical point in the story
because the group decides to run away from the rubber hunter and
return to their homes. *Mari pūricā* as object is the topic of the
sentence.
    Pūricā is also used to show contrast between inanimate objects. In
the next example the objects are mentioned within the same paragraph,
but not the same sentence. The narrator and friends have been given
toasted manioc flour mixed with water to drink. Then their host says:

Ba'ase **pūricā** *mari'i.*
food **but** there=isn't
'But there isn't any solid food' or 'Contrary to what you might
think, there isn't any solid food.'

The contrast is not overtly stated. The host did not say, 'There is toasted manioc flour to drink but there isn't any solid food.' This is a turning point in the story because, from this point on, the story is about hunting and fishing in order to get meat for the settlement.

In another text the narrator is telling what artifacts are made by the different tribes, particularly those made by the Tucano people. Then he says:

Sõ'cõro **pûricã** ũsa weetisa'a.
manioc=grating=board **but** we don't=make
'But we don't make manioc grating boards' or 'Manioc grating boards, contrary to what you might have thought, we don't make.'

This is in contrast with what 'we' do make. In this example sõ'cõro pûricã as object is the topic of the sentence. He goes on to say who does make the grating boards.

There is only one example in these texts of pûricã following a locative word. Sõ'opн 'there' is used as an object in this sentence, meaning 'that part'. Pûricã is followed by the oblique enclitic -re. The narrator is describing the various sib groups among the Tucanos. His listeners ask him more about the groups. His reply is:

Sõ'opн **pûricã-re** yн'н quē'rã masipeotisa'a.
that=part **but-oblique** I also don't=know=completely
'But I also don't know that part completely' or 'Contrary to what you might think, I don't know all that either.'

After emphasizing the fact that he didn't know any more about the sib groups but that there were others who did, he began to talk about a different topic.

2 Dependent conditional clause

Pûricã can occur following dependent conditional clauses. Only one example has been observed in the texts. In this example pûricã occurs with oblique enclitic -re. The dependent conditional clause acts much like a time phrase which may be followed by -re when time is given special attention in the sentence.

In the text about rubber hunters the narrator commands a rubber hunter to give him his own personal radio, saying:

*Tojo wegн yн¹н to mн¹н o¹o-cā **pūricā-re** waнsa¹a ni cн̆-re bujicāgн wemiwн.*

thus doing I that you give-if **but-oblique** I=will=go saying he=oblique laughing I=did

'"Therefore I'll go, if indeed you do give it to me, though I don't think you will," I said jokingly to him' or 'Therefore, contrary to what you might think, when you give it to me I'll go," I said jokingly to him.'

3 Demonstrative pronoun

Pūricā occurs following the demonstrative pronouns *te* 'those' and *to* 'that' or 'there'. It is conceivable that *pūricā* can occur with other demonstratives, but these have not been observed.

Demonstratives in Tucano are categorized according to animate and inanimate. The animate forms are further divided into masculine, feminine, and plural. There is a two-way division according to spatial placement: *a¹to* 'here' and *sō¹o* 'there'. The following are the animate demonstrative forms: *ā¹rī* 'this masculine one', *a¹tigo* 'this feminine one', *ā¹rā* 'these ones', *sī¹i* 'that masculine one', *sico* 'that feminine one', and *sōja* 'those ones'.

The inanimate demonstratives have a three-way division according to spatial or temporal arrangement: *a¹to* 'here', *sō¹o* 'there', and *to* 'over there out of sight or removed in time'. The singular forms are *a¹ti* or *a¹to* 'this', *si* or *sō¹o* 'that', *ti* or *to* 'that one removed in time or space'. *A¹to, sō¹o,* and *to* refer to a limited list of items: radios, tables, motors, benches, shelves, items of clothing, and a few others, of which *cumuro* 'bench', *casa* 'shelf', and *su¹tiro* 'clothing' are the only indigenous items. *To* can be used in a general sense referring to 'that series of events' or to 'that which was said'. *A¹ti, si,* and *ti,* which cannot occur without the nouns they modify, refer to all other objects except those that take shape suffixes. The complete paradigm of forms used for nouns having shape suffixes is not given here because it is not relevant to this paper. The following is a sample paradigm using the form *a¹ti* 'this' with the shape suffixes: *a¹ti-ga* 'this round solid object', *a¹ti-gн* 'this long or branching object', *a¹ti-wн* 'this vehicle', *a¹ti-wa* 'this strainer-like object', and *a¹ti-rн* 'this pot-shaped object'. A more complete description of Tucano demonstratives is given in my *Gramatica popular del Tucano* (1980).

The plural forms are *a¹te* 'these', *sise* 'those', and *te* 'those removed in time or space'.

Even though *te* 'those' and *to* 'that' are closely related demonstratives, *te pūricā* and *to pūricā* are not parallel in their uses. The difference between the two is based on the difference between what each is referring to. *Te* followed by *pūricā* is specific, referring to specific nominal items that are in contrast to other items. *To* can refer to a specific item, but when followed by *pūricā*, it is general in its referential scope, referring to an indefinite amount of what was said previously by one speaker in contrast with what the second speaker is about to say.

In the present data there is only one example of *te pūricāre*, occurring as topic of a sentence. *Te* by itself refers anaphorically to items mentioned earlier in the text. In this example *te* refers to the list of items given after the verb in the same sentence. *Te pūricā-re* says that these items are in contrast to items listed in the previous sentence. The narrator is speaking specifically to his hearer, and telling him what he should tell his relatives: 'This is what you will say: "The Indian people had food, houses. . . ." ' Then in contrast to this he says, 'You will say:

Te pūricā-re *dн'sawн na-re añuse su'ti añuse de'ro nise....*
those but-oblique it-lacked they-oblique good clothes good what stuff...
'But what they lacked was good clothes, nice things...' or 'Contrary to what you might expect them to have on the basis of those things I have mentioned, what they lacked was good clothes, nice things....'

To pūricā 'that but' is used to introduce alternate plans or counterproposals, and in this way acts as a connector linking the contrastive parts: what was said previously by one speaker with a new plan or proposal by a second speaker. It is as if the second speaker is saying, 'In light of what you've said, here's my proposal.' The new proposal is contrary to the expectations of the hearer. The idea of proposal and counterproposal has support in the fact that speakers of Tucano paraphrase the meaning of *to pūricā* or *to pūricāre* as *a'tiro weegнti* 'I'm going to do this', *a'tiro weerā* 'let's do this', *a'tiro weeya* 'do this', or even *a'tiro wee* 'doing this'. The proposals may or may not be carried out later by the hearer, which parallels what was said earlier about collateral information.

To *pūricā* can also occur with the oblique enclitic -*re*. Both *to pūricā* and *to pūricāre* are used exclusively in the content of direct quotations. They occur initially in the sentence or as a clarification at the end of the sentence. They may occur following vocatives or exclamations.

In the long text about conflicts with rubber hunters there are many occurrences of *to pūricā* acting as an introducer of a counterproposal. In one instance a rubber hunter wants the people to work every day, including Sundays and holidays. The narrator tells how he and his companions objected to this, saying, 'When we are in our towns, we absolutely don't work Sundays and holidays.' The expectation is that they will not have to work these days; but the rubber hunter comes up with the following counterproposal:

> *Мнsa to pūricā sorinнтн nicā da'rasīriti-rā ni'cā нʜмтн-re ocho nueve caseri mitia niwi.*
> you **that but** Sunday being not=wanting=to=work-if one day-oblique eight nine sheets bring he=said

'''However, in the light of what you said, if you don't want to work Sundays, then bring in eight or nine sheets of rubber every day,'' he said' or ' ''Contrary to your expectation that you won't work on Sundays and holidays and that you will just bring in the normal amount during the week, you will bring in eight or nine sheets of rubber every day instead of what you would normally bring in,'' he said.'

The following is another example of *to* referring anaphorically to what has just been said. The narrator has gone looking for meat for the rubber camp. The boss asks him if he got any animals. He replies that he didn't; he just got some fish. So the boss says:

> *To pūricā-re тнʜʜ ñamiacā apaturi waʜsa'a.*
> **that but-oblique** you tomorrow again you=will=go

'But tomorrow you will go again' or 'But in the light of what you said about not getting any animals, tomorrow you will go again, even though you might have expected not to have to.'

In an earlier part of the same text there is contrast between what a rubber hunter offers the people and what they really want. The rubber hunter is trying to convince the narrator to go rubber hunting by saying, 'I pay people well.' The narrator describes his response, which is in the form of a counterproposal:

> *Cʜ tojo ni-cā тнʜo yʜʜ to pūricā ʜsa po-tericjarā a'topʜ-re yʜʜ-re ni'cāro radio tocadisco me'ra niro-re yʜʜ нasa'a.*
> he thus saying-when hearing I **that but** we Indians here-oblique I-oblique one radio phonograph with being-oblique I want

'When I heard him say that I said, ''But in the light of what you say about paying us well, what we Indians here want, including me, is a radio phonograph.'' '

In another text about the death of the narrator's brother-in-law there is an example of *to pūricāre* occurring twice in the same sentence, once at the beginning and reiterated at the end. The family has planned to bury the dead man in the cemetery in another village.

But just as they are planning to leave, a big storm comes, and they decide not to go. The narrator makes a suggestion:

To pūricã-re a'to ta yaacãrã to pūricã-re.
that but-oblique here precisely let's=bury **that but-oblique**
'But let's bury him here instead' or 'In light of what you say about the rain, let's bury him here instead of taking him to Montfort as we had planned.'

The following is the only example observed of *pūricã* occurring in a question. It is a counterquestion. A rubber hunter has just asked the narrator and his friends why they aren't bringing in as much rubber as some previous workers have. The narrator challenges the rubber hunter by saying:

Dicнse mitiɾi to pūricã-re por diez.
how=many did=bring **that but-oblique** by ten
'But counting by tens how many bundles did they bring in?' or 'But in light of what you said about the previous workers how many ten-bundle lots did they bring in?'

4 Verb 'be good'

Pūricã occurs following the verb *añu* 'be good'. *Añupūricã* is a frozen expression meaning 'It's good even though I think you think it might not be'. The goodness expressed by *añupūricã* is not in the absolute sense of the word; it is toned down to mean 'It's pretty good'. I have written it as one word because it acts like a single lexical item. *Añupūricã* is commonly heard in conversation as an evaluative statement. In every example in text the meaning conveyed is an evaluation of someone or something plus the idea of counter-expectancy.

In one example a rubber hunter is trying to convince his hearers that he is different from other rubber hunters. He says:

Aperã pecasã weronojo niwe'e. Aperã na'arã nima. Yн'н pūricã añu-pūricã.
others white=men like I'm=not. others bad they=are. I but **good-but**
'I'm not like other white men. Others are bad. But I'm pretty good.'

Or the last sentence could be 'I, contrary to what your expectations might be on the basis of what you know about other rubber hunters, am pretty good.'

In another text the narrator is talking about people having left the village to go live elsewhere. The reason the people gave for leaving was that there were no more fish in the area. The narrator says that there are a few fish. Then he says:

>*Dia waro añu-pŭricā.*
>river as=for **good-but**
>'But as for the river it's pretty good' or 'Contrary to what you might think about the river because there are only a few fish in it, it's good.'

In one example *añupŭricā* occurs with person-tense suffix *-mi* 'masculine habitual', with the resultant form *añupŭricāmi* 'he's pretty good'.[6] The narrator is comparing one rubber hunter with another. He says:

>*Cŭ pŭricā añu-pŭricā-mi.*
>he but **good-but-he+habitual**
>'But he is pretty good' or 'Contrary to your expectations about rubber hunters, he is pretty good.'

In another text about two brothers, of whom the older accidentally shoots the younger, the father of the boys tells how he warned them about the gun.

>*Мнsa-re weremiwн рeсawн añu-pŭricā añu-ro pe'e.*
>you-oblique   I=tried=to=tell   gun   **good-but**   good-if
>on=the=other=hand
>'I tried to tell you that the gun is good all right, but...' or 'I tried to tell you that when the gun is good, it's good, but it is not always good.'

In this sentence he does not say what is wrong with the gun. The words *añupŭricā añuro pe'e,* which form a verb phrase doublet, give the sense that all is not well with the gun. Two sentences later he says the gun does not cock properly.

The verb phrase doublet, of which *añupŭricā añuro pe'e* is an example, is composed of a full verb as the first constituent of the phrase and a dependent verb form plus the particle *pe'e* 'on the other hand' as the second constituent. The same verb stem is used in both constituents. The whole construction gives the idea that what is being asserted in the first constituent is true even though it looks like it might not be true. The second constituent implies an ellipsis of information that may appear to negate the statement in the first constituent. Two

other examples of this type of construction are
>   Wãcu'ɪ wãcɪ- ɡɪ pe'e.
>   I=think thinking-if on=the=other=hand
>   'I do think about them all right...' or with the elliptical information
>   supplied, 'I do think about them all right, even if it does not seem
>   like it from my actions.'

The second example is

>   A'mequētiama a'mequē-rã pe'e.
>   they=didn't=fight fighting-if on=the=other=hand
>   'They didn't fight even if it looks as if they could have.'

The particle *pe'e* 'on the other hand' or 'for his part', which occurs
in the second constituent of the doublet described above, has other
uses in Tucano discourse. It occurs with much higher frequency than
pūricã does, especially at points of heavy emotional content: the
heavier the emotional content, the more instances of *pe'e*. *Pe'e* follows
simple animate noun phrases (nouns, pronouns, or demonstrative
pronouns) when these occur as subject, direct object, or indirect object
of the sentence. A noun phrase plus *pe'e* may be followed by the
oblique enclitic *-re*.

Often *pe'e* will occur in pairs, first on one participant and then on
another. It can occur on as many as four participants in any one
section of discourse, or it may occur on only one participant in which
case it singles him out for special attention. *Pe'e* spotlights in turn each
major participant at the points of heavy emotional content.

The following example of *pe'e* occurring on one participant is found
in the text about the two brothers, of whom the older accidentally
shoots the younger. Just after the father, who is the narrator, tells
about the gun going off, he says,

>   Sɪrocɪ *pe'e* aɪcɪ niwi. Cɪ acabiji *pe'e* yɪ'ɪ tacɪ Candi *pe'e* aɪcɪ
>   niwi.
>   the=one=sitting=in=back on=the=other=hand steersman he=was.
>   his younger=brother on=the=other=hand my son Candi
>   on=the=other=hand steersman he=was
>   'He, on the other hand, was the one sitting in back steering the
>   boat. His younger brother, my son, Candi was steering the boat.'

An example of *pe'e* occurring on four different participants is found
in a text where the narrator and his relatives, who have been fleeing for
days through the jungle, come upon a settlement where a relative of
theirs is living. The first occurrences of *pe'e* in this section are in

introductory or explanatory material. The first *pe'e* occurs on the relative's husband in the following sentence:

Ʉsa ñeco marapʉ niwĩ cʉ̃ pe'e.
our grandmother husband he=was he **for=his=part**
'He, for his part, was our grandmother's husband.'   The second *pe'e* occurs on their grandmother.
Co pe'e ʉsa ñeco diacʉ̃ niwo.
she **for=her=part** our grandmother true she=was
'She, for her part, was our real grandmother.'

The next sentences describe their tearful encounter. The narrator describes their reactions to her greeting:

Co tojo ni-cã ʉsa pe'e pʉru utisĩricãcati.
she thus saying-when we **for=our=part** really felt=like=weeping
'When she said that, we, for our part, really felt like weeping.'

In the next sentence *pe'e* occurs in *co marapʉ* 'her husband', who tells the others to stop talking to the narrator and his relatives because they are hungry.

Ʉsa-re tojo nitojanʉ'co co marapʉ pe'e nee na utamoticã niña yujipʉ. Nee ã'ra masa ʉjaboayʉ'rʉapara.
we-oblique   thus   saying=finishing her husband **for=his=part**
absolutely they not=talking=ones be yet. absolutely these people
they=are=very=hungry
'After she said that to us, her husband, for his part, said, "Don't talk with them. These people are starving." '

Their grandmother's husband asks them how long they have been without food. The next sentence gives their answer with *pe'e* back on the main participants in the story:

Ʉsa ticʉse nʉmʉri ʉjaboasʉ niwʉ ʉsa pe'e cʉ̃ tojo ni-cã ta.
we that=many days we=starved we=said we **for=our=part** he thus
saying=when precisely
'When he said that, we, for our part, said, "We were starving for that many days." '

A few sentences later *pe'e* occurs with *na* 'they' referring to the children of their grandmother.

Na pe'e ũsa-re po'ca mi o'owã.
they **for=their=part** we-oblique manioc=flour bringing they=gave
They, for their part, brought manioc flour and gave it to us.'

Notes

1 Tucano, of the Eastern Tucanoan language family, is spoken in the Vaupés region of southeastern Colombia and in the northwestern part of Brazil. There are approximately fifteen hundred Tucanos in Colombia, However, there are many more speakers of Tucano than there are members of the tribe, since it is the lingua franca of the Papurí River and its tributaries. The present analysis is based on texts given in the villages of Acaricuara and Montfort and in scattered settlements along the Papurí. I wish to express my thanks to those who gave the texts and have helped me to understand them.

2 The Tucano transcription reflects a sound system of voiceless unaspirated stops /p/, /t/, /k/ (written *c/ qu* as in Spanish), glottal stop written as ', voiceless aspirated stops written *pj, tj, cj,* voiced stops /b/, /d/, /g/, fricatives /s/, /h/ (written *j* as in Spanish), flap /r/ (with [ř, ň, ľ] as allophones: [ň] before nasalized vowels, [ř] following front vowels, and [ľ] elsewhere), semivowels /w/, /y/, vowels /a/, /e/, /i/, /o/, /u/, /ɨ/ (high central unrounded, written as н), and their nasalized counterparts written with ˜ over the vowel. All voiced consonants have nasal allophones preceding nasalized vowels; here *m, n, ñ* are written for /b/, /d/, /y/ before nasalized vowels as in normal Tucano orthography. Nasalization is not written on vowels following *m, n, ñ.*

3 The texts were gathered under the auspices of the Summer Institute of Linguistics between 1964 and 1976. Research for this paper was greatly aided by a concordance made on the IBM 360 computer at the University of Oklahoma by the Linguistic Information Retrieval Project of the Summer Institute of Linguistics and the University of Oklahoma Research Institute, and sponsored by Grant GS-1605 of the National Science Foundation. I am deeply grateful to Joseph Grimes for his valuable suggestions in the preparation of this paper during a linguistic workshop held in Bogotá, Colombia, from February 1977 to May 1977 at the University of the Andes. I wish to thank my co-worker Betty Welch for her aid in analysis and for helpful ideas.

4 Dependent conditional clauses normally precede independent clauses. They express the conditional sense of 'if' or 'when'. They are similar in structure to independent clauses except for the verb, which takes a dependent verb suffix. If the dependent clause refers to the same subject as the independent clause, the dependent verb suffixes are *-gн* 'masculine', *-go* 'feminine', *-ro* 'inanimate', and *-rã* 'plural animate'. The following is an example of such a dependent conditional clause in a sentence: Yн'н *pũricã нтна сно-gн añuro сно'о.* (I but men having **if+masculine +same=reference** well I=have) 'But if I have workers, I care for them well.' If the dependent clause refers to a different subject than the independent clause, the dependent verb suffix is *-cã.* The following is an example of a dependent conditional clause with such a subject: *Cн tojo ni-cã yн'н toja waнti niwн cн-re.* (he thus saying-**if+switch=reference** I return I=will=go I=said he-oblique) 'When he said that, I said to him, "I'll return." '

5 The use of the oblique enclitic *-re* indicates the element in the sentence toward which the action is directed or the element which is being given special attention, whether direct object, indirect object, time, or location. More than one element may

have -re occurring with it in one sentence.

6 There are tempting possibilities of further analysis of *pŭricā* because of some verbal forms which in part resemble *pŭricā*. One form is the verbal adjective *pŭri* 'harmful' or 'painful'. Two examples of *pŭri* are as follows: *Ujaque **pŭri** ni'i*. (fever harmful it=is) "Fever is harmful"; and *Añuro co'te-cā **pŭri**-tiaporo*. (well take=care=of-if **harmful**-it=isn't) 'If one takes good care of them it isn't harmful.' Another form that more closely resembles *pŭricā* is the verbal modifier *pŭri* 'really'. Only two examples have been observed. *Añu-**pŭri**-ro we'e тн'и нтна-re* (good-**really**-inanimate progressive your men-oblique) 'It's really good for your men.' *Нисн sijase masi-**pŭri**-we'e*. (jungle traveling know-**really**-not) 'I really don't know how to travel around in the jungle.' There is a verb suffix *-cā* or *-cā'* 'intensifier. The alternate pronunciation is based on dialect differences. An example of *-cā'* occurs in the following sentence: *Añuro wapaye peo **-cā'** - wн*. (well paying finish **intensifier**-I+past) 'I paid them all well.' An alternate spelling of the last word is *peo-cā-wн*.

References

Grimes, Joseph E. 1975. *The Thread of Discourse*. The Hague: Mouton.
West, Birdie, 1980. *Gramática popular del Tucano*. Tr. by Anne Pilat de Galvis. Bogotá: Ministerio de Gobierno and Instituto Lingüístico de Verano.

Paumarí Interrogatives

Shirley Chapman

A question in Paumarí is always begun with a question phrase. Such a phrase represents the sentence constituent about which information is being sought. Sentence constituents are nuclear (subject, object, second object), circumstantial (time, location, instrument, adjunct), and peripheral (manner, reason).

The two types of question phrase are nominal and verbal. A nominal question phrase may represent any sentence constituent except the verb, adjunct, or manner, and the verbal question phrase may represent all circumstantials, peripherals, and the main verb.

Information about the known constituents is supplied leaving the nominal question phrase to represent the most nuclear unknown constituent in the ranking. The formal properties that indicate the constituent a verbal question phrase represents are shown by affixation. These properties are transitivity or intransitivity, independence or dependence, reduplication or nonreduplication. The combination of one formal property from each set links the verbal question phrase to one particular constituent.

This paper considers what information must be given by a Paumarí[1] speaker to enable the addressee to recognize a question and to know what kind of information is expected in response.

Paumarí sentence structure in general involves a clause nucleus (subject, object, second object,[2] and verb), a clause periphery (time, location, instrument, and adjunct[3]), and a sentence periphery (dependent clauses of manner or reason). A question phrase always occurs sentence initial and represents one of the constituents. Different features within each question phrase signal the type of surface-level constituent a given question represents. Polar and rhetorical questions are sketched below (see secs. 2 and 3).

215

1 Content questions

A content question is differentiated from a noninterrogative statement by the position of the question phrase. All the question words may occur as relative pronouns in utterance-medial position in noninterrogative contexts, and under these circumstances no information is being sought by the speaker. In all questions, however, the question word is in initial position.

A sentence, represented in table 1, may contain three possible actants in its clause nucleus, and the semantic roles of each verb determine which of those slots must be filled. Optionally circumstantials of time, location, instrument, and adjunct may occur in the periphery of the clause.[4] With the exception of the adjunct, these circumstantials are represented by nominal question phrases; while the adjunct and the peripherals of manner and reason are represented by verbal question phrases.[5] There is no clear distinction made in Paumarí between reason and purpose.

actants			circumstantials				peripherals	
sbj	obj	obj2	time	loc	instr	adjt	man	reason
nominal question phrase						verbal question phrase		
nahina, hanahini, nihafori, hana						*niha-ni*		

Table 1. Relation of question phrases to
constituents of a sentence.

A question word indicates in only a general way what is being questioned:[6] *nahina* and *hanahini* generally ask about people and things, *hana* alone asks about places, *nihafori* about time and quantity, and *niha-ni* about reason, manner, and adjunct. Even though *niha* by itself is a verb root, the compound *nihafori* functions as a quantitative noun modifier or a temporal pronoun. *Nahina* may optionally substitute for *niha-ni* when information about reason is being sought.

In general, a nominal question phrase is understood to ask about a nuclear element unless all the nuclear information is present in the context;[7] in that case, it is understood to ask about a circumstantial and as a last resort about a peripheral element.

The term *question word* refers to the head of a question phrase, even though this phrase may be complex (*niha-fori-ja, hana-hi-ni*). The term *question phrase* refers to the head combined with other elements (noun, enclitic, demonstrative, or particle),[8] and these together ask for information about a constituent.

1.1 Nominal question phrases

Table 1 shows that there is no one-to-one correspondence between question words and sentence constituents. In what follows each question word is discussed in terms of the constituents it may represent and the other factors that may be relevant to make each question phrase more specific to a particular constituent of a clause.

Two of the question words are specific to location and time phrases. The first is *hana* 'where', which functions as a locative interrogative pronoun. It has an optional suffix *-ja* 'time/space' which may be reduplicated *-jaja*. No contrastive or restrictive meanings have so far been discovered to account for the presence or absence of this affix in this question word:

Hana-ja 'i-araba-ha-ja?
where-time/space you-fish-distance-independent
'Where did you go fishing?'[9]

The second question word is *nihaforija* 'when', which functions as a temporal interrogative pronoun. The time/space affix *-ja* is obligatory here and gives it temporal meaning:

Nihafori-ja 'i-'ajihi-ki-'i?
question-time/space you-depart-margin-you
'When are you going to leave?'

Nihafori, without *-ja*, may also be used as an interrogative quantifying adjective in a nominal phrase or an equational clause, and in such use it means 'how many' or 'how much':

Nihafori so'oro-ra 'i-namonaha-ja?
question basket-object you-make-independent
'How many baskets did you make?';
Nihafori vi-hi-mani-ra 'adani ija'ari vi-kha-ki?
question they-be-identification-independent plural=demonstrative people they-come-adjectival
'How many are the people who are coming?'

The more general question words *nahina* 'who, what' and *hanahini* 'which' may also be used to represent time and location phrases. In such a question phrase, the question word always functions as an

interrogative adjective and has immediately following it a noun with a
semantic component of time or location.

> *Nahina* ⎫
>   ⎬ *gora ⸀i-okha-ki-⸀i?*
> *Hanahini* ⎭
> question house you-go-margin-you
> 'What/which house are you going to?'

> *Nahina* ⎫
>   ⎬ *ahi bana ⸀i-okha-ki-⸀i?*
> *Hanahini* ⎭
> question day future you-go-margin-you
> 'What/which day will you go?'

All the remaining nominal phrases (subject, object, second object,
and instrument) may also be represented by *nahina* or *hanahini*. Which
phrase the question word is actually representing is signaled by given
information; that is, all nuclear slots are given information in an
utterance, except for the one represented by the question word. For a
question to be asked about an instrument all the nuclear slots must be
filled.

> *Nahina vani-a ⸀i-⸀avi-ja ⸀ida?*
> question   selection-circumstantial   you-drink-independent
> demonstrative
> 'From what did you drink it?' (Reply: 'A cup.')
> *Hana-ki-hi-ni-a ⸀i-okha-ki-⸀i?*
> question-*ka*=agreement-be-feminine-circumstantial   you-go-margin-
> you
> 'In what are you going?' (Reply: 'By car.')[10]

Hanahini and *nahina* are not used to distinguish nominal elements
but rather to specify known classes. If a questioner asks for
information about one member out of a class of people or things (e.g.,
which woman, which house), then *hanahini* is used. If the class is not
known, then the more general *nahina* 'what, who' is used. If the
referent is known to be plural, however, *hanahini* is used whether the
class is known or not, as *nahina* may not modify a plural noun.
Hanahini must agree in number, gender, and noun class with the noun
it represents or modifies in the following way:

> *hana-hi-ni* (question-be-3rd=sg=fem=margin)
> *hana-hi-na* (question-be-3rd-sg-masc=margin)

hana-vi-hi-na (question-they-be-3rd=pl=margin)
hana-va-ki-hi-na (question-they-*ka*=agreement-be-3rd=pl=margin)

Hi- in *hanahini* is the existential verb 'be' making the question word a nominalized equational clause. It is the question expression as a whole that means 'which', rather than a part of it. Three examples show this question phrase representing subject, object, and second object phrases:

Hana-hi-ni gamo-a bi-soko-ja ʼida prato?
question-be-feminine   woman-subject   she-wash-independent demonstrative plates
'Which woman washed the plates?' (subject);
Hana-hi-ni ʼi-ino-ni ʼida Siri-a bi-rasoha-ja?
question-be-feminine   your-tooth-noun=margin demonstrative Siri-subject she-pull-independent
'Which of your teeth did Siri pull?' (object);
Hana-hi-ni makari ʼida ʼi-ra noʼa-vini hi-ja?
question-be-feminine   cloth   demonstrative   you-object   gave-dependent=transitive be-independent
'Which cloth was it that he/she gave you?' (second object).

In this last example the surface structure of the sentence is equative due to the presence of final *hija* 'be'. In this question the object and the verb, nominalized by *-vini*, fill the complement slot. This frequently occurs when the second object (potentially tagged with *-a* enclitic) of a ditransitive verb is overtly stated.

Continuing the discussion of *hanahini* and *nahina*, although the latter may occur as an interrogative adjective, it usually functions as an interrogative pronoun and is never inflected. Its distribution is much wider than that of *hanahini* because it is the question word used in nontransitive clauses, and it is also an ordinary possessable noun meaning 'thing' in noninterrogative contexts.[11] For example:

Vakadi-nahina itxa-ni-ra na-ibavijaha-ha naothini-a...
their-things   many=small-adjectival-object   cause-put=away-independent afterwards-circumstantial...
'After she had put away her many little things....'

Three examples follow of *nahina* as an interrogative pronoun representing subject, object, and second object respectively:

(1) *Nahina 'ida kana-ni-ra nofi-ja?*
question demonstrative bathe-dependent=intransitive-object want-independent
'Who wants to bathe?' (subject);
(2) *Nahina-ra 'i-no'a-vini hi-ja 'ida ihai?*
question-object you-gave-dependent=transitive be-independent
'To whom did you give the medicine?' (object, equational);
(3) *Nahina mani 'ida Maria 'i-ra no'a-vini hi-ja?*
question identification demonstrative Mary you-object gave-transitive=dependent be-independent
'What did Mary give you?' (second object, equational).

In addition to the action clauses already discussed there are a number of types of nontransitive clauses that express relationships such as identification, possession, comparison, and referential in which *nahina* represents the unknown component. A full description of the contrastive features of these clause types is not relevant to this discussion of interrogatives, but a few examples show how *nahina* may be used to ask for information about the different relationships expressed.
Identification 'what is?':

Nahina mani 'oni?
question ∓ identification demonstrative
'What is that?'

Possession 'who owns?':

Nahina ka-so'oro mani 'oni?
question possessor-basket ∓ identification demonstrative
'Whose basket is that?'

Reply:

Kodi-so'oro mani hida.
my-basket ∓ identification demonstrative
'It is my basket' or *kodi-ani* 'Mine'.

Purpose 'what used for?':

Nahina ka-so'oro-ni mani 'oni?
question purpose-basket-margin ∓ identification demonstrative
'What is that basket used for?'

Reply:

> *Karagoahi ka-so'oro-ni mani 'oni.*
> manioc=flour purpose-basket-margin ∓ identification demonstrative
> 'The basket is used for manioc flour.'

Or,

> *Karagoahi ka-imoni.*
> 'For manioc flour.'[12]

1.2 Verbal question phrases

In the same way that a nominal question word can represent more than one kind of phrase, a verbal question word may represent more than one kind of element in a sentence (reason, manner, or adjunct). The features relating the question word to a particular element are represented by affixation on the pro-verb *ni*. These features are independent or dependent, transitive or intransitive, and reduplicating or nonreduplicating. One of each of these pairs of features is present in every pro-verb and the combinations of these choices enable the hearer to link the question phrase to the surface-level constituent.

1.2.1 Manner. Manner is indicated by reduplication in the pro-verb. When the pro-verb is **transitive,** the reduplication is of the transitivizer -*'a* to become -*'a'a*. The question phrase then has the form:

> *niha* **person-***ka-ni-'a'a-*$\left\{ \begin{array}{l} vini \\ ki \end{array} \right.$
> how person∓*ka*=agreement-DO-reduplicated+transitivizer-margin

as in:

> *Niha 'o-ka-ni-'a'a-vini koda ka-ani-ki hida 'o-kahagi?*
> how   I-*ka*=agreement-DO-reduplicated+transitivizer-
> dependent=transitive   doubt   *ka*=agreement-take=out-margin
> demonstrative my-canoe
> 'How might I take out my canoe?'

When the pro-verb is **intransitive,** the reduplication that signals manner affects the pro-verb together with the morpheme immediately preceding it. That is, in the plural, the intransitivizer *kha-* is reduplicated with the pro-verb to give *khanikhani*. Because the intransitive is realized with no explicit intransitivizer in the singular, the pro-verb and the person marker are reduplicated to give *'oni'oni* in the first person and *'ini'ini* in the second person. The third person singular intransitive prefix is also zero, so the resulting reduplication is only of the pro-verb itself, *nini*. When *ka* noun class agreement needs to be shown with a third singular subject, the allomorph *kha-* is used. This form is identical to the intransitivizer *kha*, except that the latter occurs only with plural subjects. An example of the intransitive reduplicated pro-verb is:

> *Niha nini-ni vani voroni-ja 'ida isai?*
> how reduplicated+DO-dependent=intransitive selection fall-independent demonstrative child
> 'How did the child fall?'

There are two elements in a sentence that may be represented by this form of verbal question: the main verb and peripheral manner clause. If the margin on the transitive reduplicating pro-verb of a question phrase is *-ki*, then the question phrase stands as the main verb of the sentence with the meaning 'What shall (the subject) do about the situation described in the object nominal phrase?' as in:

> *Niha 'a-ni-'a'a-ki koda hida 'arakava a-'dani-ki?*
> how we-DO-reduplicated+transitivizer-margin doubt demonstrative stativizer-break-adjectival
> 'What shall we do about the injured hen?'

The reply will be a suggestion compatible with 'do', such as:

> *'O-ka-so'oro-mani-ki hida mahija bi-va-adaha-ra-vini hida a-'dani-ni.*
> I-verbalizer-basket-identification-margin demonstrative so=that she-accompaniment-walk-negative-dependent=transitive demonstrative stativizer-break-nominalizer
> 'I will put her in a basket so that she does not walk with her injury.'

If, however, the margin on the pro-verb is dependent, then the question phrase represents a manner clause in the periphery. If the questioner is wanting information about the activity or circumstances relating to the subject of an intransitive verb or the object of a transitive verb, then the intransitive dependent margin *-ni/na* is used on the pro-verb. If, however, the information being requested is about the activity of the subject of a transitive verb, then the transitive dependent margin *-vini* occurs on the pro-verb. An example of a question about the activity of the subject of an intransitive verb:

Niha nini-na vani-a abini-ra 'ada makha?
how reduplicated+DO-dependent=intransitive selection-manner die-independent demonstrative snake
'How did the snake die?'

The reply:

'Da'di dafi hi-na vani abini-ra 'ada.
head hit be-dependent=intransitive selection die-independent demonstrative
'By his head being hit he died.'

A question about the state of the object of a transitive verb is:

Niha va-khanikhani-na vani va'ora 'i-noki-ra 'adani isai va-ka-sarampo-ki?
how they-reduplicated+intransitivizer+DO-dependent=intransitive selection them you-see-independent plural=demonstrative children they-verbalizer-measles-adjectival
'How were the children with measles when you saw them?'[13]

The number and gender agreement is between the object of the transitive verb and the pro-verb. The reply gives the requested information about the state or activity of the transitive object. The reply is:

Va-'aihota-'i-na.
they-better-completive-dependent=intransitive
'They were better.'

The final example is a question about the activity of the subject of a transitive verb:

Niha 'i-ni-'a'a-vini 'i-na-abini-ra 'ada makha?
how you-DO-reduplicated+transitivizer-dependent-transitive you-cause-die-independent demonstrative snake
'How did you kill the snake?'

There is number agreement between the subject, the pro-verb, and the main verb. The reply is a peripheral dependent clause.

1.2.2 Reason. Clauses indicating reason and purpose are interchangeable. The word *kaimoni* 'be used for', which indicates a purpose relationship between nominals, is also used within the clause to mark purpose. The presence of *kaimoni* in a question phrase generally obtains a purpose response, and the lack of *kaimoni* generally obtains a reason response.

The pro-verb in a question phrase requiring information about a reason or purpose is always intransitive and *mani* is always present. The question phrase always represents a nuclear element, that is, the main verb of an intransitive clause or the subject of an equative clause.

When the question phrase stands for an intransitive main verb, it agrees with the subject in number and gender. The intransitive subject frequently contains an adjective modifier, which may be an embedded clause and is marked by the adjectival margin -*ki*.

> Niha 'i-ni-mani-ja 'i-okha-ri-*ki*?
> why you-DO-identification-independent you-go-negative-**adjectival**
> 'Why are you not going?'

In the third person there is always a demonstrative present, and the noun and adjective are both optional:

> *Niha ni-mani-ra 'o?*
> why DO-identification-independent **demonstrative**
> 'Why does he?' 'What is the matter with him?'

When the subject noun phrase contains an embedded transitive clause in the adjectival position, an equational construction results with the embedded clause functioning as the complement.

> *Niha ni-mani-ra 'ada jorai 'i-soko-vini hi-ki?*
> *why DO-identification-independent demonstrative mat* **you-wash-dependent=transitive be-adjectival**
> 'Why the mat that you are washing it?' or 'What happened to the mat that you are washing it?'

The first example in this section, 'Why are you not going?', is a positive question seeking information about a negative fact. It is possible to negate the question word itself, under which circumstances -*mani* 'identification' is replaced by -*ri* 'negative'. These two morphemes never cooccur.

> *Niha 'i-ni-ri-ki 'i-okha-ri-ki?*
> why you-DO-negative-margin you-go-**negative**-adjectival
> 'Why are you not going?'

In the second type of reason question, the question phrase represents the subject of an equational clause. The complement is a nominalized transitive clause. The existential equational *hi* 'be' follows the nominalized clause.

The head of the question phrase may be either the verbal word *niha-ni* or the nominal word *nahina*. The question phrase with *nahina* as its head is identical to the one used for information about a second object, described earlier. The verbal word *niha-ni* is specific for asking about peripheral elements. There is agreement between the transitive object and the pro-verb. The question phrase within the subject slot is itself an embedded identificational equational clause. A tree diagram in figure 1 shows the levels of embedding.

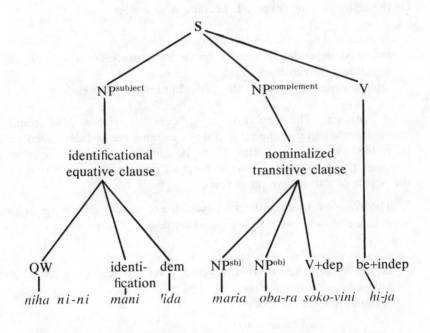

why   is   it   Mary   floor   wash   be
'Why is it that Mary is washing the floor?'

Fig. 1. Equational structure of one kind of reason question.

Niha ni-ni mani 'ida Maria oba-ra soko-vini hi-ja?
why DO-dependent=intransitive identification demonstrative Mary floor-object wash-dependent=transitive be-independent
'Why is it that Mary is washing the floor?'

When *hi* 'be' follows a transitive dependent verb (with-*vini* as margin), as in the last example, this always indicates the presence of an overt element other than subject or first object in the sentence which is associated with the transitive verb. This is a general principle, which also covers ditransitives, but is applicable here indicating the presence of a reason clause. The reply to the above question may take two possible forms:

> *Kidi-sai-a bi-ka-a'bi-vini mani 'ida bi-soko-vini hi-ja.*
> her- child- subject   she- transitivizer- vomit- dependent=transitive
> identification demonstrative she-wash-dependent=transitive be-
> independent
> 'Her child vomiting on it is the reason for her washing it.'

Or the order may be reversed, keeping *-vini* and *hi* together:

> *Bi-soko-vini hi-ki nama-ni makamaka-ni.*
> she-wash-**dependent-transitive be**-margin surface-noun=margin dirty-
> dependent=intransitive
> 'Her washing it is the result of it being dirty on the surface.'

1.2.3 Adjunct. The pro-verb in a question phrase that requires information about an adjunct is always intransitive and dependent; that is, it has the *-ni/na* margin. There is number and gender agreement between the pro-verb and the subject of an intransitive main verb or the object of a transitive main verb.

The roles of force and target, which are expressed by the adjunct phrase, are shown in the following examples:

> *Niha ni-na vani-a abini-ra 'ada abaisana?*
> how DO-dependent=intransitive selection-circumstantial die-
> independent demonstrative fish
> 'From what did the fish die?'

The reply shows a cause of death but not an instrument:

> *Akona vani-a abini-ra 'ada.*
> fish=poison selection-circumstantial die-independent demonstrative
> 'Of fish poison it died.'
> *Niha ni-na vani-a bi-vini-ra 'ada mamori?*
> how DO-dependent=intransitive selection-circumstantial he-shoot-
> independent demonstrative fish
> 'Where did he shoot the fish?'

The reply always indicates some part of the target, such as the head, side, or tail.

In order to give the above question a directional meaning, it is possible to modify it by the addition of the time/space affix *-ja* immediately following the pro-verb. *Vani* is optionally present. The answer to such a question indicates at what point or where on the target.

Niha ni-na ja vani-a a-'dani-ra 'ada 'arakava?
how DO-dependent=intransitive time/space selection-circumstantial stativizer-break-independent demonstrative cock
'How did the cock get hurt?' or 'Where was the cock hurt?'

The reply:

Pita-na ka-jaso-ni ja.
side-noun=margin adjectivalizer-left-adjectival time/space
'On the left-hand side.'

1.2.4 General verbal questions. The question phrase *nihaniki* is not associated with a particular circumstantial or peripheral element. It does not show gender agreement and always remains in the intransitive form. It may occur as an alternative to one of the more specific question phrases and in consequence the kind of information that the speaker is requesting is also less specific. The circumstances under which this question phrase is used are probably the best guide as to the kind of information the speaker is seeking.

Examples are given in which a more specific question phrase would represent a locative, instrument, adjunct, or manner element. *Nihaniki* may give information about either the subject or the object of a transitive verb because the features in the pro-verb which make this distinction (i.e., transitivity of the pro-verb) are not added; the *-ki* margin neutralizes information on both the transitivity and dependency.

Niha ni-ki-a kana-ja 'ida?
question DO-margin-circumstantial bathe-independent demonstrative
'Where/how does she bathe?'

The reply is ambiguous and could represent either location or a manner.

Gora adamini-ni-a taoba ka-nama-ni vani-a kana-ja 'ida.
house landing-noun=margin-circumstantial board adjectivalizer-surface-adjectival selection-circumstantial bathe-independent demonstrative

'At the landing place of the house on a board she bathes.'
Niha ni-ki-a kha-ja hida?
question DO-margin-circumstantial come-independent demonstrative
'How did she come here?' The reply: *Kanava* 'Canoe.'
Niha ni-ki-a 'i-khori-ja hida?
question-DO-margin-circumstantial you-dig-independent
demonstrative
'How/with what are you digging?'
Tařasařa vani-a 'o-khori-ja hida.
machete selection-circumstantial I-dig-independent demonstrative
'With a machete I am digging it.'
Niha ni-ki-a abini-ra 'ada abaisana?
question-DO-margin-circumstantial die-independent demonstrative
fish
'How did the fish die?'

The replies can be interpreted as manner, location, force, or
instrument:

> *Tapajo kaabani.*
> 'In a fish trap.' Or,
> *Kahano-na vani.*
> 'Being drunk (from fish poison).'
> *Niha ni-ki vani-a 'i-ani-ja hida viro?*
> question DO-margin selection-circumstantial you-take=out-
> independent demonstrative parrot
> 'How did you get the parrot out (from the nest)?'

The reply describes the manner in which it was done.

2 Polar questions

Polar questions do not have an interrogative word. They are
distinguished from their declarative counterparts by intonation,
affixation, and context.

A polar interrogative has a rising intonation at the end of the
utterance. A statement has a falling intonation at the end of the
utterance unless it is part of a larger intonation unit, in which case it
may be level or have a slight rise. Moreover, a question is always
followed by a pause that gives the addressee the opportunity to
respond.

There is no single affix that signals a polar question. But polar
questions usually have the particle *mani* 'identification' as a suffix in
both the question and reply, if it is not already present as a particle.

Mani seems to link two items that are in some way associated. In noninterrogative contexts *mani* is also found to link two items together such as subject and complement or command and response. The following is an example, linking a question and response:

> ʹI-nofi-**mani**-ja hida papiȓa?
> you-want-**identification**-independent demonstrative paper
> 'Do you want this paper?'

The reply:

> Haʹa, ʹo-nofi-**mani**-ja ʹoni.
> Yes, I-want-**identification**-independent demonstrative
> 'Yes, I want it.'

In another example of *mani*, it links a response and an indirect command:

> ʹOma-na bi-honoria-ha, ʹoma-**mani**-ha, raofa-na bi-honaria-ha, raofa-**mani**-ha.
> lie-dependent=intransitive he-ordered-independent, lie-**identification**-independent, jump-dependent=intransitive he-ordered-independent, jump-**identification**-independent
> 'He ordered him to lie down and he lay, he ordered him to jump and he jumped.'

The circumstances under which an utterance is made are the best indication whether it is or is not a question expecting a reply. Polar questions are frequently associated with a vocative or a second person pronoun or both, and followed by a pause. If in the course of a monologue the speaker quotes a polar question, he also gives the answer with no pause or specific reference to the audience. For example:

> Kaikahi-ʹa-ha ada hoariha, bi-ni-ʹa-hi, ʹI-ino-ni ʹbana-mani-a? Bi-ni-ʹa-mani-ha, Haʹa, ʹo-ino ʹbana-ki-ho.
> arrive-completive-independent demonstrative other, he-say-transitivizer-independent, Your-tooth-noun=margin hurt-identification-independent? She-say-transitivizer-identification-independent, Yes, my-tooth hurt-margin-I
> 'The other arrived and he said to her, "Does your tooth hurt?" She said to him, "Yes, my tooth hurts me." '

3 Rhetorical questions

Three contexts have been observed in which an utterance has the form of an interrogative but not the illocutionary force; that is, the speaker is not seeking information.

The first context is when the social situation requires some form of communication and the participants use a polar question to satisfy this requirement. The polar question that is used is identical to a real question and receives an answer as if it were a real question. For example, the normal greeting is:

'I-vani.
you-selection
'You?'

The reply is:

Ha'a, ho-vani.
yes, I-selection
'Me.'

This use extends into other areas of conversation. People ask, 'Are you eating?' 'Have you come?' when it is clear from the context that this is so.

The second context demonstrates a different kind of social pressure. When a person, usually a child, is not behaving in a socially acceptable way, the one reproving him will use a negative polar question. For example, 'Do you not have ears?' means 'You should listen.' 'Do you not have any clothes?' means 'Go and put some clothes on.' In each of these situations the negative polar question has the illocutionary force of a command.

Both positive and negative polar questions are used as real questions; and if in the context there is no social pressure as described above, the question is treated as genuine.

The third context in which a rhetorical question may be used is to express an extreme difficulty encountered by the speaker. The negativized question word *ni-nihaniki* (negative-how) is used initially as the speaker states the problem. For example, one narrative text contains: 'How is it that we cannot pass this stretch of the path: there are wasp nests hanging low in the middle of the path and snakes on both sides?' The speaker is not expecting information as to how the difficulty may be overcome and does not pause for the addressee to speak, but continues on with the narrative. Although the statement is given in an interrogative form, it has the force of 'we cannot pass'.

Notes

1 The field work on which this paper is based was carried on during the period 1964 to 1976. The Paumarí number approximately two hundred fifty people. The data represented in this paper come from a study of the speech habits of a group of about one hundred sixty living in the area of São Clemente, on the Purus River in Amazonas, Brazil. Paumarí is Arawakan. Extended contact was made possible through contracts between the Summer Institute of Linguistics and the National Indian Foundation (FUNAI) of the Brazilian Ministry of the Interior, and the National Museum, Rio de Janeiro. This paper was written at a Summer Institute of Linguistics workshop held in Porto Velho, Territory of Rondônia, Brazil, from September to December of 1976. The writer wishes to express her thanks to Joseph Grimes and Ivan Lowe for their guidance and for helpful suggestions concerning the organization and presentation of the material.

2 The term *second object* is used rather than *indirect object* because characteristically in English the indirect object refers to a beneficiary or recipient and the object refers to a patient. In Paumarí, however, the beneficiary is found in the object slot and the patient in the second object slot with ditransitive verbs.

3 The term *adjunct* here has a more restricted meaning than in much current usage. It is restricted to a single nominal phrase in the periphery of a clause with an adverbial function and containing only elements with the role of force or target.

4 The term *circumstantials* refers to four adverbial elements (time, location, instrument, and adjunct) but excludes manner and reason.

5 The verbal question word is a verb *niha* and an obligatory pro-verb *ni* 'do, be' immediately following it and glossed as 'DO'. *Niha* is one of a class of verbs that does not take affixes, the affixation being transferred to the pro-verb.

6 A manuscript by Shirley Chapman and Mary Ann Odmark describing the phonological system of Paumarí is in the archives of the National Indian Foundation of the Ministry of the Interior, Brasília. Paumarí has consonants /p t k ʔ/, /b d g/, /th kh/, /ɓ ɗ/ (voiced implosives), /č j/, /w f s š h/, /m n/, and /ř ṛ̌ (retroflexed)/. Vowels are /i a o/. There is contrastive vowel length in stressed syllables, written as a double vowel. The consonant following a stressed syllable is lengthened except for /ř ṛ̌ w/.

7 The nominal element immediately preceding the verb must be tagged with either a thematic enclitic or a demonstrative that shows emphasis. This choice is not limited to interrogative clauses but forms part of the whole staging mechanism of the language. All nominal phrases that precede the verb are in a thematic position and are tagged with enclitics as follows:

    subject-*a* transitive verb
    object-*ra* transitive verb
    subject object-*ra* transitive verb
    second object-*a* transitive verb

The subject of an intransitive verb, however, never has an enclitic. The enclitic -*a* also occurs on all the circumstantials. It is always zero following /a/.

It is possible to tag one preverbal element in a clause for special emphasis by using a demonstrative after it. The demonstrative must agree in number and gender with the head of the nominal phrase to which it is tagged. When these categories are unknown, as in many questions, the demonstrative is feminine singular. When there are two thematic elements, the one being emphasized occurs first in the following way:

    subject +demonstrative +intransitive verb
    subject +demonstrative ∓object-*ra*+transitive verb

object +demonstrative ∓subject-*a* +transitive verb
A demonstrative makes the nominal phrase to which it is tagged into an embedded identificational equational clause. *Mani* 'identification' then may optionally precede the demonstrative, except when a second nominal phrase with thematic enclitic follows immediately. Demonstratives have the additional function of standing alone as a nominal phrase with the force of a third person pronoun 'he she, they'. They are also used to distinguish time and location as shown in table 2.

	feminine singular	masculine singular	plural
near speaker/now	*hida*	*hada*	*hadani*
near addressee/now	*'oni*	*'o*	*va'oani*
distant from speaker and addressee, not now or time not signaled	*'ida*	*'ada*	*'adani*

Table 2. Paumarí demonstratives

8 A number of optional particles express time, order, and speaker's viewpoint within a nominal phrase and therefore, at times, within an interrogative phrase. The time particles *bana* 'future permissive' and *koda* 'future dubative' and the speaker viewpoint particles *mani* 'identification' and *vani* 'selection' occur in this paper. *Mani* functions like a verb 'be', but is never inflected as a verb root. It also occurs as a verb suffix. It is not restricted to interrogative contexts, but serves generally as a link between two items like question and reply, comr and and response, or subject and complement. *Vani* generally serves to indicate one out of a group of known possibilities. In narrative it shows contrast and counterexpectation. It may follow a sentence-initial noun, phrase, or clause and frequently occurs in interrogative utterances after a circumstantial or peripheral element.

9 Independent is a kind of margin that is the final affix occurring on all verbs, most adjectives, and some nouns. The margin that occurs on nouns, occasionally on adjectives, and on dependent intransitive verbs and intransitive nominalized clauses is -*ni/na*. -*ni* occurs on second singular and plural and third singular feminine stems, -*na* elsewhere. The margin that occurs on adjectives and on verbs that give descriptive, explanatory, collateral, and background information is -*ki*. It is neutral regarding transitivity or dependency and is glossed 'margin'. The margin which occurs on dependent transitive verbs and on transitive nominalized clauses is -*vini*. -*ja/ra* occurs only as a verb margin in independent clauses. -*ra* is used for the third singular masculine and the third plural, -*ja* elsewhere. It is used for the immediate tense and therefore is found frequently in dialogue. -*hi/ha* is the event line margin in narrative. It occasionally occurs in third person interrogative contexts when the action is in present time but remote in location from the conversation. -*ha* occurs in the third singular masculine and third plural, -*hi* elsewhere.

10 There is a small class of nouns in Paumarí called the *ka*- class. When such a noun occurs, any other noun or adjective within the same nominal phrase is required to have a *ka*- prefix. When a *ka*- noun occurs in a nuclear nominal phrase, the *ka*- prefix also occurs on the verb in that clause. For example, *vanami* 'paddle' is a *ka*-class noun. *'O-ka-noki-ki 'oni vanami ka-karaho.* (I-ka=agreement see-margin demonstrative paddle ka=agreement-large) 'I see that large paddle.' Canoes, cars, and planes are all members of this class, and when a ka- prefix occurs on a verb of motion, even though the vehicle is not stated, it is understood that travel is by such

means. *ka-* has morphologically conditioned allomorphs *ki-, ko-, a-,* and *kha-*. *Kha-* occurs with the reduplicating pro-verb *ni-; a-* occurs with *kha-* 'motion' in 'I/you/we/they come by canoe' and 'he goes by canoe'; *ko-* occurs with *'avi-* 'drink' *baranaha-* 'call', *'bai-* 'eat', *dora'* 'gather up', *fini-* 'fear', *o'oi-* 'enter', *'oma-* 'lie down' *sa-* 'take', *saka-* 'harpoon', *sona-* 'throw'; *ki-* occurs with *hi-* 'arrive', *hi-* 'be'; and *ka-* with all other verb roots.

11 **Nontransitive** is used in preference to **equational** to describe clauses that have a subject and complement (identification, possession, purpose, comparison, reference, and existential) because many action clauses are also expressed as surface-level equational clauses.

12 The *ka-* prefixes glossed 'possession' and 'purpose' are identical in the third person when preceded by a noun, but they represent different paradigms:

possession		**purpose**	
kodi-ani	'mine'	*kodi-imoni*	'for me'
kada-ani	'yours'	*kada-imoni*	'for you'
kidi-ani	'his'	*kidi-imoni*	'for him'
noun + *ka-ni*	'a person's'	noun + *ka-imoni*	'for a person'

13 The pronoun *va'ora* obligatorily precedes the verb when the object is third plural animate. This rule applies even if the object occurs preceding the verb (object-*ra va'ora* verb), or following the verb (*va'ora* verb object), or if the object is left implicit (*va'ora* verb).

Summer Institute of Linguistics
Publications in Linguistics

(* = in microfiche only   ** = also in microfiche)

1. **Comanche Texts** by E. Canonge (1958) *
2. **Pocomchi Texts** by M. Mayers (1958) *
3. **Mixteco Texts** by A. Dyk (1959) *
4. **A Synopsis of English Syntax** by E. A. Nida (1960) *
5. **Mayan Studies I** by W. C. Townsend et al. (1960) *
6. **Sayula Popoluca Texts, with Grammatical Outline** by L. Clark (1961) *
7. **Studies in Ecuadorian Indian Languages I** by C. Peeke et al. (1962) *
8. **Totontepec Mixe Phonotagmemics** by J. C. Crawford (1963) *
9. **Studies in Peruvian Indian Languages I** by M. Larson et al. (1963) *
10. **Verb Studies in Five New Guinea Languages** by A. Pence et al. (1964) **
11. **Some Aspects of the Lexical Structure of a Mazatec Historical Text** by G. M. Cowan (1965) *
12. **Chatino Syntax** by K. Pride (1965) *
13. **Chol Texts on the Supernatural** by V. Warkentin (1965) *
14. **Phonemic Systems of Colombian Languages** by V. G. Waterhouse et al. (1967) *
15. **Bolivian Indian Tribes: Classification, Bibliography and Map of Present Language Distribution** by H. and M. Key (1967) **
16. **Bolivian Indian Grammars I and II** by E. Matteson et al. (1967) *
17. **Totonac: from Clause to Discourse** by A. Reid et al. (1968) *
18. **Tzotzil Grammar** by M. M. Cowan (1969) **
19. **Aztec Studies I: Phonological and Grammatical Studies in Modern Nahuatl Dialects** by D. F. Robinson et al. (1969) **
20. **The Phonology of Capanahua and its Grammatical Basis** by E. E. Loos (1969) **
21. **Philippine Languages: Discourse, Paragraph and Sentence Structure** by R. E. Longacre (1970) **
22. **Aztec Studies II: Sierra Nahuat Word Structure** by D. F. Robinson (1970) **
23. **Tagmemic and Matrix Linguistics Applied to Selected African Languages** by K. L. Pike (1970) **
24. **A Grammar of Lamani** by R. L. Trail (1970) **
25. **A Linguistic Sketch of Jicaltepec Mixtec** by H. C. Bradley (1970) **
26. **Major Grammatical Patterns of Western Bukidnon Manobo** by R. E. Elkins (1970) **
27. **Central Bontoc: Sentence, Paragraph and Discourse** by L. A. Reid (1970) **
28. **Identification of Participants in Discourse: A Study of Aspects of Form and Meaning in Nomatsiguenga** by M. R. Wise (1971) **
29. **Tupi Studies I** by D. Bendor-Samuel et al. (1971) **
30. **L'Enonce Toura (Côte d'Ivoire)** by R. Bearth (1971) **
31. **Instrumental Articulartory Phonetics: An Introduction to Techniques and Results** by K. C. Keller (1971) *
32. **According to Our Ancestors: Folk Texts from Guatemala and Honduras** by M. Shaw et al. (1971) *
33. **Two Studies of the Lacandones of Mexico** by P. Baer and W. R. Merrifield (1971) **
34. **Toward a Generative Grammar of Blackfoot** by D. G. Frantz (1971) *
35. **Languages of the Guianas** by J. E. Grimes et al. (1972) *
36. **Tagmeme Sequences in the English Noun Phrase** by P. Fries (1972) **
37. **Hierarchical Structures in Guajajara** by D. Bendor-Samuel (1972) **